NEW AGE TECHNOLOGY IN SUPPLY CHAIN MANAGEMENT

Digital Transformation Tools in Perspective

NEW AGE TECHNOLOGY IN SUPPLY CHAIN MANAGEMENT

Digital Transformation Tools in Perspective

Mohammed Majeed, PhD
Editor

AAP | APPLE ACADEMIC PRESS

First edition published 2025

Apple Academic Press Inc.
1265 Goldenrod Circle, NE,
Palm Bay, FL 32905 USA

760 Laurentian Drive, Unit 19,
Burlington, ON L7N 0A4, CANADA

CRC Press
2385 NW Executive Center Drive,
Suite 320, Boca Raton FL 33431

4 Park Square, Milton Park,
Abingdon, Oxon, OX14 4RN UK

Apple Academic Press exclusively co-publishes with CRC Press, an imprint of Taylor & Francis Group, LLC

Library and Archives Canada Cataloguing in Publication

CIP data on file with Canada Library and Archives

Library of Congress Cataloging-in-Publication Data

CIP data on file with US Library of Congress

ISBN: 978-1-77491-882-1 (hbk)
ISBN: 978-1-77491-883-8 (pbk)
ISBN: 978-1-00360-525-6 (ebk)

About the Editor

Dr. Mohammed Majeed, DBA, PhD (Dr^2)
Senior Lecturer, Tamale Technical University, Tamale, Ghana

Mohammed Majeed, PhD, DBA, is a distinguished academic and researcher currently serving as a Senior Lecturer at Tamale Technical University, Ghana, where he holds the position of Head of the Department of Logistics and Procurement Management. With an impressive academic background, Dr. Majeed has earned two doctoral degrees—a Doctor of Business Administration (DBA) and a Doctor of Philosophy (PhD) in Marketing, earning him the title "Dr^2."

Dr. Majeed is also known for his strong presence in the publishing world, collaborating with eminent academic publishers and contributing articles featured in renowned academic publications from Emerald, Wiley, Taylor & Francis, Springer, Cogent, Routledge, and Apple Academic Press. His research interests span several vital areas in contemporary marketing and business, such as value co-creation, digital marketing, green and sustainable practices, branding, and consumer behavior.

In addition to his role at Tamale Technical University, Dr. Majeed lectures at prominent institutions across Ghana, including the University for Development Studies (UDS), Kwame Nkrumah University of Science and Technology (KNUST), and the University of Cape Coast (UCC). His prolific contributions to academic literature include six published books, with ten more in production with leading publishers such as Springer, Apple Academic Press, and Bentham Science. Furthermore, Dr. Majeed has authored over 40 book chapters, solidifying his influence as a scholar and thought leader in his field.

Furthermore, his experience as a department head in Logistics, Procurement, and Marketing has enriched his academic perspective, bridging theoretical insights with real-world applications.

Contents

Contributors

Mustapha Abdul Aziz
Department of Logistics and Procurement Management, Tamale Technical University, Tamale, Ghana

Stanley C.
Hospitality and Tourism Management Department, Tamale Technical University, Tamale, Ghana

Alhassan F.
Hospitality and Tourism Management Department, Tamale Technical University, Tamale, Ghana

Abdul Ganiw Hussein
Department of Logistics and Procurement Management, Tamale Technical University, Ghana

Anass Issah
Northern Electricity Distribution Company, Ghana

Abukari Inusah
Department of Logistics and Procurement Management, Tamale Technical University, Tamale, Ghana

Cruickshank Festus Nii Lante
Total Energy Oil, Ghana

Bilkisu Maijamaa
Department of Statistics, Faculty of Natural and Applied Sciences, Nasarawa State University Keffi, Nigeria

Mohammed Majeed
Marketing Department, Tamale Technical University, Tamale, Ghana

Clement Nangpiire
SDD University of Business and Integrated Development Studies, Ghana

Kwasi Nkayi
Tamale Teaching Hospital, Ghana

David Inusah Offei
Automotive Engineering Department, Tamale Technical University, Tamale, Ghana

Adam Osman Oscar
Department of Logistics and Procurement Management, Tamale Technical University, Tamale, Ghana

Abas S.
Hospitality and Tourism Management Department, Tamale Technical University, Tamale, Ghana

Jayadatta S.
KLE's Institute of Management Studies and Research (IMSR), Hubli, Karnataka, India

Sumaila Seidu Salaam
Procurement Directorate, Tamale Technical University, Tamale, Ghana

Gordon Sabutey Terkpeh
University for Development Studies, Ghana

Jonas Yomboi
University for Development Studies, Ghana

Preface

This book, *New Age Technology in Supply Chain Management: Digital Transformation Tools in Perspective,* explores the effects of IT and digital transformation tools on supply chain management, which is key to organizations. Such technologies include big data, robotics, artificial intelligence (AI), machine learning (ML), blockchain, and Internet of Things (IoTs).

In all, the book presents nine chapters, which include four empirical papers and five review chapters. Each chapter is structured to give readers an introduction to IT and supply chain management (SCM) and explain how IT/digital transformation tools mentioned above affect SCM and procurement at different types of industries and markets. The book also provides ample information supporting the importance of certain technologies, methods, and requirements for efficient and effective implementation in workplaces and businesses.

This book will represent the gold standard in the field of purchasing and SCM literature. Aspiring industry executives and students preparing for certification from the Chartered Institute of Logistics and Transport (CILT) and the Chartered Institute of Procurement and Supply (CIPS) (all levels) will find this book invaluable in their pursuit of knowledge. This book presents a truly global perspective on procurement and supply chain by using detailed real-world examples to bring the subject matter to life. As a result, many other sectors, including the hospitality, retail, petroleum, health care, and others are impacted.

CHAPTER 1

Artificial Intelligence on SCM in the Hospitality Sector

MOHAMMED MAJEED[1], ALHASSAN F.[2], ABAS S.[2], and STANLEY C.[2]

[1]*Marketing Department, Tamale Technical University, Tamale, Ghana*

[2]*Hospitality and Tourism Management Department, Tamale Technical University, Tamale, Ghana*

ABSTRACT

Organizations are projected to move toward more technological ways of working, managing, organizing, and supporting change in different organizational processes due to technological breakthroughs made possible by the digital economy. Human resource management (HRM) plays a crucial role in ensuring that businesses are able to attract and retain top personnel, but the widespread use of artificial intelligence (AI) and robots in the global economy is predicted to have far-reaching effects on the character, structure, and terms of employment. The goal of this chapter is to provide a literature assessment on the impact of AI on supply chain management in the hotel industry. Thanks to AI-enhanced hotel and tourist operations and management systems, the hospitality industry has been rebranded as an intelligent hotel and tourism business. Since this technological advancement enables customers to access reliable and accurate information that allows them to personalize their requests, make reservations, and purchase hotel and tourism products and services directly through technological platforms, it has also reshaped the models of tourism and hoteling by disrupting the traditional system.

New Age Technology in Supply Chain Management: Digital Transformation Tools in Perspective.
Mohammed Majeed (Ed.)

1.1 INTRODUCTION

One of the world's largest and fastest-growing industries is the hospitality and tourist sector (Ruel and Njoku, 2020). At a compound annual growth rate (CAGR) of 7.0% between 2012 and 2023, the worldwide hospitality market expanded from $4390.59 billion in 2012 to $4699.57 billion in 2023. It seems likely that the chances of a global economic recovery from the COVID-19 epidemic have been hampered, at least in the medium term, by the conflict between Russia and Ukraine (Hospitality Global Market Report, 2023). Artificial intelligence (AI) implementation is crucial in today's information age. Since its debut, it has presented both opportunities and challenges for company activities, such as supply chain management (SCM), and other businesses, such as the hospitality sector. As the globe has become more interconnected over the past few decades, supply chains (SC) have evolved into intricate networks involving numerous companies. Recent years, and 2021 in particular, have shown that there are several potential causes for SC disruptions and shortages (Hang et al., 2022). The introduction of cutting-edge technologies in the SC sector appears to be a game changer for many businesses. AI of Things (AioT) was presented by Nozari et al. (2022) to eliminate the need for human operators of machines and to speed up production through the use of computers; however, implementing this vision faces considerable obstacles including a lack of adequate infrastructure, security, and expertise. Modern robots equipped with an AI platform can observe their environments, process that data, and then make a rational, data-driven decision on what to do next. These machines are programmed to recognize things or sounds with high accuracy based on large data sets from which they learn how to make decisions (Esteva et al., 2017). In a similar vein, AI must be taken into account while implementing innovation in a global economy (Limna, 2022). There have been several advances in AI-powered technologies that could help the economy and raise people's level of living (Koo et al., 2021; Limna et al., 2021). New technologies, consumers who expect exceptional service, customers who act as a substantial source of innovation, and the problems of growing expenses all contribute to a highly competitive climate for today's hospitality business. Technologies such as AI have shown to be quite useful to SCM in recent years (Mnih et al, 2015). While AI is one of the trendiest subjects in technology, the field is still in its infancy when it comes to the possibilities it presents for SCM and procurement. AI is frequently hailed as a miraculous new approach to solving difficult issues (Sievo, 2022). Since AI reliability has increased, more businesses are beginning to adopt the technology, including the hotel sector. One day, all hotels will need to implement some form of AI to lower their maintenance expenses (Allam, 2016). By using AI, businesses can raise their profits through increased consumer satisfaction, brand recognition, and loyalty. AI can be implemented in the hospitality business in the form of personal assistants, room control systems, robots, and unified services (HR, finance, etc.) (tesseract.academy, 2022).

Studies have shown that algorithms can help boost SCP thanks to AI-enabled technologies by encouraging new approaches (Baryannis et al. 2019a; Nayal et al. 2021). New technologies including AI, product tracking sophisticated applications, and additive manufacturing hold great promise for SC risk analytics, which may be used to improve SCR and project management (Ivanov et al., 2019). In today's era of ubiquitous computing, AI implementation is essential. The purpose of this chapter is to assess AI in the hospitality industry from a SCM viewpoint.

1.2 CONTRIBUTION

This chapter was created to assist policymakers in identifying and overcoming some of the obstacles associated with integrating AI into the global hospitality and tourism industry. This chapter contributes to the body of knowledge by analyzing the potential benefits and costs involved with travel, tourist, and hospitality industries adopting AI and service automation. It demonstrates that the benefits are extremely diverse, and managers must analyze each one before determining whether or not to use the new technology. The use of exaggerated technological hysteria, premonitions, or decision-blinding technophobia are not effective methods for determining whether AI will be beneficial to the company. This study contributes to the SCM literature by documenting the extent to which hotel enterprises in hotels utilize SCM-related AI and the outcomes of such implementation. It also gives useful practical implications by demonstrating the kind of benefits hotels often obtain from implementing the stated technologies, which may play a role in motivating hoteliers to adopt SCM-related AI. This chapter offers a significant contribution to the hospitality and tourism literature as it examines how AI technologies are deployed to improve hotel workers' talent management.

1.3 LITERATURE

1.3.1 AI

The term "AI" is a portmanteau of the words "artificial," which denotes a human-made entity, and "intelligence," which describes an independent mode of thought (Limna et al., 2021). AI is the practice of programming a computer to perform tasks normally requiring human intelligence (Wang et al., 2020). What we mean by "AI" is that machines can mimic human intelligence. Although the idea of AI has been around since the 1950s, it is only in the most recent years that the technology has matured to the point where it can be regarded as trustworthy enough to be employed for critical business operations. AI is the subfield of computer science that focuses on building intelligent machines to carry out jobs traditionally performed by people. The purpose of this is to make software that can accurately simulate human behavior. Simply put, AI allows a machine to perform any cognitive tasks that humans were responsible for before through self-awareness and self-learning. The goal of AI is to program computers to act and think like humans do to solve problems (Min, 2010). AI is thus crucial for the digitalization and automation of SC processes, which in turn increases SC productivity (Dolgui and Ivanov 2021). In particular, incorporating AI into SCM has the potential to drastically alter the way businesses operate and the duties of managers.

1.3.2 HOSPITALITY INDUSTRY

The term "hospitality" is used to describe the industry of catering to travelers' needs through running lodgings, eating establishments, and drinking establishments. Four main sectors—the food and beverage sector, the travel and tourism sector, the accommodation sector, and the recreation sector—make up the hospitality industry, a sizable subset of the service sector. Food and beverage (F&B) establishments, bars, and food trucks fall under this category; Transportation (travel agencies) and lodging (hotels, motels, and hostels) fall under the travel and tourism umbrella; and recreation (sports, health, and leisure) falls under the recreation umbrella. While every industry depends on and affects the others, rapid changes are occurring in many areas of the hospitality industry as a result of factors such as technological advancements and shifting consumer preferences (Hospitality Global Market Report, 2023). Hotels, restaurants, bars, event organizing, amusement parks, transport, travel agencies, and other tourism-related sectors are all included in this industry. Most commonly associated with the hospitality industry is the provision of both lodging and food and drink for those who are not staying overnight. Inns, motels, and other similar establishments are what the nonresidential accommodation services offer to guests such as tourists and businesspeople. Chained and independent ownership structures are two examples (Hospitality Global Market Report, 2023). Over the past decade, there has been a 31% rise in international arrivals, from 900 million to more than 1.3 billion. In addition to increasing the total number of available rooms, this has also had a significant impact on the number of available jobs around the world (EHL Isight, 2023). With one billion fewer foreign visitors and US$1.1 trillion in lower international tourism receipts, 2020 is widely regarded as the worst year in tourism history. According to the most recent numbers from the World Tourism Organization (UNWTO, 2023), tourism has dropped by almost 74% from its peak 30 years ago. The Hospitality Global Market Report (2022) forecasts that the worldwide hospitality industry will increase from $3.952 billion in 2021 to $4.548 billion in 2022, a CAGR of 15.1%. Due in part to the rebound from international travel restrictions, we are experiencing such rapid expansion. At a CAGR of 10.2% from 2018 to 2026, the market is projected to reach $6715.27 billion.

1.3.3 AI IN SCM

The purpose of SCM is to ensure customer satisfaction by coordinating the flow of goods and services from point A to point B in the SC, as well as the exchange of information between the many entities involved in this process. An SC is a system used in commerce to coordinate the delivery of materials, cash, or data from the point of origin to the point of sale. Companies' methods of transferring data and products to one another and their supply chain partners are always evolving in response to technological advances. One such developing technology that is altering the SC across many industries is AI, which is having a particularly profound effect on the production of automobiles. In a warehouse setting, AI can be used to do automated checks for damage or flaws in both equipment and stock. This lessens the likelihood of machinery failure or damaged products being shipped to consumers. In today's modern SCs, AI-enhanced solutions are being utilized to improve efficiency, mitigate the effects of a global labor shortage, and uncover new, more secure means of transporting commodities. AI applications can be found at every stage of the SC, from production to final delivery. To monitor the condition of their pricey trucks and other transportation equipment and to keep tabs on their whereabouts at all times, shipping companies are increasingly turning to AI and Internet of Things (IoT) devices.

All the while learning, improving, and optimizing the process, AI may use the data generated by the machines and the staff to remove bottlenecks, strengthen supplier and customer relationships, and speed up delivery. Warehouse security can be further enhanced by incorporating machines into procedures. Accident rates can be lowered by using AI robots to operate risky machinery and stock items in inconvenient locations (Singh, 2022). The likelihood of human injury in the event of an accident has been greatly diminished. In this approach, each participant may make timely deliveries of products and services without maintaining unnecessary stocks for unexpected fluctuations in demand, all thanks to the real-time access to information between partners made possible by AI. SCM has evolved from manual, mechanization-focused maximization to sophisticated web-based and automated synchronization of the supply chain components (Ivanov, 2021; Lee et al., 2022), which is vital in coping with the rising complexities of today's global SCs (Ma et al., 2021).

To provide a comprehensive perspective of the hotel's warehouse and SC, AI can deliver better quality data and analysis. AI's scenario-running capabilities mean it can reveal insights into the best stock levels for satisfying customer demand. Since the study is performed daily, hotels will be able to tell whether and when they need to adjust their business plan in response to the ever-changing hotel industry (Singh, 2022). One way in which hotels can respond to fluctuating demand is by increasing or decreasing the rate at which they process orders.

1.3.4 AI IN HOSPITALITY

The term "AI" refers to a computer's or robot's ability to do jobs that would typically be done by a human. Using robotics and big data, the hospitality industry can provide a more customized experience for guests. Many of these companies fail or succeed based not just on their current financial situation, but also on their capacity to evolve and grow in response to market demands (Van Niekerk, 2016; Wikhamn, 2019). AI-enhanced hotel and tourist industry management and management solutions provide information to the hospitality business, rebranding it as the intelligent hotel industry (Ruel and Njoku, 2021). In addition, the hospitality sector has integrated digital processes and AI into its many systems, including property management, revenue management, and customer relationship management, to aggregate KPIs (Mariani et al., 2018). Therefore, the hotel sector is capitalizing on cutting-edge technology such as AI to improve service and experience for guests. Smart tools for customer service have been developed from these technical breakthroughs, and they are being used to enhance the client experience (Goel et al., 2022).

1.3.5 HOW AI IS TRANSFORMING THE HOSPITALITY SECTOR

The hospitality sector is swiftly gaining traction due to the disruption caused by AI-powered services in other sectors. As a result of early technological advancements, it is now possible to plan an entire trip, including flights, hotels, and car rentals, using nothing more than your phone. Businesses in the hotel industry that are short on personnel or funds may benefit from the use of AI. Managing inventory and SCM, menu optimization, guest profiling, and crowd management are just some of the back-of-the-house and front-of-the-house processes that can benefit from AI-based solutions offered by a growing number of organizations. Accommodations that cater to a global clientele no longer have to stress over language barriers. Instead, inquiries from guests are addressed in their native tongue thanks to real-time translation software. Concierge services that recall guests' breakfast preferences are being replaced with chatbots that can make educated guesses based on previous stays but still check in to see if they'd want anything different this time around.

1.3.6 BENEFITS OF AI IN HOSPITALITY

Utilizing AI in this way will improve procurement processes and the company as a whole. There are several main SCM areas where AI has proven useful.

Concurrently, AI has the potential to lead to the replacement of human talent with technology, which could require the tourism and lodging industries to rethink their organizational structures and procedures (Saini and Bhalla, 2022). Enhanced quality management, advancement, deployments, and profitability in human resource management are additional benefits of employing digital analytics and AI tools to manage and monitor the performance of human talent (Hecklau et al., 2017). AI provides a cloud-based software platform that streamlines data created by hotels and enables customers in the chain to customize and maximize the visitor experience by adapting encounters and interactions to specific guests (Nocker and Sena, 2019). Because of the importance of employee participation, recruitment, and productivity to service quality and customer happiness, there is a growing interest in studying the effects of AI technology in the hotel and tourism industries (Ruel and Njoku, 2021). Automating warehouse processes can help ensure that goods are quickly and easily retrieved from storage, allowing them to continue on their way to the end consumer without any hiccups. There are many problems that AI systems can handle in a warehouse, and they can do it much faster and more correctly than a human being could. Automating warehouse processes with the help of AI can not only save time, but also drastically cut down on the number of workers required there.

Utilizing user data, social media information gathered about prospective guests and market data, AI-based hyperdynamic pricing can be utilized in tandem with booking engines to automatically adjust prices and show rates that will maximize revenues. It's easy to make real-time adjustments to reflect shifting market conditions. The aim is to leverage the user's social media profile information to suggest hotel rooms or deals that are more likely to be of interest to the user's intended audience, and the software is becoming better all the time to make this possible (Lacalle, 2021). Better operational, inter-departmental, human–machine, and machine-to-machine interfaces might be possible with the use of AI technology. AI can tackle challenges that are much above the capabilities of a human brain. Market-wide, common AI applications include card and bar code scanning, fingerprint, and facial recognition. Since AI is not hindered by human feelings, it can make extreme decisions and do complex computations far more quickly (Yian, 2021).

As a result, the room service employees will be able to take more orders and get them done faster, leading to more money made from extra services. Similarly, automated menu ordering, available in many restaurants in the United States (Ivanov et al., 2017), has not replaced the waiters but has improved restaurants' operational efficiency by saving waiters' time and allowing some steps of the service process to be transferred to the guest and implemented simultaneously rather than sequentially (e.g., a waiter can deliver an order to one table while the customers on another table order through the automated menu). Since this is unlikely to happen anytime soon, businesses in the tourist and hospitality industries will instead use AI to boost productivity and serve more consumers with the same number of workers (Jacobs, 2022).

Reduced reliance on human labor for routine hotel operations can cut costs, improve quality of service, and reduce the likelihood of human error. Gatekeeper AI helps hotels swiftly and easily respond to client requests, giving guests the impression that their requirements are being handled and freeing up human concierges to tackle more complex demands (Lacalle, 2021). Whether at the call center or the warehouse, automation and AI can do their tasks more efficiently and for longer periods of time while minimizing human mistakes and the resulting costs. Robots in warehouses improve efficiency thanks to their rapid movement and pinpoint accuracy (Jacobs, 2022).

The use of AI in hotel engineering has the potential to improve analysis and pinpoint the sources of SC flaws. By taking preventative measures such as lowering SCM's energy and water use, they can aid in lowering operating costs. AI is used in the hospitality business, and one use is in providing superior in-person client service (Revfin, 2023). There is a tremendous amount of room for growth in this field, as evidenced by the rapid progress being made in the creation of intelligent robots around the world. It can already handle simple interactions with customers. The increasing preference of both consumers and service providers for innovative technical service solutions is expected to fuel the market's expansion. Preferences to isolate oneself from others and keep a safe distance to prevent the spread of disease are predicted to boost the industry's growth in hospitality settings such as restaurants and hotels (Global Market Estimates, 2023). Using AI has several potential advantages for the industry, not the least of which is enhanced analytics based on user behavior, patterns, and inputs. Optimal resource utilization and minimal waste can be achieved through better decision-making that is guided by actual, real-time data and analytics. By reducing the need for human intervention, AI systems can improve efficiency, safety, and overall process quality. Because of this, we are better able to meet our promise of on-time delivery to the consumer. Warehouses can more easily meet delivery deadlines, thanks to automated solutions that speed up manual processes, freeing up space, and reducing wait times for all parties in the value chain (Jacob, 2022).

AI could communicate in a variety of languages, although human hospitality workers often only speak a small handful of them. In addition, AI can add value for customers by making the service delivery (SCM) process exciting (see Ivanov and Webster, 2019 for a discussion of the incorporation of "fun" into technological acceptance models). The adoption of AI helps workers become more efficient, which in turn improves corporate outcomes, and necessitates the growth of a wide range of skillsets, from technical know-how to interpersonal and conceptual talents (de Leede, 2016). However, AI has the potential to supplant human talent with machines, which will force the hotel and tourism industries to rethink their organizational structures and operational processes (Prentice et al., 2020). The time that AI would free up for workers from completing mundane and repetitive jobs may be put to better use in other areas, such as innovation and revenue generation (Ivanov and Webster, 2017). The business that decides to use AI will gain a reputation as an industry leader in innovation and technological advancement, which will boost its brand awareness and revenue.

In terms of public perception, the hospitality sector excels. With the use of deep learning, hotels in the SC may now examine the reviews and comments left by guests across a wide range of social media sites and other review websites. What consumers are saying about the company is a valuable source of information. Brand reputation can be boosted by positive feedback, while consumer complaints can be used to improve services (Ivanov and Webster, 2017). It is expected that many parks will have trouble filling positions this summer, and one way to compensate for the resulting drop in revenue is for parks to charge higher admission rates and limit visitor numbers (Sherry, 2021). It's an ideal solution for time-consuming, manual SCM processes, with the potential to significantly reduce labor expenses while also resolving the shortage of available workers. Even when "working" under extreme stress, AI doesn't need to take a break. As a result, it can continuously execute the SCM processes. As a result, the company's SCM efficiency and performance will improve (Yian, 2021). Guest wait times are cut in half because of the AI-powered chat-bots stationed at the front desk. Such a feature enables hotels to track guest comments and questions to better prepare for their guests' needs.

One of the most difficult aspects of hotel customer service is getting back to guests promptly when they have questions, but thanks to AI, hoteliers now have another tool at their disposal to help them out. In addition, it may help with things such as data analysis, and it can collect data to learn and react to customer interactions (Brian, 2019). Since AI is fundamentally concerned with data, it can process any kind of record or set of data. Incorporating AI into data processing has the potential to reduce human error and improve data precision (Yian, 2021). AI technology is now commonplace, and companies use a variety of customer service methods to connect with their clientele. Today, digital marketing accounts for over 25% of all marketing spending, and nearly 80% of marketing companies invest in technology-related capital purchases (most often hardware and software) (Foo et al 2018, Sterne, 2018).

SCM, digital advertising purchases (programmatic buying), website administration and optimization, search engine optimization (SEO), outbound e-mail marketing (outbound e-mail), lead filtering and scoring, and many other marketing chores are all aided by AI (Sterne, 2018).

1.4 DISCUSSIONS

The use of AI is no longer the stuff of science fiction. Economic growth is dependent on the application of AI. What's more, digital assistants based on AI technologies are becoming increasingly common. The following are a few of the ways they assist hospitality businesses: enhanced customer satisfaction, increased efficiency, and reduced overhead. However, there are also potential drawbacks to AI development, including the loss of jobs in low-tech industries, the rise of robot autonomy, and worries over personal security and privacy (Limna, 2022). When compared to their more innovative competitors, traditional hotels lack online visibility and brand identification. Some companies have historically been successful in developing their own markets thanks to a large number of properties or an exceptional service offering. This pattern, however, has been upended by the advent of the internet and the subsequent growth of OTAs. With so many similar hotel names on the market, traditional hotel chains have a hard time competing with Internet travel and booking companies (EHL, Insight, 2023). AI technologies are already present in many areas of the hospitality and tourism industry, including the hotel and restaurant business. The use of AI is both strategic and crucial to the progress of the economy. Improvements in customer service, increased operational capacity, and decreased expenses are just some of the ways in which AI helps firms in the hospitality industry. Some dangers posed by AI development, however, include employment loss in low-tech areas, robot autonomy leading to a loss of control, and safety, security, and privacy worries. Dora et al. (2021) argue that using AI in SCs can help hotels deal with the special problems of food safety, quality, and waste.

1.5 IMPLICATIONS

This article added to the body of knowledge on the topic of AI implementation in the hotel sector. This means that it might be used to inform the direction of future studies on the impact of AI on the hospitality sector. It could also help researchers consider more variables in their work. If you're interested in learning more about how AI is being used in the hotel business, this article is a good place to start. In addition, the application of AI could help business owners, managers, and marketers in the hotel industry (or any other) achieve and improve high SCM performance by adopting effective methods to fulfill the requirements of customers and staff. Insights provided in this chapter can be used by policymakers in the hospitality and tourism industries wherever in the globe to better understand and address the barriers to using AI into SCM. Hoteliers can stay competitive by providing memorable stays for each visitor and boosting their loyalty by learning more about their preferences and habits. However, many hotel owners mistake personalization for a means to merely sell upgrades or enhance their e-mail marketing strategies. Hotel owners should be realistic about the obstacles they face, but not disheartened; there are many options for staying competitive.

Traditionally, the primary emphasis of revenue management has been on pricing and utilizing available rooms to maximize income. These are no longer the limits of a successful Revenue Management plan, and modern revenue managers must instead seek out novel data integration strategies for optimizing revenue growth and profitability. As a result of this technology's enhanced capacity to do human tasks, hotels can enhance their operations and the quality of their guests' experiences to retain more customers and generate more revenue. Using AI to improve the service provided to guests is a no-brainer for the hotel sector. As a result, hotel managers can provide service that is above and above their guests' expectations by learning more about their clients. Voice-activated services, data analysis, and chatbots that can act as concierges are just a few examples of the ways that AI is changing the hotel sector. If you're interested in learning more about how AI is being used in the hotel business, this article is a good place to start. To better understand and implement appropriate strategies to meet the wants and expectations of not just the consumers but also the staff, the implication might be applied to business owners, managers, and marketers in the hospitality industry or any sector that makes use of AI. Good results for the company's bottom line are a natural consequence. Additionally, the literature on the subject of AI implementation in the hotel sector was expanded upon in this review paper. This means that it might be used to inform the direction of future studies on the impact of AI on the hospitality sector. It could also help researchers consider more variables in their work. The hotel sector makes use of AI in the areas of revenue management, guest experience, and the automation of routine tasks. As new technologies appear on the market daily, hotel managers using AI must carefully weigh their available budget, guest feedback, and expansion plans to determine where their investment will have the largest impact.

1.6 FUTURE OF AI IN HOSPITALITY

In the last two years, the hotel sector has been among the areas most affected by the global coronavirus pandemic. Since many formerly closed regions are now accessible, the tourism sector has a unique chance to recover and thrive with the aid of AI. Global Market Estimates (2021, 2023) predicts rapid expansion in the application of AI in the hotel industry in the coming years. From 2021 to 2026, the analysts project a CAGR of 10%. (Mahendra, 2022). The primary factors that will lead to its expansion are the hospitality and food industries. Even though the majority of current tech deployments are in the food and beverage industry, the hotel industry is predicted to see a far faster rise of AI inside the sector (Global Market Estimates, 2023). From 2021 to 2026, the lodging and accommodation sector will develop at the fastest rate of any sector (Global Market Estimates, 2023). AI use in this sector will be bolstered by changes to business SC operations and a focus on standardizing methods. Industry SC growth will be supported by the increasing need to limit human contact and preserve social distance to reduce the spread of infectious diseases (Global Market Estimates, 2021, 2023). The future of SCM in the hospitality industry is driven by digitization (particularly AI) and innovation. During COVID-19, activities relied heavily on the incorporation of new technologies. The genuine victors during the pandemic were online shopping, contactless technologies, food delivery, and SCM services. Forty-five percent of airline travelers are open to using electronic passports instead of paper ones (EHL Insight, 2023). The lack of qualified workers is seen by 89% of tourism businesses as a hindrance to the introduction of cutting-edge technologies (EHL Insight, 2023).

Business models, sales processes, customer service alternatives, and consumer behavior are just some of the areas that Davenport et al. (2020) predict will be profoundly affected by AI's introduction into the marketing mix. How AI will affect marketing plans and tactics; how customers' habits will shift; and concerns over data privacy, prejudice, and ethics are three main areas to explore. The ability to collect and keep data effectively is becoming increasingly important for businesses. Using big data analytics, businesses can determine with greater accuracy whether or not high-spending customers are treating themselves to an extravagant meal or drink because they are celebrating a particular occasion. The value of a customer to a business can be calculated with data like this.

1.7 CONCLUSION

Improved data analytics, consumer behavior pattern analysis, and a more direct connection to customer needs are driving AI's rising profile in the hospitality industry. It has been demonstrated that AI technologies are superior at handling the needs of end-user customers. Numerous sizable consumers are making investments in these technologies to improve and expand their operations. The use of AI in the hospitality business has several potential benefits. AI is now integral to running a business and has several uses in SCM. AI has a significant impact on SCM because of its potential to capture synergy from close cooperation between SC participants. This, in turn, improves the SC's responsiveness to the needs of final customers, flexibility, resilience, cost savings, innovation, and, ultimately, competitiveness and profitability. It is helpful to get an empirical estimate of the effects of technology solutions developed to aid SCM. It can be used to improve service and the overall customer experience by providing a more in-depth understanding of the customer journey, improved guest profiling, and the identification of visitors' wants and needs. Reasons for the widespread use of AI in this sector include its capacity for real-time data analytics, the accuracy of its findings, and its efficiency.

Since AI provides substantial competitive advantages, many organizations are using it throughout large swaths of their value chains. They have been able to eliminate several layers of manual activities, such as promotions, assortments, and SC, with the use of AI technologies. The e-commerce sector is increasingly utilizing AI to foresee future trends, streamline warehouse and shipping operations, determine appropriate pricing, and tailor promotions to individual customers. Some companies even go above and above by anticipating customers' needs and delivering products before they have even received confirmation of their order. However, several shifts are required to effectively reap AI's benefits; more crucially, the shifts will drive many businesses (hotels, retail and manufacturing spheres) to embrace new tactics, such as room designs, reshaping their industrial footprints, and developing novel SC models. In conclusion, the hospitality industry is one of the most notable places where AI is reshaping the SC. AI is assisting hotels in many ways, including streamlining operations, planning service delivery, reducing the risk of SC, minimizing SC disruption, overcoming language barriers, enhancing customer service and quality control, and better-anticipating consumer demand.

1.8 PROPOSED FUTURE RESEARCH

To start, researchers in the future will need to investigate how the public's perception of AI will affect the rate at which new technologies are adopted. It's important to get feedback from people who'll be utilizing AI services by conducting surveys to find out what people like and don't like about AI. Consumers may be resistant to some forms of technology while readily adopting others. Because consumers' openness to, or resistance to, new technologies can pose significant barriers to their widespread adoption, understanding consumer preferences should be an early and ongoing priority for AI businesses. The report suggests thinking about conducting quantitative research on the uptake of AI in the hospitality industry and other areas. Moreover, a qualitative method may provide a more complete picture of the findings from an investigation, which is useful for developing follow-up research.

KEYWORDS

- **hospitality**
- **hotel**
- **AI**
- **SCM**
- **technology**
- **industry**

REFERENCES

African Business. How Can Africa Monetise Big Data? *African Business*, 2020. https://african.business/2020/12/technology-information/how-can-africa-monetise-big-data/

Baryannis, G.; Dani, S.; Antoniou, G. Predicting Supply Chain Risks Using Machine Learning: The Trade-Off Between Performance and Interpretability. *Futur. Gen. Comput. Syst.* **2019,** *101*, 993–1004.

Brian, L. Demand for Data Scientists Is Booming and Will Only Increase. Search Business Analytics, Jan 2019. http://searchbusinessanalytics.techtarget.com/feature/Demand-for-data-scientists-is-boomingand-will-increase

Davenport, T.; Guha, A.; Grewal, D.; Bressgott, T. How Artificial Intelligence Will Change the Future of Marketing. *J. Acad. Market. Sci.* **2020,** *48* (1), 24–42.

de Leede, J. (Ed.) *New Ways of Working Practices*; Advanced Series in Management, Emerald Group Publishing Bingley, **2016**.

Dolgui, A.; Ivanov, D. 5G in Digital Supply Chain and Operations Management: Fostering Flexibility, End-to-End Connectivity and Real-Time Visibility Through Internet-of-Everything. *Int. J. Prod. Res.* **2021,** 1–10. DOI:10.1080/00207543.2021.2002969.

Dora, M.; Kumar, A.; Mangla, S. K.; Pant, A.; Kamal, M. M. Critical Success Factors Influencing Artificial Intelligence Adoption in Food Supply Chains. *Int. J. Prod. Res.* **2021,** 1–20. DOI: 10.1080/00207543. 2021.1959665.

Esteva, A.; Kuprel, B.; Novoa, R. A.; Ko, J.; Swetter, S. M. et al. Dermatologist-Level Classification of Skin Cancer with Deep Neural Networks. *Nature* **2017,** *542* (7639), 115–118.

EHL Insight. Hospitality Industry: All Your Questions Answered, **2023**. https://hospitalityinsights.ehl.edu/hospitality-industry

Foo, K. L.; Virzi, A. M. Marketing Data and Analytics Survey 2018: Messy Data and Mismatched Resources Undermine Marketing Teams. Gartner Research, 19 July 2018.

Global Market Estimates. AI in Hospitality Market, **2023**. https://www.globalmarketestimates.com/market-report/ai-in-hospitality-market-3546

Hangl, J.; Behrens, V. J.; Krause, S. Barriers, Drivers, and Social Considerations for AI Adoption in Supply Chain Management: A Tertiary Study. *Logistics* **2022,** *6*, 63. https://doi.org/ 10.3390/logistics6030063

Hospitality Global Market Report. Hospitality Global Market Report 2023—By Type (Non-Residential Accommodation Services, Food and Beverage Services), By Ownership (Chained, Standalone)—Market Size, Trends, and Global Forecast 2023–2032, **2023**.

Hospitality Global Market Report. The Overall Growth in the Travel and Tourism Industry Stands at 15.1%, **2022**.

Ivanov, D.; Dolgui, A.; Sokolov, B. The Impact of Digital Technology and Industry 4.0 on the Ripple Effect and Supply Chain Risk Analytics. *Int. J. Prod. Res.* **2019,** *57* (3), 829–846.

Ivanov, D. Digital Supply Chain Management and Technology to Enhance Resilience by Building and Using End-to-End Visibility During the COVID-19 Pandemic. *IEEE Trans. Eng. Manag.* **2021**. https://doi.org/10.1109/TEM.2021.3095193

Ivanov, S.; Webster, C. Adoption of Robots, Artificial Intelligence Automation by Travel, Tourism and Hospitality Companies: A Cost-Benefit Analysis. In: *International Scientific Conference Contemporary Tourism—Traditions and Innovations*, Sofia University, 19–21 October, **2017**.

Ivanov, S.; Webster, C. Conceptual Framework of the Use of Robots, Artificial Intelligence and Service Automation in Travel, Tourism, and Hospitality Companies. In: *Robots, Artificial Intelligence and Service Automation in Travel, Tourism and Hospitality*; Ivanov S., Webster C., Eds.; Emerald Publishing: Bingley, **2019;** pp pp. 7–37.

Jacobs, T. *The Evolving Landscape of Artificial Intelligence (AI) in Supply Chains & Logistics*; Throughput Inc, 2022. https://throughput.world/blog/ai-in-supply-chain-and-logistics/#AI_in_Supply_Chains_%E2%80%93_The_Business_Advantages

Lacalle, E. How Is Artificial Intelligence Changing the Hospitality Industry? *Mews* **2021**. https://www.mews.com/en/blog/artificial-intelligence-hospitality-industry

Lee, K.; Romzi, P.; Hanaysha, J.; Alzoubi, H.; Alshurideh, M. Investigating the Impact of Benefits and challenges of IOT Adoption on Supply Chain Performance and Organizational Performance: An Empirical Study in Malaysia. *Uncertain Supply Chain Manag.* **2022,** *10* (2), 537–550. https://dx.doi.org/10.5267/j.uscm.2021.11.009

Limna, P. Artificial Intelligence (AI) in the Hospitality Industry: A Review Article. *Int. J. Comput. Sci. Res.* **2022**. DOI: 10.25147/ijcsr.2017.001.1.103

Limna, P.; Siripipatthanakul, S.; Phayaphrom, B. The Role of Big Data Analytics in Influencing Artificial Intelligence (AI) Adoption for Coffee Shops in Krabi, Thailand. *Int. J. Behav. Analyt.* **2021,** *1* (2), 1–17.

Ma, S.; He, Y.; Gu, R.; Li, S. Sustainable Supply Chain Management Considering Technology Investments and Government Intervention. *Transp. Res. Part E: Logist. Transp. Rev.* **2021,** *149*, 102290. https://doi.org/10.1016/j.tre.2021.102290

Mahendra, S. Future of Hospitality with Artificial Intelligence, 2022. https://www.aiplusinfo.com/blog/future-of-hospitality-with-artificial-intelligence/#:~:text=The%20Value%20of%20AI%20in%20Hospitality&text=The%20researchers%20foresee%20a%2010,drivers%20of%20the%20predicted%20growth.

Mariani, M.; Baggio, R.; Fuchs, M.; Höepken, W. Business Intelligence and Big Data in Hospitality and Tourism: A Systematic Literature Review. *Int. J. Contemp. Hosp. Manag.* **2018,** *30* (12), 3514–3554.

Mnih, V.; Kavukcuoglu, K.; Silver, D.; Rusu, A. A. et al. Human Level Control Through Deep Reinforcement Learning. *Nature* **2015,** *518* (7540), 529–533.

Nozari, H.; Szmelter-Jarosz, A.; Ghahremani-Nahr, J. Analysis of the Challenges of Artificial Intelligence of Things (AIoT) for the Smart Supply Chain (Case Study: FMCG Industries). *Sensors* **2022,** *22*, 2931.

Nayal, K.; Raut, R. D.; Queiroz, M. M.; Yadav, V. S.; Narkhede, B. E. Are Artificial Intelligence and Machine Learning Suitable to Tackle the COVID-19 Impacts? An Agriculture Supply Chain Perspective. *Int. J. Logist. Manag.* **2021**. 10.1108/IJLM-01-2021-0002

Prentice, C.; Dominique Lopes, S.; Wang, X. The Impact of Artificial Intelligence and Employee Service Quality on Customer Satisfaction and Loyalty. *J. Hosp. Market. Manag.* **2020,** *29* (7), 739–756.

Ruel, H.; Njoku, E. AI Redefining the Hospitality Industry. *J. Tour. Fut.* **2021,** *7* (1), 53–66.

Revfin. How to Use Artificial Intelligence in the Hospitality Industry, 2023. https://www.revfine.com/artificial-intelligence-hospitality-industry/

Saini, A.; Bhalla, R. Artificial Intelligence and Automation: Transforming the Hospitality Industry or Threat to Human Touch. In: *Handbook of Research on Innovative Management Using AI in Industry 5.0*, **2022,** 88–97.

Sherry, B. 3 Ways AI Is Transforming the Hospitality Industry. How Restaurants, Hotels, and Other Businesses Are Using Artificial Intelligence to Create Better Customer Experiences. Inc. Africa, **2021**. https://incafrica.com/article/ben-sherry-artificial-intelligence-hospitality-industry

Sievo. AI in Procurement, **2022**. https://sievo.com/resources/ai-in-procurement/ (accessed 3 Dec 2020).

Singh, R. Artificial Intelligence and Machine Learning In Supply Chain Management. Eazystock, **2022**. https://www.eazystock.com/blog/artificial-intelligence-and-machine-learning-in-supply-chain-management/#What_is_artificial_intelligence

Sterne, J. From Programming to Statistics to Machine Learning for Marketing. *Appl. Market. Anal.* **2018,** *3* (4), 298–305.

tesseract.academy. Artificial Intelligence and Data Science in the Hospitality Sector, 2023. https://tesseract.academy/artificial-intelligence-in-the-hospitality-sector/

Wang, C. X.; Di Renzo, M.; Stanczak, S.; Wang, S.; Larsson, E. G. Artificial Intelligence Enabled Wireless Networking for 5G and Beyond: Recent Advances and Future Challenges. *IEEE Wireless Commun.* **2020,** *27* (1), 16–23.

Yian, T. L. Artificial Intelligence (AI) in Procurement for the Hotel Industry, 31 Jan 2021. https://publication.sipmm.edu.sg/artificial-intelligence-ai-procurement-hotel-industry/

CHAPTER 2

Electronic Procurement and Procurement Performance in the Oil and Gas Industry: A Case Study of Total Oil Service Stations in Tamale

MOHAMMED MAJEED[1], CRUICKSHANK FESTUS NII LANTE[2], and SUMAILA SEIDU SALAAM[3]

[1]*Marketing Department, Tamale Technical University, Tamale, Ghana*

[2]*Total Energy Oil, Ghana*

[3]*Procurement Directorate, Tamale Technical University, Tamale, Ghana*

ABSTRACT

The purpose of this quantitative, cross-sectional study is to understand, test, and measure the impact of e-procurement practices on procurement performance among total oil service stations in Tamale. The methodology offers an explanation of the research design (correlation), strategy (quantitative), approach (deductive), respondents, data collection, instrumentation (questionnaire), and analysis of data (SPSS-AMOS) used in the present study. Also, the findings revealed that all the e-procurement dimensions—e-payment, e-sourcing, e-ordering, and e-requisition—are effective tools to improve procurement in the oil and gas sectors. The findings from the multivariate data analysis provide a better understanding of e-procurement system dynamics and are helpful to key decision-makers. There are limited studies available in the existing e-procurement literature using the resource-based view theory to understand procurement performance. This study will offer a comprehensive understanding to readers in this gap and relatively new concept.

New Age Technology in Supply Chain Management: Digital Transformation Tools in Perspective. Mohammed Majeed (Ed.)

It is concluded that e-procurement management systems help to increase procurement performance amongst the oil and gas firms, especially service stations in Ghana.

2.1 INTRODUCTION

2.1.1 BACKGROUND OF THE STUDY

The sale of fuel at the service stations is the basis of this study. Those service stations buy and resell fuel and related products to different customers. As procurement and supply chain competitiveness approaches in the fuel sector, strategic sourcing and electronic procurement have become essential strategies in recent years (Cardo and Biazzin, 2020). Due to the fact that the discovery and exploration of oil in Ghana was accomplished only approximately half a decade ago, the Ghanaian oil and gas industry is still considered a young industry. However, the general public has a high expectation that the economic benefits of the discovery would be realized in the shortest amount of time (Niboi, 2018). Meanwhile, the industry must deal with the issue of environmental safety while simultaneously ensuring that shareholders receive a positive return on their investment. President Kuffour (2000–2008) declared confidently in 2007 that "with oil as a shot in the arm, we're going to fly" (BBC News, 2007).

A multitude of transaction methods are used in the oil and gas procurement process to facilitate communication amongst the many stakeholders involved in the procurement process. It covers the use of mail, phone, and fax, and, more recently, email and the Internet, among other technologies (Bittok, 2017). The procedure, as it was carried out prior to the advent of e-procurement, was manual, involved a great deal of paper work, and was prone to corruption, in addition to being time-consuming. It was because of this lack of efficiency that the practice of e-procurement was developed, in which electronic transactions are employed to support all types of transactions that facilitate the procurement process (Vaidya, 2006).

The implementation of e-procurement processes in Africa is a result of the desire to reduce corruption, increase transparency, and ensure accountability in public procurement activities. Most African countries have resorted to legal reforms in order to streamline public procurement and the adoption of procurement frameworks, with the exception of Ghana. E-procurement systems, for example, were mandated by the government of Tanzania to ensure that all public procurement transactions were well-integrated and conducted online. This included allotment, advertisement, contracting, submission, communication, checking, invoicing, valuation, and monitoring to ensure that all public procurement transactions were open and transparent (Mwangi et al., 2018). According to a study conducted by Harelimana (2018) in Rwanda, e-procurement has significantly improved the public performance of the Ministry of Economics and Finance, which has decreased its total cost expenses to 18.6 million in 2016 from 24.4 million in 2015.

Much research has been done in Africa, as well as other regions of the world, on the impact of electronic procurement on the general performance in many industries. An investigation by Azanlerigu and Akay (2015) in Ghana on the prospects and problems of e-procurement in some chosen public institutions indicated that a lack of staff competency has hampered the seamless implementation of e-procurement in public institutions. Despite the fact that the vast majority of firms are committed to the development of e-procurement skills, training is not without flaws. Evidently, personnel play an important role in the adoption of e-procurement, and their skills, abilities, and training have the potential to have a significant impact on the adoption and implementation of e-procurement in the institutions under the Ministry of Finance's jurisdiction. Similarly, a study conducted by Laryea et al. (2014) on electronic procurement in the Ghanaian construction sector found that the paper-based method is susceptible to manipulation, delays in approval, poor record keeping, and resource loss, resulting in shorter procurement lead time. The usage of electronic systems in the procurement of works was found to be restricted, with the call for tenders and the payment of contractors being the two primary activities carried out utilizing electronic databases and software, respectively, in the procurement process. According to the findings of the study, effective implementation of e-procurement is essential for public institutions to achieve optimal performance. The results of a study conducted by Harelimana (2018) on the influence of e-procurement on the performance of public institutions in Rwanda found that the installation of ERP increases flexibility, which in turn translates into better earnings control and management. Aside from enhancing flexibility, ERP systems also improve management accounting and decision-making, which in turn improves management's capacity to control accruals and other issues that may impede organizational skills, such as shorter procurement lead times.

2.1.2 PROBLEM STATEMENT

Since the inception of the internet, it has offered a platform for the development of a new generation of business enterprises. It is altering the way businesses are conducted across all industries (Pavel and Vitek, 2016). The World Wide Web has evolved into a valuable source of information, goods, and services for people throughout the world (Bittok, 2017). In practice, this has resulted in the development of software-based systems. They are important because they provide information that organizations require in order to be more effective, efficient, and accurate while also saving time and money. The applications of these systems range from allowing organizations to keep track of records and trends, among other things, to allowing organizations to save time and money (Pavel and Vitek, 2016). With the advent of electronic systems in the new millennium, oil marketing firms have been compelled to shift their operations from the traditional way to e-business. This has resulted in a significant increase in global competition, which threatens existing businesses and forces them to modernize their business practices (Farrington and Lyson, 2016).

A considerable reform is underway in the Ghanaian public sector, which is also experiencing intermittent change, particularly in the deployment of integrated new technology (Jomo, 2016) to streamline and close loopholes in public procurement procedures. The implementation of e-procurement in Ghana is unavoidable because the government is concerned about preventing public resources from being plundered by government personnel working in partnership with ill-intentioned providers.

Online searching for products and services, submission of requisitions, online approval, transmission of purchase orders, online advertisement, invoicing, and payment processing are all examples of procurement processes that have been automated. Oil and gas (OG) firms in industrialized countries have been able to reduce delivery times of SCM from eight weeks to four weeks through the use of electronic procurement, while the accuracy of deliveries has increased (Afshin et al., 2006). When it comes to OG procurement, the use of online technology (also known as e-procurement) tries to eliminate face-to-face interactions in order to promote market openness while also fostering trust and limiting fraud and corruption (Vaidya et al., 2016). There are a plethora of potential benefits of e-procurement according to Neupane et al. (2014). These include standardizing and monitoring procurement, increasing transparency, decreasing personal discretion in purchasing decisions, increasing fair competition among bidders, eliminating human interference, and optimizing value for money.

In the opinion of Boariu (2018), e-procurement contributes to cost reduction through the prevention of duplication and the removal of paper work. This is due to the fact that supplies (oil marketing companies—OMCs) are stored electronically, making the recovery of older orders easier.

Pre-e-procurement, strategic procurement was frequently responsible for administrative regular work as well, such as individual transactions, transforming purchase requests into purchase orders, and ensuring that incoming bills were correctly allocated to the appropriate accounts. When it comes to procurement, strategic considerations are typically overlooked, with the buyer having little influence over the selection of suppliers (OMCs) and the products purchased (Dameri et al., 2012).

There has been some investigation into the extractive industry in Ghana, a country that is wealthy in natural resources. As a result, most of these studies (Institute of Economic Affairs-Ghana, 2010; Ndaba, 2010) have focused on the mining and nonoil-extractive industries, as the oil and gas resource was only discovered in 2007 and extraction began in 2010, and to a large extent on the socioeconomic issues associated with Ghana's extractive resource industry.

Governments from numerous nations, including Ghana, have adopted e-procurement methods as a means of improving the efficiency of public procurement as a response to a growing number of inefficiencies in the sector (Suleiman, 2013). The studies on e-procurement have been conducted by a number of researchers, but they have fallen short of examining the effect of e-procurement practices on the procurement performance (Mahmood, 2013; Mohammed, 2011; Mchopa, 2013), particularly in assessing cost reduction, time reduction, and customer satisfaction as primary indicators of effectiveness in procurement. A large number of past studies have focused on the issues of drivers and barriers to e-procurement as their area of interest, which is understandable given the advent of a new technology at the time of their publication. Suleiman (2013), Mahmood (2013), Mohammed (2011), and Mchopa (2013) are some of the most significant studies. Therefore, they do not provide information on the impact of e-procurement on the performance of procurement.

A surprising lack of research has been done on the overall procurement performance (environmental, economic, and social) of the industry, let alone procurement in Ghana's upstream oil and gas industry, despite the industry's significance to the country's development. Much of the conversation in the business has centered on the predicted social advantages of the industry, with little attention being paid to the industry's procurement performance as a whole from a holistic perspective. Therefore, to close the knowledge gap, the study investigates the effect of electronic procurement on procurement performance in the oil and gas industry with special emphasis on total oil service stations in Tamale.

2.1.3 RESEARCH OBJECTIVES

2.1.3.1 MAIN OBJECTIVE

The main objective of this study is to investigate the influence of electronic procurement on procurement performance in the oil and gas industry.

2.1.3.2 SPECIFIC OBJECTIVES

The study was guided by the following specific objectives:

1. To assess the relationship between e-requisition and procurement performance in the total oil service station;
2. To assess the relationship between e-sourcing and procurement performance in the total oil service station;
3. To assess the relationship between e-ordering and procurement performance in the total oil service station; and
4. To evaluate the relationship between e-payment and procurement performance in the total oil service station.

2.1.4 RESEARCH QUESTIONS

The following research question will be used in order to make this investigation and will help in answering the questions regarding electronic procurement on procurement performance in the oil and gas industry.

1. Is there any relationship between e-requisition and procurement performance in the total oil service station?
2. Is there any relationship between e-sourcing and procurement performance in the total oil service station?
3. What is the relationship between e-ordering and procurement performance in the total oil service station?
4. What is the relationship between e-payment and procurement performance in the total oil service station?

2.1.5 SIGNIFICANCE OF THE STUDY

It is the purpose of this study to determine the impact of e-procurement procedures on reducing procurement fraud in the oil and gas procurement industry in Ghana. The following are some of the specific contributions made by this study: On the knowledge contribution front, this study provides insight into the impact of e-procurement processes on the prevention of procurement fraud in the oil and gas industry. In the first scenario, information on the extent to which chosen oil and gas companies are utilizing e-procurement methods is presented. Using e-procurement procedures, the study uncovers information about cost reduction, time reduction, and customer satisfaction. In terms of policy contribution, this study serves as a reference material that policymakers may use as a starting point for revising existing procurement regulations and developing better policies that can cut costs and time, thereby assuring value for money in oil and gas procurements.

The study may also assist in identifying the flaws in e-procurement that have been identified at the Ghanaian procurement authority in terms of procurement performance, as well as recommendable techniques for addressing the weaknesses that have already been identified at the same organization. The findings of the study are anticipated to give the finance and audit staff the ability to review some of the policies controlling financial and procurement management and determine whether they are achieving the intended outcomes. These policies may then be modified to meet the needs of the various stakeholders, resulting in improved procurement performance for those who use them as a starting point.

According to the researchers, this study provides valuable information on the impact of e-procurement practices on the performance of public entities in terms of the extent to which e-procurement practices—cost reduction, time reduction, and customer satisfaction—can be gauged among the public entities that were selected. As a result, the findings of this study provide a platform for other researchers to undertake additional studies on e-procurement from a variety of perspectives.

The findings of the survey will provide organizations with clear insights into the elements that will influence the adoption of e-procurement by their employees in the future. The findings of this study will also be valuable for future research into the e-procurement process in order to gain a better understanding of the factors that influence it. As a source of knowledge, the study will also be beneficial to research scholars who are interested in undertaking research in e-procurement and related areas as a result of its findings. The study will also be useful to policymakers in organizations, both in the private and public sectors, who will be able to redefine the procurement department in order to achieve more efficient performance through the application of e-procurement. The researcher believes that this study provides valuable information on the impact of e-procurement practices on the performance of procurement, specifically the extent to which e-procurement practices, cost reduction, time reduction, and customer satisfaction can be measured among the selected oil and gas entities.

2.2 LITERATURE REVIEW

2.2.1 RECOURSES OF THE GHANA OIL AND GAS

In accordance with Article 257(6) of the Ghanaian Constitution of 1992, "every mineral in its natural state found in, under, or upon any land in Ghana; rivers, streams, and water courses throughout Ghana; the exclusive economic zone; and any area covered by the territorial sea or continental shelf shall be the property of the Republic of Ghana and shall be vested in the President on behalf of and in trust for the people of Ghana" (The Constitution of the Republic of Ghana, 1992). The rights to offshore oil exploration and production (also known as blocks) were sold to a number of international firms in 2004, but Ghana retained ownership of the rights until 2006. The next year, in July 2007, Tullow Oil and Kosmos Energy discovered oil in economic amounts in the western part of Ghana, which was previously undiscovered. The region was given the name "Jubilee Field." It was not long before the construction of the production facility began, and oil production was formally inaugurated in December 2010. Since then, further discoveries have been made that extend the previous findings. The Tweneboa Field appears to be the site of a second significant finding.

The amount of oil predicted in the Jubilee field has fluctuated over time according to various estimates. According to reports from offshore oil exploration and production businesses and stakeholders such as Ghanaian newspapers, there are between 1 and 2 billion barrels of crude oil in the world's oceans and on the continent. On the other hand, it is frequently unclear whether the writers are referring to the entire amount or the recoverable amount, and it is only reasonable to conclude that the total amount is being referenced. When you consider that only 30–50% of a total field amount will be retrieved, this might make a significant impact.

According to the Central Intelligence Agency's 2017 version of the World Factbook, Ghana had a total oil reserve of 660 million barrels of oil as of January 1, 2016 according to the agency (World Factbook, 2017). It is light and sweet in taste, and it comes from the Jubilee field. Quality is determined in the oil refining industry by the lightness and sweetness of the oil, and sweet and light oil indicates excellent quality. Accordingly, crude oil has an API gravity of 37.6 degrees and a sulfur level of 0.25% (weight), according to an independent laboratory investigation, and it does not exhibit any peculiar characteristics. In addition, because of its high quality, this sort of crude oil is highly sought after by refineries around the world. So, the Jubilee oil can be marketed at the same price as the international price reference oils and compete with them for the market share.

The Ghanaian oil and gas business is comprised of a complex supply network including several levels of tiers and linkages, as well as a diversified supplier base, which contributes to its complexity (local and locally owed suppliers, foreign and foreign-owned suppliers, local and foreign supplier partners, smallscale suppliers, largescale suppliers, marginalized supplier groups such as female-owned, etc.). As a result, for the purposes of this study, suppliers in the Ghanaian oil and gas industry are restricted to the first-tier supplier organizations that are fully locally owned or local–foreign partnership and joint venture suppliers of the case study organizations, which are Tullow Oil Ghana and TOR. In the following step, the potential supplier responders were chosen from a list based on references from the case study organizations as well as from a search list compiled from the internet and other sources of organization information such as the telephone directory and Yellow Pages.

2.2.2 GHANA OIL AND GAS SUPPLY CHAIN AND INDUSTRY PLAYERS

A recent study, published in Niboi (2018), found that, like any other oil and gas industry supply chain, the Ghanaian petroleum industry's supply chain includes the global processes of exploration and extraction as well as refining and transportation of petroleum products, marketing, and distribution. Upstream, midstream, and downstream are the three key components of the sector according to most definitions. In some circles, the upstream industry is referred to as the exploration and production (E&P) sector, and it is comprised of companies engaged in the activities of discovering and producing crude oil and natural gas. A critical link between remote oil-producing areas and the urban areas where the majority of consumers live, the midstream transports petroleum products from point A to point B. The midstream industry is responsible for the processing, storing, marketing, and transportation of commodities such as crude oil, natural gas, natural gas liquids (NGLs, mostly ethane, propane, and butane), and sulfur, among others (Niboi, 2018). Oil refineries, petrochemical factories, petroleum products wholesalers, retail shops, and natural gas distribution businesses are examples of activity in the downstream industry.

2.2.3 NATIONAL PETROLEUM AUTHORITY

It was founded by an Act of Parliament (the National Petroleum Authority Act, 2005; ACT 691) with the mission of regulating, supervising, and monitoring the downstream petroleum business in Ghana. As a regulator, the Authority guarantees that the downstream petroleum business operates efficiently, profitably, fairly, and at the same time provides value for money to its customers and the general public. It is the downstream petroleum industry in Ghana that includes all activities associated with the refining and importation of crude oil, as well as the marketing, sale, and distribution of refined petroleum products throughout the country. The petroleum industry engages in a variety of commercial activities, including the importation, exportation, processing, refining, storage, sales, marketing, distribution, shipment, and transportation of crude oil and refined products. The downstream petroleum industry is one of the country's most important subsectors and a significant contributor to the country's Gross Domestic Product (GDP). According to 2014 estimates, the sector currently employs over 5000 service providers and generates annual revenues of over GHS12 billion (US$4.01 billion), accounting for approximately 10% of the country's gross domestic product. The sector collaborates closely with international suppliers such as Vitol, BP, Trafigura, Glencore, and others, who account for around 80% of the country's petroleum product requirements (NPA, 2017).

2.2.4 PROCUREMENT POLICY OF THE GHANA OIL AND GAS INDUSTRY

According to Vestre (2016), the oil and gas industry forms part of a broader energy industry, which includes the power generation section, the nuclear section, and the renewable section. The importance of this industry cannot be understated as it contributes significantly to the Gross Domestic Product (GDP) of every country. The International Energy Agency's World Energy Outlook (2009) identified the energy industry as one of the fastest-growing industries because of the increased demand from emerging countries. The projection in demand for energy was seen as a major opportunity for companies because meeting this projected demand will require huge investments and efforts with guaranteed returns.

The sustainable national development of Ghana, like many other countries throughout the world, is tied to sustainable procurement in the country's major economic sectors, including the oil and gas industry, the mining industry, agriculture and cash crops, and the government sector. A number of factors represent the relationship between a country's national development and sustainable procurement, including laws and regulations that guide, protect, promote, and ensure sustainable procurement in these areas. The Petroleum (Local Content and Local Participation) Regulations 2013, L.I. 2204 and the Ghana Petroleum Commission Act, 2011 are two of the most notable of these regulations (Act 821). All of these laws and regulations are intended to use the procurement and supply chain management operations of the oil and gas industry as a stimulus for economic growth in their respective countries. Sustainability in procurement in this sector can therefore be considered a strategic means of helping the government achieve its long-term economic development objectives.

2.2.5 TULLOW OIL GHANA (UPSTREAM CASE STUDY ORGANIZATION)

In the oil and gas industry, the upstream sector includes a wide range of activities such as searching for potential underwater or underground oil and natural gas reserves, drilling and exploratory wells, and then drilling and operating the wells that recover and bring the crude oil or raw material gas to the surface. There are majors (such as ENI Petroleum Co. Inc.), independent oil businesses (such as Hess, Anadarko, Tullow, and Kosmos), a national oil company (PetroSA), as well as local Ghanaian companies involved in exploration and production (E&P) and service providers (including a petrochemical company) (GNPC, 2016). Tullow was designated as the Jubilee Field Operator in October 2008, and the company immediately began working with the government of Ghana and the other partners on developing the field in order to provide Ghana with its first significant oil output. The Jubilee Field Phase 1 Development Plan and Unitization Agreement, which was approved by the Minister of Energy in Ghana on behalf of the Government of Ghana in July 2009, was the first step in the process.

A successful development effort, which included the construction of a floating production storage and offloading facility (FPSO), resulted in the first oil being produced from the Jubilee field in November 2010. This was accomplished within 40 months after the initial discovery well, making it the fastest thorough fullscale deepwater development ever accomplished (Tullow Oil, 2017). Tullow Oil has been the primary operator of the Jubilee Field since that time. Tullow Ghana has been chosen as the case study for the upstream sector because it is the "lead operator of the first and second oil fields" in the Ghanaian oil fields (Graphic, 2017). Tullow Oil is a significant independent oil and gas exploration and production business focused on oil and gas exploration and production. As of December 31, 2018, the Group has an interest in 90 exploration and production licenses in 16 countries, which are managed by three Business Delivery Teams: West African Exploration and Production Licenses, East African Production Licenses, and New Ventures (Tullow, 2018b).

2.2.6 TEMA OIL REFINERY (DOWNSTREAM CASE STUDY ORGANIZATION)

Tema Oil Refinery is located in Tema, Ghana (downstream case study organization). Downstream oil and gas industry activities include the refining of petroleum crude oil and the processing and purification of raw natural gas, as well as the marketing and distribution of products derived from crude oil and natural gas. The downstream sector of the oil and gas industry is comprised of companies that refine petroleum crude oil and process and purify raw natural gas. So, the downstream sector of Ghana's oil and gas industry is made up of organizations involved in the numerous operations that occur across the industry's value chain. Oil refineries and processors such as the Tema Oil Refinery (TOR) and Bulk Oil Storage and Transportation (BOST), which are responsible for the planning and development of a national transmission system to meet national demands as well as the development of strategic pipelines and storage facilities, are among the organizations involved.

Again, due to the limited availability of resources for this research and the need to tailor the selection organization and activities to the research interest and research questions, the oil refinery and processing industry has been selected as the case study organization of the downstream sector. This is due to the limited availability of resources for this research and the need to tailor the selection organization and activities to the research interest and research questions. This is due to the fact that the oil and gas processing activity of the downstream sector encompasses activities that not only have a significant influence on the environment but also have the potential to significantly increase local employment and development opportunities.

The Tema Oil Refinery (TOR), which is controlled by the government of Ghana, is the country's main and only refinery. In 1963, the refinery was built, and it was one of the first eight refineries in Africa at the time of its construction. There are 45,000 barrels per stream day (BPSD) of capacity at the state-owned refinery, which supplies this number out of a total demand of 65,000 barrels per stream day (BPSD) at the refinery. A wide range of petroleum products are refined and distillated at Tema Oil Refinery Limited, including gasoline (petrol), liquefied petroleum gas (LPG), kerosene, gas oil (diesel), aviation turbine kerosene (Jet A1), naphtha, premix, fuel oil, and cracked fuels. Tema Oil Refinery Limited is a subsidiary of Tema Oil Limited (TOR, 2017).

TOR has positioned itself to improve and expand its infrastructure in response to the discovery of oil and gas in Ghana. This will ensure the availability of petroleum products on the Ghanaian market and the reliability of TOR as a major producer of petroleum products in the ECOWAS subregion. To achieve this, TOR aspires to become the preferred supplier of finished petroleum products to Bulk Distribution Companies (BDCs). The refinery has increased its present capacity for producing and storing petroleum products, as well as its storage capacity. The total storage capacity of the refinery, which includes both crude oil and finished petroleum products, has increased from 340,000 metric tonnes to 1,000,000 metric tonnes, and the storage capacity of LPG has increased from 7560 to 10560 metric tonnes according to the refinery. A price is charged to Bulk Distribution Companies for storage services provided by the refinery, which is dependent on the availability of storage space (TOR, 2017).

2.2.7 TOTAL PETROLEUM GHANA LIMITED

A subsidiary of the global Total Group, Total Petroleum Ghana Limited is a petroleum company based in Ghana (the fourth largest publicly traded integrated international Oil and Gas Company in the world). The company's operations in Ghana have spanned more than 60 years during which time it has experienced a number of acquisitions and mergers (Total Ghana, 2020). These improvements, combined with the company's commitment to safety and quality, have contributed to the company's enviable reputation in the oil marketing business (Total Ghana, 2020). Total has a 14% market share as of December 2013, with its closest competitors, Shell and Goil, each holding 12 and 11% of the total market share, respectively, according to the latest statistics (Boadu, 2016). National Petroleum Authority statistics on the performance of oil marketing companies (OMCs) for 2017 show that TPGL is the third best market shareholder in the industry, with 11% of the market (National Petroleum Authority, 2017).

This represents a decline from the first to the third best market shareholder in the industry in just four years. Although other variables, such as marketing decisions and industry issues, may have contributed to the reduction in TPGL's market share since 2013, the company's operational performance can be examined to establish whether or not it played a role in the decline. In light of the high number of outsourced operational activities, such as network equipment maintenance (for example, fuel dispensers, generators, electrical installations, and so on), as well as the distribution of petroleum products, understanding the impact of service providers' performance on the company's performance is critical. In general, new arrivals into the oil marketing industry have resulted in a little decrease in the market share of the top three oil marketing companies in Ghana. The purpose of this study is to investigate the impact of e-procurement on the performance of service stations, which operate as oil marketing firms.

2.2.8 PETROLEUM SECTOR POLICY

When Quaye-Foli (2006) was conducting research in the petroleum industry, he had a primary focus on arranging information and data for the purpose of educating and informing energy policymakers, regulators, legislators, academics, the media, and research institutions. Natural gas usage principles are covered in terms of the globe and Ghana, with an emphasis on major regulators, actors, and other energy agencies. The information obtained includes the following: Aside from that, Adams (2009) contributed new knowledge to the industry debate in 2009. He discovered that the business was confronted with challenges in upstream development in terms of investment, petroleum economics, a lack of clearly defined environmental legislation, and fiscal petroleum policy, among other things. The article then recommended that Ghana engage international oil companies for both investment and technology transfer, that environmental laws be revised, and that a new Petroleum Regulatory Authority be established in order to avoid the Ghana National Petroleum Commission (GNPC) from serving as both a player and a regulator in the petroleum sector.

Furthermore, Research (2015) performed a study on the issue of "Fueling Ghana's Growth, Oil, and Gas Industry," in which they found Production, exports, contribution to gross domestic product, market structure, and industry regulation were all investigated in the study. According to the findings of the research, the downstream sector in petroleum refining was underdeveloped, faced obstacles such as a shortage of skilled workers and marine boundary issues, and needed to be expanded further. The research also highlighted that the local sector lacked funding in order to look for new petroleum reserves. Furthermore, African Trade Policy Notes (2011) looked into topics such as institutional, public financial management, and macroeconomic challenges, as well as policy tradeoffs, among other things. According to the findings and recommendations of the paper, Ghana should promote openness in oil income management, restore fiscal sustainability and responsibility, remove bottlenecks in nontradeable industries, and boost the proportion of agricultural items in the country's exports.

Other studies have been carried out by White (2011, 2015) and Bedwei (2017), who investigated the tax policy framework for petroleum operations, specifically the taxation of income from oil and gas in Ghana. The papers were primarily concerned with Ghana's tax policy, which included everything from upstream to downstream sectors. The studies combined all tax regulations into a single document without necessarily examining their ramifications for the entire industry. As a result, this research did not contribute to the advancement of knowledge in the business in terms of policy suggestions for policymakers. In a similar vein, Kastning (2010) explored the fundamentals of Ghana's nascent oil business, which he found to be rather interesting. The petroleum revenue management bill, the government's oil policy, and the major players in the upstream industry were the primary topics of discussion in this article. According to the findings of the study, this was the first time Ghana had discovered oil. The populace had higher expectations, and it was impossible to directly attract investment from oil revenues into the infrastructure of the sector, as was the case in the past. The document also pointed out that Ghana had already begun to comply with the Extractive Industries Transparency Initiative (EITI), which was published in 2012. The Energy Group Africa Region World Bank (2013) conducted a study on the topic of electrifying economic growth in Ghana, ensuring that the electricity and petroleum sectors are up to the task of achieving this.

An investigation of this topic was carried out by the Energy Group Africa Region of the World Bank in 2013. This research was primarily concerned with electricity demand and supply, generation, transmission constraints, and reforms in the power distribution industry, among other things. In addition, they looked into the natural gas industry. Consequently, demand and supply analyses, institutional problems on the part of the Ghana National Gas Company (GNGC) and the Bulk Oil Storage and Transportation (BOST), and lastly the upstream oil and gas sector are all covered. According to the findings of the study, the government had postponed investment in gas supply and power generation, and Ghana was unable to attract private sector investment in the industry because the country's current gas pricing strategy was unattractive to investors. Further research found that the state-owned energy companies were inefficient in their day-to-day operations. However, the study was unable to provide adequate new knowledge on the subject matter of petroleum midstream transportation. Again, Adam (2014), Amoako-Tuffour (2011), Ofosu-Peasah (2017, 2018), Centre for Policy Analysis (CEPA) (2010), and United Nations (2012) papers discussed the Petroleum Revenue Management Act, annual budget funding amount, domestic investments, and crude oil prices, as well as the United Nations Sustainable Development Goals. In the course of their research, they discovered that Ghana's petroleum revenue management had been both recommendable and consistent with the Petroleum Revenue Management Act of 2011. However, they discovered a lack of responsibility on the part of the policy's implementing authorities.

2.2.9 E-PROCUREMENT

In the context of procurement, e-procurement refers to the use of electronic information and communication technologies (ICTs) to carry out individual or all stages of the procurement process. These stages include search, sourcing, negotiation, ordering, receipt, and postpurchase review. In the context of technology, e-procurement refers to the acquisition of goods and services by a private or public organization via the internet (Croom and Jones, 2013). Furthermore, according to Samoei and Ndede (2018), electronic procurement (e-procurement) is the use of the internet and related technologies to perform purchasing activities (such as purchasing products and services over the internet) by "automating the entire purchasing process and making orders and requisitions of the information available throughout the entire supply chain." It is the electronic integration and control of all procurement activities, including purchase requests, authorization, ordering, delivery, and payment of a supplier, which is known as e-procurement (Kohli, 2012). With regard to the definitions provided above, it should be noted that researchers have slightly different perspectives on e-procurement than one another. For example, the definition provided by Croom and Jones (2013) describes e-procurement as a technology that facilitates the acquisition of products and services over the internet without mentioning the processes that are involved. Specifically, Samoei and Ndede (2018) provide detailed information on the e-procurement process, which allows readers to gain an understanding of what e-procurement is all about. Kohli (2012) also provides detailed information on the e-procurement process, which allows readers to gain an understanding of what e-procurement is all about.

2.2.10 DIMENSIONS OF E-PROCUREMENT

Additionally, Lindskog and Wennberg (2002) define e-procurement as the use of web-based technology to support key procurement processes.

2.2.10.1 E-REQUISITIONING

E-requisitioning is an electronic system that assists in the management of requests for goods and services by the user, including the definition of specifications and other information about the item that is requested by the user (Farrington and Lyson, 2016). The technology enables users to efficiently request goods and services to be purchased—allowing orders to flow from their personal computers through computerized material management systems and into the procurement department in a timely fashion. As soon as the procurement department receives clear specifications of requirements from user departments, it will reply to the order as quickly as possible by interacting with them and organizing sourcing logistics if the item is to be procured from a third-party vendor. Because the entire process is completed online, it allows both the procurement department and the user department to monitor the transaction and make required changes, allowing them to provide clients with high-quality and cost-effective service on a timely basis (Farrington and Lyson, 2016).

This system is divided into two major stages: First and foremost, procurement requirements must be recognized. It is with this in mind that the public procurement process begins when the needs or requirements of the users are identified and presented to the procurement department. The requirements are often recognized at the conclusion of the financial year, allowing for the formulation of an annual procurement plan and the appropriate approvals to be obtained. A procurement strategy is required since it aids in the determination of requirements and budgets as well as the avoidance of unnecessarily expensive emergency purchases. Second, the establishment of specifications; following the identification and assessment of procurement requirements, the procurement department, in collaboration with the user department, identifies specifications, a schedule of requirements, terms of reference, and procurement methods to be used in the supply of various goods and services based on the annual procurement plan.

2.2.10.2 E-SOURCING

This entails online identification/solicitation of a specific supplier, evaluation of the supplier, and lastly contracting with the supplier to deliver the products/services that are required (Florian et al., 2016). This refers to the process of identifying new potential suppliers through the use of Internet technologies, with the goal of reducing search expenses as much as possible (Ombat, 2015). Essentially, it relies on a web-based platform to support all steps in the sourcing process, including expenditure analysis, demand aggregation, requirement definition, supplier discovery, negotiations (request for proposal or quotation), reverse auctions, bidding evaluations, and contract administration. E-sourcing is a website that allows purchasers to select goods and services from a large number of providers all at once. Using this method, customers can evaluate possible suppliers for a certain product or service by supplying information on what and where to purchase the product or service. The buyer can access potential suppliers' products and services through the use of this system, which is integrated with the suppliers' automated system (Farrington and Lyson, 2016). Product catalogs or product lists, which are printed, contain specifications, prices, and images of the things that providers are able to supply.

When opposed to the manual approach, which is slow in giving pricing information, the advantage of adopting this system is that it is easier to update price changes in a dynamic marketplace. As a result, an e-sourcing system assists procurement officers in obtaining quick information on a variety of products sold by suppliers on the internet. Because the system compels all interested suppliers to be registered in the system, it allows real-time two-way contact between buyers and sellers while also minimizing maverick buying in the public sector according to the system's designers. This makes the purchasing process easier and faster than it would be if the old traditional techniques were used. When opposed to a manual technique of evaluation, this system makes it easier to evaluate possible suppliers for a certain product or service by utilizing software that can be installed on a computer rather than applications that must be downloaded (Farrington and Lyson, 2016).

The use of e-sourcing significantly minimizes the amount of money that buyers must spend in order to receive information about product features and costs. Information on these topics can be found in online product overviews and particular websites that are designed to compare pricing between different merchants. This information is factual, accurate, and inexpensive. Due to the fact that e-sourcing lowers the costs of searching, it significantly increases their economic efficiency (Fernandes and Vieira, 2015). Prices in various marketplaces can now be discovered using numerous methods, thanks to the advent of electronic sourcing (e-sourcing). Examples of such mechanisms include online auctions, which are used to sell the items of a product or service that are currently available, or buyers listing their product specifications and the price they are willing to pay, and then making offers to participating sellers based on their specifications. Due to the fact that information exchange in search of goods and services does not impose any logistical expenses at all because the internet can accomplish this fully autonomously, e-sourcing has made significant contributions to lowering the cost of logistics (Fernandes and Vieira, 2015).

According to Mongina (2015), e-sourcing has made it feasible for businesses to reach a greater number of suppliers at no additional expense because they no longer require a physical encounter or because the business does not rely solely on suppliers who can be visited. The informed benefits of e-sourcing include a simplified supplier sourcing process, lower relative pricing as a result of increased supplier competition, and the creation of a repository of online supplier sourcing information (Masheti, 2016).

When compared to the past, where geographical limitations were an impediment to locating suppliers, e-sourcing is more efficient because e-mailing serves as an intermediary in locating suppliers as well as obtaining other worldwide information via the internet, making the exercise more efficient overall. E-sourcing has made it feasible for businesses to reach a greater number of suppliers at no additional expense because they no longer require a physical encounter or because the business does not rely solely on suppliers who can be visited. The internet has made it feasible for people to do online sourcing and obtain all of the information they require just by hitting a button on their computers while sitting in the comfort of their own offices. Organizations, for the most part nowadays, communicate with potential suppliers through the internet, and they can obtain whatever vital inputs they require to improve their operations (Laudon and Laudon, 2016). When it comes to tracking supplier information specifics during the purchase process, computers can be used effectively, and this lowers unnecessary costs by simply investing in computers and internet technology subscriptions at a low cost (Davenport and Harris, 2017).

2.2.10.3 E-ORDERING

This is the procedure by which the buyer makes a commitment to purchase products or services from the supplier online using a purchase order document that has been accepted by the provider (Farrington and Lyson, 2016). E-ordering is the process of placing orders for and receiving things through the use of software that is based on the internet. When using this system, you submit your orders online, and after detailing the essential information, you click on the button that says "Place Order." You will subsequently receive an electronic order confirmation. Ordering online saves time and is more dependable due to the fact that the successful supplier is given an order or contract for the supply of products or services by entering into an agreement utilizing the agreed-upon terms and conditions, which are acknowledged and accepted by both sides (Farrington and Lyson, 2016). In e-procurement systems, data security is crucial due to the sensitivity of the information and the legal nature of the orders and payments that are processed. When it comes to ensuring security, the system must have procedures for identifying and verifying the buyer who submits an order so that the supplier knows it is safe to proceed with completing the order.

Fernandes and Vieira (2015), for example, suggest that e-ordering systems and processes require protection because they include a financial transaction and may be susceptible to fraud. It is vital for both buyers and suppliers to have total confidence and trust in the underlying security infrastructure in order to encourage them to engage in e-ordering activities. Because it processes information in a short amount of time and at the lowest possible cost, this system contributes to more effective procurement by lowering the overall transaction costs in procurement (Fernandes and Vieira, 2015).

Another advantage of using an e-ordering system in the public sector is the reduction of paperwork in procurement when compared to the manual ordering system, which involves the use of hard documents such as Local

Purchase Orders and Quotation forms, which must be approved and authorized by several offices in the organization and must pass through several offices before being approved and authorized by the appropriate office.

After being signed, these documents are frequently submitted manually to the supplier at a late stage, resulting in a delay in the procurement process. Another disadvantage of manual ordering is the accumulation of documents in the office as a result of their frequent use, increasing the likelihood of damage and misplacement of the documents. As a result, employing electronic order processing, which allows for the fast authorization of papers through the use of digital signatures, such an issue can be avoided (Vaidya et al., 2006). Because information is saved in a computer, it is possible to maintain the security and accuracy of information while also conserving office space and saving money. E-ordering is a process of purchasing products and services from outside providers that make use of internet technology. A buyer can electronically order a variety of products from sellers in the marketplace utilizing catalogs offered by merchants in the marketplace. The ordering catalog system is an electronic catalog that contains specific specified (contracted) suppliers, selected products and services, as well as the agreed-upon purchasing rates for those products and services, among other things.

2.2.10.4 E-PAYMENT

This refers to the settlement of claims/invoices from suppliers who have delivered items or given a specific service to the organization through the use of an online payment system. Using the system, an electronic invoice can be provided to the buyer, which is then compared with other internal documents such as requisitioning forms, local purchase orders, and Goods Received Notes before authorizing the payment to the supplier (Farrington and Lyson, 2016).

Electronic payment refers to a system in which an order receipt and invoice must be processed online by generating an electronic message that authorizes the payment procedure and is sent to the supplier. The system operates by incorporating a purchase card into computer software, and it is also referred to as an online payment system. It is possible to send an electronic invoice to the buyer, which will be matched with the order and receive information through the internet, and then generate an electronic message authorizing the payment process, which is then provided to the supplier, thanks to the system (Farrington and Lyson, 2016). According to this viewpoint, the e-payment system is more efficient than the manual system when it comes to processing supplier payments. It has been overemphasized by various schools of thought, including the World Bank (2017), which states that organizations should link their electronic procurement systems to their financial management systems in order to facilitate the process of making online payments to suppliers because the system can reduce processing time and costs. The World Bank (2017) states that organizations should link their electronic procurement systems to their financial management systems in order to facilitate the process of making online payments to suppliers because the system can lower processing time and costs. It is required under this system that the buyer verifies several types of certifications, such as acceptance certificates, quality certifications, performance of services, or execution of work, as well as other relevant papers, before allowing online payment of bills.

2.2.11 PROCUREMENT PERFORMANCE

Performance refers to the actual output or outcomes produced by an organization as compared to the expected outputs (goals and objectives) produced by the organization (Farrington and Lyson, 2016). Financial performance (profits, return on assets, return on investment, and so on), product market performance (sales, market share, and so on), and shareholder return (total shareholder return, economic value added, and so on) are the three specific categories of business outcomes that are measured (Gonzalez et al., 2019).

When it comes to procurement performance in the public sector, Henderson (2014) asserted that there should be a broader conversation about what comprises the important success criteria in order to aid the development of procurement performance across the information economy. In spite of the tremendous benefits of using procurement performance to improve government operations, its adoption has been sluggish and, in some cases, impossible. Therefore, there is a knowledge gap about the elements that influence procurement performance implementation in government ministries (Bhote, 2014). Because it aids in the coordination of procurement activities, procurement performance is more likely to be advantageous in scattered supply chains than in centralized ones. When it comes to procurement performance, different actors in supply networks have different levels of influence, legitimacy, and urgency to implement it, and procurement performance can have an impact on confidence in supply chain relationships. Different industries demonstrate varying proclivities to embrace procurement performance measures, which may be traced back to the use of information exchange infrastructures prior to the introduction of the internet (Burt, 2013). In order to reap the best benefits from procurement performance management, it must be properly integrated throughout the whole supply chain (Venable et al., 2005).

The adoption of procurement performance is more likely to occur if it is perceived that suppliers are capable of dealing with it according to some research. It has been demonstrated in a number of studies that the procurement performance has significant potential (Nakumara, 2013). In accordance with this research, procurement performance systems enable firms to decentralize operational procurement procedures while centralizing strategic procurement processes as a result of the increased supply chain transparency given by these systems. Because the actions and priorities in these two areas are completely different, a company's procurement function is divided into two categories: strategic processes and operational processes. Prior to delivering on procurement performance, strategic procurement was frequently tasked with dealing with administrative mundane duties, such as single transaction processing. The process of translating purchase requests into purchase orders as well as the process of ensuring that bills received are properly allocated. As procurement performance has gained popularity in recent years, firms are confronted with a variety of issues that are related to the introduction and use of procurement performance in various industries. In order to meet the performance objectives of the company, it is necessary to manage procurement performance adoption effectively. In order to be successful, an organization must consider numerous important elements, including the competency of the procurement performance service given by an online auction intermediary as well as the business's own internal skills.

According to Johnston (2005), one of the most important success factors pertaining to procurement performance is the technological capability of the procurement system, technical service quality in terms of system quality (security, dependability, ease of use, and accessibility), and service quality in terms of customer satisfaction (e.g., responsiveness of service). In addition, trust in the service provider is a critical success factor in the adoption of electronic services. Clients can access the internet at any time and from any location because of the increased level of convenience provided by procurement performance. Furthermore, the instance of computer access is regarded as an indicator of relative advantage in a variety of contexts

(Daniel, 1999; Black et al., 2001; Polatoglu and Ekin, 2001; Gerrard and Cunningham, 2003). However, according to Johnston (1995), there are some service quality determinants that are predominantly satisfiers and others that are predominantly dissatisfiers, with the main sources of satisfaction being attentiveness, responsiveness, care, and friendliness.

The integrity, dependability, responsiveness, availability, and usefulness of a system are the most common sources of dissatisfaction. Karin and colleagues (2013) identified nonadherence to electronic procurement procedures as a major hindrance to the development of procurement in Kenya. He did not, however, disclose at what level of the procurement process this occurred. As much as the studies mentioned above emphasize the importance of good need assessment as a foundation for effective procurement, they fall short of bringing to light the relationship between need assessment and performance in the context of performance. The importance of procurement as a moral and ethical concern is also emphasized by Karin, who recognizes that administrative action is permeated by moral choices and that procurement professionals serve as role models for not only technical and professional competencies but also for moral behavior (Schlosser, 2013). Ahmed (2014), in his study on e-procurement, also found that many organizations, on the other hand, are unable to provide services to their constituents. He discovered that this could be due to a lack of financial resources or a lack of capacity to give a high-quality service at a reasonable price. As a result, these organizations should seek alternative means of ensuring that services are improved and that they reach the individuals who are most in need of them.

2.2.12 RESOURCE-BASED VIEW (RBV) THEORY

It is the belief of RBV that a firm's internal resources and competencies are the most important source of competitive advantage over its competitors. The firm is viewed as a collection of assets or capabilities, and the performance of companies is determined by the extent to which those assets or capabilities are unique to the organization (Bhandari et al., 2020). According to RBT, a firm has a long-term competitive advantage when it is implementing a value-creating strategy (value) that is not being implemented by other competitors at the same time (a rarity) and when these other competitors are unable to duplicate the benefits of this strategy (imperfect imitability) (Barney et al., 2011). As posited by academics and scholars, a firm's resources and capabilities are what enable it to attain growth, competitive advantage, and long-term viability in the marketplace (Bhandari et al., 2020; Celec and Globocnik, 2017). Resource capacity refers to the combination of land and labor that enables a firm to manufacture products and provide services, whereas capability capacity refers to the combination of human, physical, and technical resources that a firm's members possess as well as higher-order systems that can be deployed as processes (Sims et al., 2016). Business executives in small and medium-sized enterprises (SMEs) employ resources and competencies to design strategies and gain strategic positions for their competitive advantage in order to earn business contracts that will ensure their profitability and long-term viability (Chen and Schiele, 2017).

In order for resources to make a substantial contribution and obtain competitive advantages, they must be exploited in groups rather than individually (Bridoux, 2015). With this in mind, it follows that using technical resources, such as e-procurement, allows the organization to perform better than other organizations that do not make use of the technology. In order to achieve a sustainable competitive advantage and achieve superior performance, the organization can make use of tangible and intangible resources such as computer programs and physical assets, organizational processes, firm attributes, information knowledge, capabilities, knowledge, and skills, among other things. However, when seen from a critical perspective, while it is evident that resource-based theories of competitive advantage can have significant managerial implications, it also demonstrates that resource-based theories of competitive advantage have significant prescriptive limitations. Because causally ambiguous resources are at the heart of a firm's competitive advantage, managers in that firm will never be able to pinpoint which of their resources is responsible for generating that competitive advantage. This has the potential to considerably restrict the prescriptions that can be obtained from the theory. Second, no theories of sustainable competitive advantage can be used by managers in organizations that do not have the ability to generate sustainable competitive advantages in the process of developing these advantages. As a result, where the possibility for sustainable competitive advantages does not exist, resource-based logic cannot be employed to generate such advantages. In addition, the RBT has been used the most commonly in three areas: marketing strategy, international marketing, and marketing innovation, among others (Irina et al., 2013). However, market-based resources frequently differ from resources studied in nonmarketing contexts, making the application of the theory in other situations, such as public procurement, difficult or impossible (Fang et al., 2011). In the case of the RBT, for example, there are two major assumptions: resource heterogeneity, which necessitates a distribution of resources and capabilities that is uneven across enterprises. It is also known as resource immobility, and it states that resources are not easily transferrable across organizations (Barney et al., 2011).

When it comes to applying the idea in different circumstances, this poses difficulties in conceptualizing the phenomenon. Furthermore, little study has been done to verify the underlying resource requirements that are critical to resource-based performance forecasts, which has resulted in some research being unable to demonstrate theoretical robustness (Irina et al., 2013). RBT, on the other hand, can provide extremely valuable information about priceless goods. For this reason, the researcher considers this theory relevant in investigating the impact of e-procurement on the performance of public procurement, with the goal of determining whether technology as a resource has enabled public entities to improve performance in procurement and gain competitive advantages or whether this has not been the case.

2.2.13 STUDY FRAMEWORK

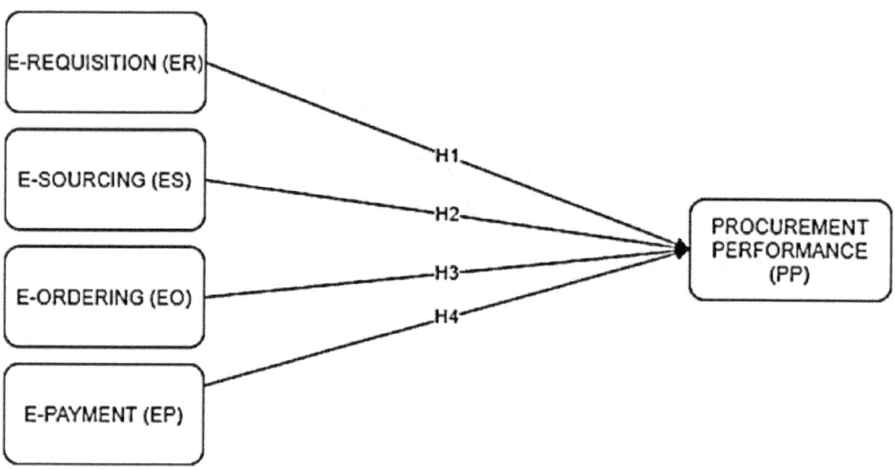

FIGURE 2.1 Conceptual framework.

2.2.14 E-PROCUREMENT AND PROCUREMENT PERFORMANCE

According to the findings of a study conducted by Quesada et al. (2016), e-procurement has a direct impact on procurement practices and has a positive impact on procurement performance. Then there are other researchers, such as Aryati and Gapur (2015), who discovered that e-performance exists. According to Van Weele (2012), purchasing performance can be divided into two categories: purchasing effectiveness and purchasing efficiency. Organizations use performance to assess how well they are progressing toward their predetermined objectives, identify areas of strength and weakness, and make decisions about future initiatives with the purpose of determining how to initiate performance improvements. Thus, purchasing performance is not an aim in and of itself but rather a means to more effective and efficient control and monitoring of the purchasing function (Lardenoije et al., 2011). Edwardsson (2013) argues that specification is an inherent component of the procurement process and should be treated as such. Without a quality specification, the purchasing department may encounter a number of snags and roadblocks during the procurement process.

A distinction should be made between purchasing efficiency and purchasing effectiveness, which represent two distinct talents and capacities for the purchasing function, according to CIPS. Therefore, an organization can be both effective and inefficient at the same time; the problem is to strike a balance between the two. Amaratunga and Baidry (2011) argue that performance is a critical factor in any organization's ability to shift its focus and become more competitive and that its absence or inappropriate use of performance measures can act as a barrier to change and result in the deterioration of the procurement function. Purchasing decisions must be made in an inexpensive and effective manner according to the Procurement Act of 2003. In other words, they should be based on market prices and should be able to generate savings, among other things. Furthermore, it means that improper practices, such as careless procurement leading to waste, wear and tear of stocks, overinvoicing, unplanned expenditure, a scarcity of items when needed, poor quality products, and other concerns, should be avoided.

Therefore, the following hypotheses have been formulated:

H1: There is a significant positive relationship between e-requisition and procurement performance in the total oil service station.

H2: There is a significant positive relationship between e-sourcing and procurement performance in the total oil service station.

H3: There is a significant positive relationship between e-ordering and procurement performance in the total oil service station.

H4: There is a significant positive relationship between e-payment and procurement performance in the total oil service station.

2.3 RESEARCH METHODOLOGY

2.3.1 STUDY AREA

Ghana is a West African country located between Cote d'Ivoire and Togo, bordering the Gulf of Guinea, with a population of over 30 million people. Despite the fact that it is seen as a beacon of democracy in the subregion, the country has maintained political stability and peace since the establishment of constitutional democratic governance in 1992. Since then, the country has had a quarter-century of reasonably competent economic management, a competitive business climate, a steady drop in poverty levels, and a general improvement in the overall economic situation. Ghana, which is rich in natural resources and has a market-based economy with few trade and investment restrictions compared to other countries in the region, is a promising investment destination. Agriculture employs more than half of the workforce, which is primarily comprised of small landowners, and accounts for approximately 20% of GDP. Exports of gold, cocoa, and oil are among the most important sources of foreign cash. Timber, tuna, bauxite, aluminum, manganese ore, diamonds, and horticulture items are among the other things exported from the country. Accra's economic growth has been further bolstered in recent years by the rise of the country's burgeoning oil industry; however, the drop in oil prices since 2015 has cut Ghana's oil revenue by more than half. The country's gross domestic product (GDP) is predicted to be $120.8 billion in 2016 (World Factbook, 2016). There is widespread recognition of Ghana's mining potential as well as its contribution to world mineral output, particularly in the gold sector. The mining industry made a significant contribution to the excellent 14.4% GDP growth that the economy achieved last year. Approximately 40% of total mechanized exports in 2011 were accounted for by the mining industry according to the Bank of Ghana (Ghana Chamber of Mines, 2011), an economic boom peak that was largely attributed to the commencement of oil production in Ghana (Ndaba, 2010).

In spite of the significant contribution that mining (mineral extraction) makes to the Ghanaian economy, the sector has a long history of conflict in the country. Mining has been viewed with suspicion and attacked for a variety of reasons, including the following: (1) the charge that the industry's adverse environmental and social effects are hardly ever addressed and most often ignored, resulting in detrimental consequences on the health, lives, and livelihood of local mining communities; (2) the charge that mining has failed to make the necessary positive impact on the environment and social conditions (Institute of Economic Affairs-Ghana, 2010). Unquestionably, the mining industry, which is Ghana's most important source of wealth, has not received the greatest amount of support from the general population, particularly from the local mining communities. Ghana has lately added oil resources to its already extensive collection of natural resources. President Kuffour (2000–2008) declared confidently in 2007 that "with oil as a shot in the arm, we're going to fly" (BBC NEWS, 2007). Since then, there has been a flurry of public debate around the country: What amount of money will be generated by the oil production? What will be the social ramifications of the finding of oil? What is the best way to prevent the dreaded 'Resource Curse'? By revenue value alone, the oil and natural gas business is among the world's largest industries and is a significant contributor to global economic growth.

According to Ernst and Young (2016), global oil and gas activity reached $395 billion in 2016, representing a 14% rise over the previous year's figure. Countries have benefited greatly from the oil and gas industries, which have generated substantial revenue and contributed significantly to the gross domestic product (GDP) of producing countries. Through nearly 40 years of operations, the oil and gas industry has contributed more than NOK 7000 billion (about $700 billion) to the Norwegian economy in current dollars. In 2008, the oil and gas sector generated 26% of total national value creation, which was three times more than the value created by land-based industries and approximately 23 times larger than the overall value created by primary industries (FACTS, 2009). The worldwide oil business also generates considerable revenues, taxes, and employment opportunities. According to the International Labor Organization (2016), an estimated 6 million people are directly employed by the petroleum sector, with an additional 60 million or so jobs being created indirectly by the business. Despite the increasing level of employment, the petroleum industry continues to suffer from a scarcity of highly skilled personnel. Because of this, the industry has a greater possibility to create jobs (both directly and indirectly). Women are also finding increased employment opportunities in the petroleum business, though at a far slower rate than men. It is possible that this is due to the difficult working conditions in the sector. Thus, it is not unexpected that governments that make fresh oil discoveries tend to have high expectations for the advantages that will accrue from this natural resource in the near future. It goes without saying that oil and gas production has considerable and diverse negative effects and costs on the environment, human health, and cultural heritage as well. This is why pollution is often referred to as the most pervasive and deadly consequence of the oil and gas industry's operations.

All activities involved with the oil and gas industry's production chain, from upstream exploration to downstream refining, are related to pollution, and this is true for virtually all of the industry's activities. Gas emissions, wastewater, solid waste, and aerosols generated during drilling, production, refining, and transportation total more than 800 different chemicals, the majority of which are oil and petroleum products, of which oil and petroleum products are the most prominent. These environmental consequences can be disastrous in some cases, and the costs (environmental, social, and economic) can last for a substantially longer period of time. For instance, the Deepwater Horizon Oil Spill (also known as the BP oil spill or the Gulf of Mexico oil spill) is an industrial disaster that began on April 20, 2010, in the Gulf of Mexico on the BP-operated Macondo Prospect and ended on April 22, 2010. In what has been dubbed "the greatest marine oil leak in the history of the petroleum industry," the United States government assessed the total discharge to be 4.9 million barrels of oil. The spill lingered for months, fouling beaches throughout the region, killing coastal and marine creatures, harming flora, and causing significant damage to the fishing industry in the process. BP, the company that operated the well, was fined more than $18 billion. It is estimated that the disaster cost BP more than $50 billion in fines, settlements, and clean-up expenditures, in addition to the costs of the leak itself.

Worldwide, there is a consensus that human industrial and economic activities are depleting the earth's environmental health and that the world urgently needs to protect the environment from further environmental damage. As a result of their report (1987), which was one of the first to look in detail at the challenges and effects of climate change, as well as the need to preserve earth's resources for future generations, the Brundtland and Khalid Commission emphasized the importance of economic development in a sustainable manner that did not deplete natural resources to unsustainable levels or place undue pressure on the environment. The petroleum sector is distinguished by its complexity of operation, high level of financial investment, and high degree of risk. Due to the challenging environment of extreme locations, marginal oilfields, new global business trends, new technological developments, and the volatility of oil and gas prices, the oil and gas industry is faced with the challenge of seeking better solutions to overcome these challenges, which includes developing and implementing new and innovative procurement strategies, among other things. As a separate and complicated enterprise, the oil and gas industry must be recognized as such. The direct application of procurement lessons learned in other industries, such as construction, may be inappropriate because the oil and gas industries differ in many aspects relating to the operation, construction, and maintenance phases between the two industries. The oil and gas industries also differ in many aspects relating to the construction phase (Mohammad and Price, 2004). A faster global transition to sustainable development has pushed environmental, social, and economic sustainability onto government agendas around the world, with governments linking their sustainable national development goals to environmental, social, and economic sustainability in the key sectors of their economies (Walker et al., 2012). Because the public sector spends a significant amount of money on products and services, sustainable procurement is becoming an increasingly crucial part of the route toward national sustainable development goals for governments. In 2013, governments spent an average of 29% of overall general government expenditure on public procurement according to the Bureau of Economic Analysis (OECD, 2015). Because of the enormous volume of spending that it represents, procurement, like the public sector, is a critical pillar of service delivery in the oil and gas business. Procurement in the oil and gas business may play a significant role in improving the efficiency of the sector while also gaining the trust and support of the general public. In addition, well-designed procurement procedures in the sector can aid in the achievement of important policy objectives such as innovation, environmental protection, job creation, and the growth of local communities and small and medium-sized firms.

Ghana, like many other countries around the world, links its sustainable national development to the procurement of sustainable goods and services in the country's major sectors of the economy, including the oil and gas industry, the mining industry, agriculture and cash crops, as well as the government. A number of factors represent the relationship between a country's national development and sustainable procurement, including laws and regulations that guide, protect, promote, and ensure sustainable procurement in these areas. The Petroleum (Local Content and Local Participation) Regulations 2013, L.I. 2204 and the Ghana Petroleum Commission Act, 2011 are two of the most notable of these regulations (Act 821). All of these laws and regulations are intended to use the procurement and supply chain management operations of the oil and gas industry as a stimulus for economic growth in their respective countries.

2.3.2 RESEARCH DESIGN

Researchers select a design based on its appropriateness for the desired population (Robson and McCartan, 2016). Quantitative designs can be experimental, quasiexperimental, or nonexperimental, which include correlational, descriptive, and evaluation methods (Gabbiadini and Greitemeyer, 2017). Qualitative designs consist of grounded theory, ethnography, phenomenological study, narrative, and case study methods (Ahmed and Ahmed, 2014). A correlational model was the most appropriate quantitative design for this study. Bettany-Saltikov and Whittaker (2014) stated researchers should use correlational designs when measuring two or more quantitative variables (e-procurement and procurement performance) from the same group of participants to find a relationship between those variables. Therefore, I used this design to examine the relationship between independent variables of e-procurement (e-requisition, e-sourcing, e-ordering, and e-payment) and the dependent variable of procurement performance.

2.3.3 RESEARCH STRATEGY

To obtain meaningful results, a researcher must select the right method for the line of inquiry (Yin, 2018). The three available methods for conducting research include qualitative, quantitative, and mixed methods, with each method resulting in different types of information (McLaughlin et al., 2016; Yin, 2018).

The researchers found a quantitative strategy to be suitable for this study since the goal is to establish relations. McCusker and Gunaydin (2015) explained that in quantitative research, several features of the study are designed before the data collection process. The researcher understands the research objective and can remain separate and impartial from the subject matter (McCusker and Gunaydin, 2015). Quantitative data are precise but lack contextual detail (McCusker and Gunaydin, 2015), which does not help the researcher deeply understand an issue. Qualitative researchers explore the complexities of an issue or reexamine an issue from a different perspective (Marshall and Rossman, 2016). Using a qualitative approach enables obtaining in-depth data by allowing participants to describe experiences in their words (Marshall and Rossman, 2016). Pursuing a qualitative approach requires a method of data collection that helps identify and explore the underlying dynamics of an issue (Merriam and Tisdell, 2015). Using a mixed-method approach, combining qualitative and quantitative designs adds credibility to a qualitative study, but the researchers did not seek to obtain in-depth data or request participants to describe experiences in their words. So, the researcher neither uses a mixed nor a qualitative strategy.

2.3.4 POPULATION

Study participants consisted of individuals who were at least 18 years of age and were full-time with at least 1 year of employment in a total oil service station in Tamale, Ghana. Proper and ethical selection of participants with experience in the area under study is imperative to the success of this project work (Montalvo and Larson, 2014). The target demographic is front desk and customer service employees from procurement, front desk customer service employees, pump attendants, managers, IT personnel, as well as suppliers from the oil and gas industry.

2.3.5 SAMPLE SIZE

The study targeted 200 respondents drawn from front desk customer service employees, pump attendants, managers, IT personnel, and suppliers of the 31 service stations in Tamale-Ghana. Limiting the sample to one company has the potential of bias as a result of the influence of one company's internal culture (Ho, 2017). The simple random sampling technique will be used to select a sample of 139 respondents from the population, purposely to solicit the required information from them to help achieve the objectives of the study. Due to the nature of the population of Tamale service stations, the simple random sampling technique is more appropriate to ensure that each and every respondent has an equal chance of being selected in the sample.

2.3.6 DATA COLLECTION TECHNIQUE

This study adopted an online survey. Online surveys are a quick and reliable method of gathering quantitative data (Basil, 2017). We gathered data via hosting an online survey made using the Qualtrics website, rather than using survey vehicles like paper, email, or social media, which have lower response and completion rates, as well as greater expenses, as stated by Basil (2017). The advantages of online surveys were their ease of use, rapid deployment, cheap cost, respondent convenience, and short response time (Walsh and Brinker, 2014), making them an agreeable medium for data collection (Alwin, 2014). Low response rates, sample bias, inability to reach persons with restricted Internet access, and the possibility of survey fraud are among potential drawbacks of online surveys (Middleton et al., 2014).

Another downside of internet surveys is that respondents can exit at any time, leaving questionnaires unfinished (Middleton et al., 2014). After weighing the benefits and drawbacks of online surveys and other data collection methods, management researchers consistently choose them (Walsh and Brinker, 2014). Online surveys are the most successful and efficient technique to collect data in quantitative research according to Bryman and Bell (2015). The validity of a study is supported by the use of a pre-established instrument with appropriate reliability and validity values (Ertürk, 2014; Hom et al., 1984; Kihm et al., 2014). A pilot study evaluates time, cost, statistical variability, and predict validity by testing the design of a fullscale investigation on a smaller sample (Denscombe, 2014). Because we used an existing survey, I did not need to conduct a pilot study.

2.3.7 SOURCES OF DATA COLLECTION

The sources of data used for the research methodology comprise primary data to formulate a questionnaire.

2.3.7.1 PRIMARY DATA

These are the data collected from the field to address the specific research questions or to find solutions to the problems at hand (Cooper and Schindler, 2006). Hence, data was collected from the field of businesses within the Ghanaian oil and gas, precisely all the total oil service stations. Questionnaires designed were sent out via online to service station managers and front desk customer service employees, pump attendants, IT personnel, and suppliers. Thus, the researcher went to the field of corporate firms, predominantly service stations, to solicit data such as key employees to aid the research work. Moreover, the researcher took time to observe and monitor the administering of all such procedures regarding the questionnaires.

2.3.7.2 SECONDARY DATA

The secondary data was collected via literature from journals and databases (Scopus, Web of Science). Data was also gathered from the government.

2.3.8 INSTRUMENT OF DATA COLLECTION

Instruments of data collection include questionnaires, interviews, focus groups, surveys, observations, etc. Even though data collection can be conducted through various tools, a particular instrument to be adapted depends purposely on the kind and type of research. A questionnaire was the basic instrument used for eliciting data from the service station employees. The study used a five-point Likert scale. Participants indicate their degree of agreement or disagreement with each of the statements using the following scales: 1 = strongly disagree, 2 = disagree, 3 = neutral, 4 = agree, and 5 = strongly agree (Weiss et al., 1967). The close-ended questions in the questionnaires had their own answers, while the open-ended questions also demanded opinions and views from the respondents. The study adopted only the close-ended questions since this is a quantitative study.

2.3.9 DATA ANALYSIS

IBM SPSS Version 24.0 and Amos Version 22.0 for Windows are statistical and graphical data analysis programs (Green and Salkind, 2016). To describe the general distributions by frequency and percentage, this software includes Pearson's correlation coefficient analysis, descriptive statistics, and structural equation modeling (Green and Salkind, 2016). AMOS is a powerful tool for analyzing huge datasets and predicting direct and indirect correlations between various independent and dependent variables (Brezavscek et al., 2014). The correlations between the independent variables of e-procurement components and dependent variables of procurement performance were investigated using SPSS-Amos. As a result of inferences formed about participant replies, three alternative hypotheses will be approved or rejected. SEM analysis is a statistical technique for evaluating the relationships between multiple independent variables and a dependent variable, explaining variances among independent variables and their relationships to a dependent variable, and evaluating explanatory variables when used to predict the outcome of a response variable (Chen et al., 2014).

Identifying measures of central tendency, such as minimums, means, maximums, and standard deviations, is possible with descriptive statistics (Green and Salkind, 2016). Understanding each variable's frequency and percentage level aids in determining its general distribution (Green and Salkind, 2016). Descriptive statistics were utilized to examine the survey's demographics and to provide a visual relationship between participant responses and research variables. Missing data is unavoidable in computerized surveys according to Bryman (2015). Any incomplete surveys were deleted from the analysis to accommodate missing data.

2.3.10 MEASURES

All the measures in this study were adapted from literature using the five-point Likert scale. All four constructs of e-procurement were adapted from Salisu and Bakar (2019), while procurement performance items were adapted from Radomska et al. (2019).

2.4 DATA ANALYSIS AND RESULTS

2.4.1 DESCRIPTIVE ANALYSIS

Descriptive statistics refers to a process for measuring the central tendency of a specific variable using minimum, median, maximum, and standard deviation (Green and Salkind, 2016). The study conducted analysis on the study variables (e-requisition, e-paying, e-sourcing, and e-ordering) and procurement performance. The descriptive statistics that summarized major characteristics of the study variables were mean scores and standard deviation.

TABLE 2.1 Descriptive Statistics.

Constructs	Items	N	Maximum	Minimum	Mean	SD
E-requisition (ER)						
	ER1	127	1	5	3.33	1.347
	ER2	127	1	5	3.12	1.740
	ER3	127	1	5	3.02	1.567
	ER4	127	1	5	3.01	1.840
	ER5	127	1	5	3.12	1.821
Average ER		127	1	5	3.14	0.915
E-sourcing (ES)						
	ES1	127	1	7	3.23	1.730

TABLE 2.1 *(Continued)*

Constructs	Items	N	Maximum	Minimum	Mean	SD
	ES2	127	1	7	3.74	1.521
	ES3	127	1	7	3.51	1.580
	ES4	127	1	7	4.01	0.912
	ES5	127	1	7	3.12	1.347
	ES6	127	1	7	3.42	1.650
	ES7	127	1	7	3.81	1.721
Average ES		127	1	7	3.97	1.033
E-ordering (EO)						
	EO1	127	1	5	3.54	1.347
	EO2	127	1	5	3.12	1.740
	EO3	127	1	5	3.65	1.821
	EO4	127	1	5	3.21	1.580
	EO5	127	1	5	3.41	1.712
Average EO		127	1	5	3.17	1.071
E-payment (EP)						
	EP1	127	1	5	4.54	1.347
	EP2	127	1	5	3.56	1.740
	EP3	127	1	5	3.72	1.821
	EP4	127	1	5	3.29	1.580
	EP5	127	1	5	3.41	1.712
Average EP		127	1	5	3.52	1.071
Procurement Performance (PP)						
	PP1	127	1	5	3.84	1.347
	PP2	127	1	5	3.12	1.740
	PP3	127	1	5	3.22	1.821
	PP4	127	1	5	3.51	1.580
	PP5	127	1	5	4.01	1.712
Average PP		127	1	5	3.33	1.12

Sources: Researcher's fieldwork (2021).

It was observed in Table 2.1 that IT systems had a mean score of 3.14, which suggests that IT capability was adopted in service stations in Ghana to a moderate extent. The respondents were relatively in agreement in their responses, as shown by a low standard deviation of 0.915. On the individual measures of e-sourcing, it was established that service station website information had the highest mean score of 3.97, while e-ordering had the least score at 3.17. The moderate adoption of e-procurement in service stations suggests that most hoteliers have recognized the opportunities that arise as a result of the automation of processes and interconnecting hotel departments through computer networks. Consequently, service stations need to invest significantly on e-ordering which would enable the service stations to improve on business spanning, increase staff competences, and adopt a proactive stance in providing solutions to emerging challenges.

Also, Table 2.1 shows that the average mean score for procurement performance was 3.33, which alludes to the fact that procurement performance was moderately adopted in service stations in Tamale. At the same time, the results showed that the respondents varied significantly in their agreement on the adoption of procurement performance, as shown by a high standard deviation of 1.12.

2.4.2 RELIABILITY AND VALIDITY

Both Cronbach's alpha (α) and composite reliability (CR) have acceptable values in Table 2.2. All of the variables have a Cronbach's alpha value greater than the allowed 0.6 (Hair et al., 2017). Similarly, the 0.70 composite reliability requirement for all variables has been created. The table also shows that the average variance recovered from each variable is more than the acceptable convergent validity criterion of 0.50 (Hair et al., 2010). As a result, the discriminant validity of the variables under study is evaluated using the Fornell and Larcker (1981) criterion to guarantee that each variable represents a separate phenomenon.

TABLE 2.2 Reliability and Validity.

Constructs	Items	Loadings	α	rho_A	CR	AVE
E-requisition (ER)			0.93	0.94	0.94	0.68
	ER1	0.77				
	ER2	0.87				
	ER3	0.74				
	ER4	0.75				
	ER5	0.71				
E-sourcing (ES)			0.95	0.93	0.95	0.56
	ES1	0.82				

TABLE 2.2 *(Continued)*

Constructs	Items	Loadings	α	rho_A	CR	AVE
	ES2	0.75				
	ES3	0.76				
	ES4	0.73				
	ES5	0.77				
	ES6	0.71				
	ES7	0.72				
E-ordering (EO)			0.94	0.89	0.82	0.72
	EO1	0.82				
	EO2	0.75				
	EO3	0.72				
	EO4	0.73				
	EO5	0.70				
E-payment (EP)			0.88	0.92	0.89	0.69
	EP1	0.84				
	EP2	0.72				
	EP3	0.70				
	EP4	0.70				
	EP5	0.75				
Procurement Performance (PP)			0.92	0.94	0.93	0.76
	PP1	0.82				
	PP2	0.75				
	PP3	0.77				
	PP4	0.72				
	PP5	0.72				

Sources: Researcher's fieldwork (2021).

2.4.3 CORRELATION ANALYSIS

We run correlation analysis so as to ascertain the direction and the strength of the association of variables in the study, as opined by Jobson (2012). The results of the correlation analysis were as shown in Table 2.3. The discriminant validity and convergent validity were established because the value of each pair of constructs is greater than the value of the square correlations between the pairs of constructs, as shown in Table 2.7.

TABLE 2.3 Discriminant Validity and Correlation.

	AVE	ER	ES	EO	EP	PP
ER	0.68	**0.82**				
ES	0.56	0.65	0.75			
EO	0.72	0.58	0.59	**0.85**		
EP	0.76	0.55	0.60	0.65	**0.83**	
PP	0.67	0.71	0.69	0.75	0.73	0.87

Sources: Researcher's fieldwork (2021).

A confirmatory factor analysis (CFA) was used to test the construct's reliability and validity in order to assure measurement quality. CFA is a method of determining how well a set of measured variables accurately represents a set of constructs (Hair et al., 2010). Table 2.3 shows that the average variance extracted (AVE) for all factors is more than 0.5, demonstrating that the measurement indexes are convergently valid. To demonstrate discriminant validity, AVE values for two factors should be greater than the square of the correlation between the two factors (Hair et al., 2010). As seen in Table 2.3, AVE values between constructs are greater than squared correlation, indicating discriminant validity.

2.4.4 HYPOTHESIS RESULT

The study tested the three hypotheses using the structural equation modeling technique in Amos. The indicators used to measure the relations were t-tests, beta values (β), and probability values (p).

TABLE 2.4 Hypothesis/Paths.

Paths	Hypothesis	Original sample	Sample Mean (M)	SD	t-statistics	β	p-value
ER → PP	*H1*	0.193	0.202	0.060	12.47	0.45	0.002
ES → PP	*H2*	0.613	0.546	0.056	16.26	0.62	0.000
EO → PP	*H3*	0.611	0.603	0.076	13.42	0.51	0.001
EP → PP	*H4*	0.198	0.651	0.082	12.56	0.36	0.001

Sources: Researcher's fieldwork (2021).

Reports from the analysis from Table 2.4 show that e-requisitions have a significant and positive relation with procurement performance ($t = 12.47$, β

= 0.45, and p = 0.002). Hence, hypothesis one (H1) is supported. Secondly, reports from the analysis from Table 2.6 show that e-sourcing have significant and positive relation with procurement performance (t = 16.26, β = 0.62, and p = 0.000), supporting hypothesis two (H2). Finally, reports from the analysis from Table 2.6 show that e-ordering has a significant and positive relation with procurement performance (t = 13.42, β = 0.51, and p = 0.001), which confirms hypothesis three (H3). Finally, e-payment also has a significant and positive relation with procurement performance (t = 12.56, β = 0.36, and p = 0.001). The study therefore says that e-procurement has the ability to make oil and gas achieve procurement performance in Ghana.

2.5 SUMMARY OF FINDINGS

Furthermore, the study concludes that e-procurement had some impact on the number of suppliers as it makes the procurement process easy, reduces supply loss, enhances transparency in tender competition, increases transaction speed, standardizes supplies, reduces errors for supplier records, and ensures better services to suppliers. Reports from the analysis from Table 2.9 show that e-requisitions have a significant and positive relation with procurement performance (t = 12.47, β = 0.45, and p = 0.002). Hence, hypothesis one (H1) is supported. Secondly, reports from the analysis from Table 2.6 show that e-sourcing has a significant and positive relation with procurement performance (t = 16.26, β = 0.62, and p = 0.000), supporting hypothesis two (H2). Finally, reports from the analysis from Table 2.6 show that e-ordering has a significant and positive relation with procurement performance (t = 13.42, β = 0.51, and p = 0.001), which confirms hypothesis three (H3). Finally, e-payment also has a significant and positive relation with procurement performance (t = 12.56, β = 0.36, and p = 0.001).

2.6 CONCLUSIONS

The goal of this study was to unveil the effect of e-procurement on procurement performance in the oil and gas sector. It was shown in this study's findings that several aspects influence the deployment of e-procurement in the oil and gas firm sector. These factors include cost effectiveness; fewer errors; time savings; promotion of accountability; increased efficiency; transparency; and assurance of value for money. According to the findings of the study, the e-contract management and e-tendering programs were the two e-procurement initiatives that failed owing to inadequate technology. Finally, the study discovered that the impact of e-procurement on those involved in procurement includes the following: it simplifies the procurement process, reduces supply loss, increases transparency in tender competition, increases transaction speed, standardizes supplies, reduces errors in supplier records, and ensures better services to vendors. Oil and gas firms should put more emphasis on e-payment, e-ordering, and e-requisition since they lead to the procurement performance of their various service stations and other partners.

2.7 RECOMMENDATIONS

From the conclusions made above, the following recommendations are made: Oil and gas companies should increase their investments in e-procurement since it improves performance in oil and gas firms because it is cost effective, reduces errors, saves time, promotes accountability, increases efficiency, promotes transparency, and assures value for money.

The service stations should ensure that the automated procurement process should be specific to requisition, tendering, contract warding, and payment. The goal of the e-procurement in the institution should be to enhance the quality of service delivery and to provide timely, transparent, and accurate financial and accounting information. Further, it is recommended that the OMCs and service stations adopt a user-friendly information system that all suppliers can use with ease. This will reduce the bias on the use of electronic procurement, and all will embrace it.

Furthermore, improvements in technology, particularly in information and communication technology (ICT) infrastructures, should be advocated in order to make the e-procurement process easy and efficient. According to the findings of the study, service stations and suppliers (OMCs) should be educated on the importance of e-procurement because it simplifies the procurement process, reduces supply loss, increases transparency in tender competition, increases transaction speed, reduces errors in supplier records, and ensures better services.

APPENDIX: QUESTIONNAIRE

TAMALE TECHNICAL UNIVERSITY
SCHOOL OF BUSINESS
CENTER FOR PROFESSIONAL STUDIES (CPS)
ELECTRONIC PROCUREMENT AND PROCUREMENT PERFORMANCE IN THE OIL AND GAS INDUSTRY (A CASE STUDY OF TOTAL OIL SERVICE STATIONS IN TAMALE)

We are the final year Advanced Diploma in Chartered Institute of Logistic and Transport (CILT) of Tamale Technical University undertaking a research on the topic: *Electronic Procurement and Procurement Performance in the Oil and Gas Industry (A Case Study of Total Oil Service Stations in Tamale).*

This study serves in partial fulfillment for the award of Chartered Institute of Logistic and Transport. All information provided by the respondent will be used for academic purposes, and their privacy is highly guaranteed. Kindly provide the researchers with the needed information.

Thank you.

INSTRUCTION: Please tick (√) in the box and write wherever necessary.

Section 1

Gender	**Please tick**
Male	
Female	
Age	
21–25	
36–40	
26–30	
31–35	
41–44	
45 and above	
Working experience	
Less than 5 years	
6–10 years	
11–15 years	
18 and above years	
Education	
Diploma	
Degree	
Masters	
PhD	

Section 2

Please, in the following table, indicate your level of agreement or disagreement with the statement relating to e-procurement and procurement performance.

Constructs	1	2	3	4	5
E-requisition (ER)					
Eliminated long procedures in procurement					
Increased speed in the requisitioning process					
Enabled fast communication with suppliers					
Reduced time in procurement					
Reliability of spending information					
E-sourcing (ES)					
Reduces theft					
Reduces corruption					
Integrity in procurement has increased					
Lesser physical interaction between buyer and supplier					
Improved strategic procurement					
Improved procurement planning					
E-ordering (EO)					
Eliminated paper works					
Improved buyer/supplier relationship					
Improved procurement lead time					
E-payment (EP)					
Ensures transparency					
Fast payment for fuel and goods					
Easy to make payment to suppliers					
Customers get the flexibility to pay					
We hold less cash					
Procurement Performance (PP)					
Cost reduction					
Time reduction					
Increased speed in service delivery					
Activities are done quickly					
Responsiveness in obtaining supplies has increased					

Note: 1=strongly disagree, 2=disagree, 3=neutral, 4=agree, and 5=strongly agree.

KEYWORDS

- **E-procurement**
- **performance**
- **service**
- **sector**
- **gas**
- **e-payment**
- **e-sourcing**
- **e-ordering**
- **e-requisition**

REFERENCES

Ablo, A. D.. Local Content and Participation in Ghana's Oil and Gas Industry: Can Enterprise Development Make Difference? *Extract. Ind. Soc.* **2015,** *2* (2), 320–327.

Adam, M. A.. *Three Years of Petroleum Revenues Management in Ghana; Transparency Without Accountability*. African Centre for Energy Policy (ACEP), Accra, Ghana, 2014.

Adams, M. A.. Investment Challenges in the Oil and Gas Industry. Centre of Energy Economics and Policy, Accra, Ghana, 2009. https://www.ghanaweb.com/GhanaHomePage/features/InvestmentChallenges-In-The- Oil-And-Gas-Industry-170750.

African Trade Policy Notes. The Challenges of Ghana's Offshore Oil Discovery. http://Siteresources.worldbank.org/Intafrregtoptrade/Resources/14GhanaOilpolicynoteREVISED.pdf.

Afriani, Y.; Laba, A. R.; Aswan, A. The Effect of Managerial Ownership, Financial Performance, Corporate Competition on Stock Prices with Capital Structure as the Intervening Variable in the Coal Mining Companies Listed on the Indonesia Stock Hasanuddin. *J. Bus.Strat.* **2020,** *2* (1), 24–33.

American Petroleum Institute's Report. U.S Oil and Gas Infrastructure Investment Through 2035: An Engine for Economic Growth. American Petroleum Institute's: Washington, DC., 2017. https://www. icf.com/./reports./2017/us-oil-and-gas-infrastructure- investment-throug.

Amoako-Tuffour, J.. How Ghana Plans To Manage Its Petroleum Revenue. A Step Towards Transparency, Accountability and Government Standards. Institute of Economic Affair Ghana (IEA Monograph, no.26), 2011.

Amoako-Tuffour, J. et al.. Ghana's Petroleum Industry: The Prospects and Potential Impediments Towards Good Governance Standards. Ghana Policy, 2010.

Amponsah, O. Ghana's Downstream Petroleum Sector: Assessment of Key Supply Chain Challenges and Prospects for Growth. *Int. J. Manag. Bus. Stud.* **2014,** *7* (3), 441–448.

Ahi, P.; Searcy, C. A Comparative Literature Analysis of Definitions for Green and Sustainable Supply Chain Management. *J. Clean. Produ.* **2013,** 329–341.

Aliyu, A. A.; Muhammad, U. B.; Rozilah, K.; Ma, D. Positivist and Non-Positivist Paradigm in Social Science Research: Conflicting Paradigms or Perfect Partners? *J. Manag. Sustain.* **2014,** *79*.

Anadarko. Funnet June 30, 2017, 2016. https://www.anadarko.com/content/documents/apc/Operations/2016-AnnualReport.pdf

Anand, S.; Sen, A. *Human Development and Economic Sustainability*; World Development, 2000; pp 2029–2049.

Anderson, M. G.; Katz, P. B. Strategic Sourcing. *Int. J. Logist. Manag.* **1998,** *9* (1) 1–13.

Bai, C.; Sarkis, J. Integrating Sustainability into Supplier Selection with Grey System and Rough Set Methodologies. *Int. J. Prod. Econ.* **2010,** 252–264.

Bailey, K. D. *Methods of Social Research*, Redigert av 3rd.; The Free Press: New York.

Ball, A.; Broadbent, J.; Jarvis, T. Waste Management, the Challenges of the PFI and 'Sustainability Reporting. *Bus. Strat. Environ.* **2006,** 258–274.

Barraket, J.; Weissman, J. Social Procurement and Its Implications for Social Enterprise: A Literature Review [Working Paper No. CPNS48].» The Australian Centre for Philanthropy and Nonprofit Studies, 2009.

Bedwei, A. Tax Guide for Petroleum Operations in Ghana. Price Water Coppers (PWC), 2017. https://www.pwc.com/gh/en/assets/pdf/2017-tax-guide-for-petroleum-operations-in-ghana.pdf

Cardoso, A. L.; Biazzin, C. What Is the Value of E-Procurement for Suppliers? The Drivers, Barriers and Opportunities for Engaging MRO Suppliers. *Int. J. Procurement Manag.* **2020,** *5* (7), 1–20.

Centre for Policy Analysis (CEPA). Ghana: The Emerging Oil Economy Prospects and Challenges. No. 22, 2010. http://www.cepa. org.gh

Central Intelligence Agency. World Factbook. Funnet July 31, 2017. https://www.cia.gov/library/publications/the-world-factbook/fields/2244.html.

CEO, Tullow. Sustainability. Funnet May 20, 2018. https://www.tullowoil.com/sustainability.

Charmaz, K.; Belgrave, L. L. Grounded Theory, 2015. https://doi.org/10.1002/9781405165518.wbeosg070.pub2.

Cho, J.; Kang, J. Benefits and Challenges of Global Sourcing: Perceptions of US Apparel Retail Firms. *Int. Market. Rev.* **2001,** 542–561.

Ghana National Petroleum Corporation. Introduction to Ghana Oil and Gas Industry; Framework for Oil and Gas, 2015. https://www.gnpcghana. com/speeches/gnpcug.pdf.

Ghana National Petroleum Corporation. Ghana's Oil and Gas Industry; History, Current & Future Trends. https://www.gnpcghana.com/speeches/gnpcug. pdf (accessed on 4 Dec 2017).

Ghana Statistical Service. Annual Gross Domestic Product (accessed on 10 Nov 2017).

Harelimana, J. B. The Impact of E-Procurement on the Performance of Public Institutions in Rwanda. *Glob. J. Manag. Bus. Res.: D Account. Audit.* **2018,** *18* (2).

Institute of Economic Affairs-Ghana. *Natural Resource Management in Ghana: A Case for Constitutional amendment*; Accra, 2010.

Kituzi, A. E. Influence of E-Procurement on Organizational Performance: The Case of Kenya Association of Manufacturers Firms in Nairobi County, Kenya. Master's Thesis, University of Nairobi.

NPA. NPA. Funnet August 7, 2017. http://www.npa.gov.gh/about-npa.

Ombat, K. O. The Relationship Between Procurement Systems and Performance of Procurement Function in Commercial Banks in Kenya. *Int. J. Econ. Comm. Manag.* **2015,** *3* (12), 697–723.

Ofosu-Peasah, G.. Mapping Ghana's Oil and Gas Revenue to Expenditure: The Case of the Heritage Fund, 2017. www.reportingoilandgas. org/wp-content/uploads/Mapping-Ghanas-Oil2017–11–15.

Ofosu-Peasah, G. Budget Analysis on the Upstream Oil and Gas Sector: Gaps, Red Flags, and Implications, 2018. at http://www.reportingoilandgas.org/rog- publications/budget-analysis-onthe-upstream-oil-and-gas-sector-gaps-red-flags-and-implications/

Petroleum (Local Content and Local Participation) Regulations 2013, L.I 2204. Funnet June 10, 2017. http://www.petrocom.gov.gh/pdfs/13-Local-Content-and-Local-ParticipationRegulations-L_I-2204.pdf

Petroleum Commission Ghana. Funnet August 7, 2017. http://www.petrocom.gov.gh/index.html.

Pezzey, J. Economic Analysis of Sustainable Growth and Sustainable Development (Environment Department Working Paper No. 15); World Bank: Washington, DC.

Phillips, N.; Hardy, C. *Discourse Analysis: Investigating Processes of Social Construction*; Sage: London.

Poch, M.; Comas, J.; Rodriguez-Roda, I.; Sanchez-Marre, M.; Cortés, U. Designing and Building Real Environmental Decision Support Systems. *Environ. Model. Softw* **2004,** 857–873.

Porter, M. E. America's Green Strategy. *Sci. Am.* **1991,** *96.*

Public Procurement Act 2003, Act 663. Funnet May 16, 2018. https://www.ppaghana.org/documents/Public%20Procurement%20Act%202003%20Act %20663.pdf

Public Procurement Act 2016, Act 914 (Amendment). Funnet May 16, 2018. http://www.ppaghana.org/documents/ACT663_RePrinted.pdf.

Putnam, R. *Bowling Alone*. Simon and Schuster: New York, 2000.

Rao, P. Greening the Supply Chain: A New Initiative in South East Asia. *Int. J. Oper. Prod. Manag.* **2002,** 632–655.

Republic of Ghana. Petroleum (Local Content and Local Participation) Regulations. Funnet July 5, 2017, 2013. http://www.petrocom.gov.gh/pdfs/13-Local-Content-and-LocalParticipation-Regulations-L_I-2204.pdf

Supply, Chartered Institute of Purchasing. *Supply Chain Diligence*; Profex Publishing Limited, 2012.

The Constitution of the Republic Of Ghana. Funnet June 30, 2017, 1992. http://www.jsg.gov.gh/constitution/chapter/chap_21.htm.

TOR. Funnet August 5, 2017. http://www.tor.com.gh/about-tor/company-profile/.

Tullow. Funnet May 25, 2018. https://www.tullowoil.com/about-us; Funnet June 20, 2018, 2015. https://www.tullowoil.com/Media/docs/defaultsource/3_investors/financials/2015/tullow- oil-five-year-financial-summary.pdf?sfvrsn=2.

Tullow Ghana. Tullow Oil. Funnet June 30, 2017. http://www.tullowoil.com/operations/west-africa/ghana.

Tullow. Local Content Q&A. Funnet April 20, 2018. https://www.tullowoil.com/suppliers/local-content-q-a

Tullow Oil PLC. Funnet June 30, 2017, 2015. https://www.tullowoil.com/Media/docs/defaultsource/3_investors/2015-annual- report/tullow-oil-2015-annual-report-andaccounts.pdf?sfvrsn=2.

Tullow Oil. TEN Field. Funnet June 29, 2017. http://www.tullowoil.com/operations/westafrica/ghana/ten-field

Tullow Oil. Funnet July 30, 2017. http://www.tullowoil.com/operations/westafrica/ghana.

Tullow Oil, Plc. Code of Ethical Conduct. 1 Oct. Funnet April 16, 2018, 2015. https://www.tullowoil.com/Media/docs/default-source/1_About_us/tullow-oilcode-of-ethical-conduct.pdf?sfvrsn=2.

Tullow. Sustainability. Funnet May 10, 2018. https://www.tullowoil.com/sustainability

United Nations. Ghana Sustainable Energy for All Action Plan, 2012. www.energycom.gov.gh/files/Se4all-Ghanaactionplan.pdf 2017–12–13.

White, D. Tax Guide for Petroleum Operations in Ghana. Price water Coppers (PWC), 2011, 2015. https://www.pwc.com/gh/en/pdf/ghana-petroltax-guide-2011.pdf.

World Bank Team. International Development Project Appraisal Document, Ghana, 2015. http://documents.worldbank.org/.../PAD1373-PAD-IDA-R2015- 0095–1-P151447- Box3914.

Vestre, V. H.. *A Critical Assessment of Outsourcing in the Oil & Gas Industry*; University Of Stavanger: Stavanger, 2016.

CHAPTER 3

Blockchain (BC) on Supply Chain Management (SCM)

ADAM OSMAN OSCAR, MUSTAPHA ABDUL AZIZ, and ABUKARI INUSAH

Department of Logistics and Procurement Management, Tamale Technical University, Tamale, Ghana

ABSTRACT

The purpose of this chapter is to discuss the benefits of blockchain (BC) on supply chain management. A BC is a distributed ledger that records transactions between users in a way that is both permanent and decentralized. BC, at its core, eliminates the need for third-party middlemen in the validation and recording of transactions. Businesses may ensure continued rapid expansion by developing supply networks that can easily adjust to the ever-shifting demands of the market. Our findings underline the importance of digital leadership in explaining the contribution of various BC technology characteristics to trust-building and supply chain flexibility and lend support to the hypothesis that the transparency and security of information provided by BC technology has an impact on both. BC technology is being implemented for the sake of absolute transparency.

3.1 INTRODUCTION

The term "supply chain management (SCM)" refers to the coordination of the flow of goods, money, and data from their point of origin to the end user. Procurement, shipping, inventories and warehousing administration, border checks, and distribution are all components of SCs (Fernandez, 2022). Organizations, ministries, and various divisions within each contribute to the smooth operation of the SC. However, 62% of businesses said they have

New Age Technology in Supply Chain Management: Digital Transformation Tools in Perspective. Mohammed Majeed (Ed.)

poor visibility into their SCs (Delfis, 2017). BC, in principle, is a decentralized digital record stored in cryptocurrency that may be used for tracking, exchanging commitments, creating smart contracts, and making payments. The blocks that eventually form a BC are where the transactions are stored. BC technology helps eliminate disputes that occur when several edits are made simultaneously from various machines inside a distributed database (Peters and Panayi, 2015). Both BCs and distributed databases have similarities, including their reliance on a network of computers for their functionality and upkeep. Global trade relies on physical papers such as letters of credit (LC) and intermediaries involved in such operations enable the functioning of trade. By removing the need for brokers and physical document verification, BC technology has the potential to revolutionize the global SC ecosystem.

The management of the SC has been increasingly digitized by businesses and governments since the end of the 20th century (Fernandez, 2022). Changes in the SC can be made for the better thanks to new technologies. The implementation of BC technology in the SC could increase SC visibility and traceability while decreasing overhead (Laaper, 2023). Scholars, managers, and professionals from all around the world are interested in BC technologies (Wamba et al., 2020). It is widely understood by these actors that BC is not a buzzword, but a highly disruptive technology that is already reconstructing the businesses and their SC business models. Despite significant progress over the past few years, BC applications pertaining to operations and supply chain management (OSCM) are still in their infancy and should investigate potential uses (Fernandez, 2022; Ismagilova et al., 2019; Zhao et al., 2016; Yli-Huumo et al. 2016).

Moreover, the majority of the literature we analyzed focused on BC technology in the context of Bitcoin and other cryptocurrencies. However, previous academic research has rarely touched upon other applications of BC technology, particularly corporate applications. As a result, a deeper investigation into the potential benefits of BC technology for various commercial applications is warranted.

3.2 LITERATURE

3.2.1 BC

Simply put, BC is a decentralized, encrypted, and consensus-based database that may be used to store any kind of transactional data or other information (Swan, 2015). It is a data structure that combines data records, called blocks, in a chain and was developed in 2008 by Satoshi Nakamoto, the anonymous author of the Bitcoin white paper. The "chain" is a digital distribution database or list of entries that users or members maintain over a distributed computing network. When it comes to processing and verifying ledger transactions, BCs rely on encryption. BC is an immutable digital ledger of transactions that is distributed across a network and protected by sophisticated cryptography (Pilkington, 2016). BC technology is an additional layer of the web. Each "block" is connected to the next through a chain. Like database records, data is organized into sets within a block. While there may be multiple data sets within a block, for the sake of clarity this chapter will assume that there is only one data set per block. All three of BC's defining characteristics—decentralization, verification, and immutability—are highlighted in this concise explanation. The BC can be thought of as an extra layer that can be added to preexisting enterprise resource planning systems. Proof-of-provenance, for instance, is a digital enterprise platform that has been helping companies increase the visibility and traceability of their products and SCs thanks to BC technology since 2013. It aids companies in being open and honest on three fronts: with customers, with their products, and with individual items. Using Provenance's (2015) immutable data ledger, businesses are able to quickly and easily collect data, open data, and verify crucial information. According to Provenance, "a six-month pilot for tracking responsible sourcing of tuna

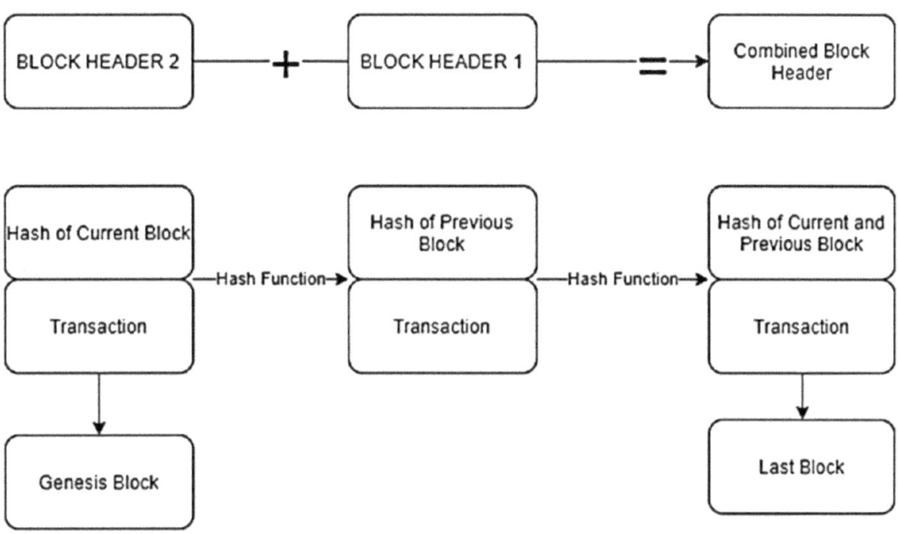

FIGURE 3.1 Framework of BC architecture.

Source: Adapted from Giri and Manohar (2021, p. 3).

in Indonesia via BC" is now complete (Laaper and Fitzgerald, 2017). Important data for all parties can be updated in real time, eliminating the need for time-consuming and prone-to-error reconciliation processes with each party's internal records (Casey and Wong, 2017). As a result, everyone in the network has much better and more up-to-date insight into what's going on. For this reason, SCM scholars are focusing a lot of their attention on this area because it can be a source of large data that is extremely useful to businesses and SCs (Kache and Seuring, 2017).

3.2.2 *SCM*

By managing the entire production process, from the procurement of raw materials to the distribution of the finished product or service, we refer to this as SCM. It also manages the transfer of money, communications, and resources related to a product or service. Although logistics is an integral aspect of the SC, it is easy to overlook this fact because of its frequent association with the SC (Singh, 2022). Planning, sourcing, producing, distributing, and after-sales support are all components of conventional SCM systems that provide for centralized control of the SC. Further, due to its immutable ledger, BC may be issued to track and trace the origin of products, as well as to detect counterfeits and other forms of fraud across the SC. Business owners face challenges when transporting temperature-sensitive goods like cheese (Singh, 2022).

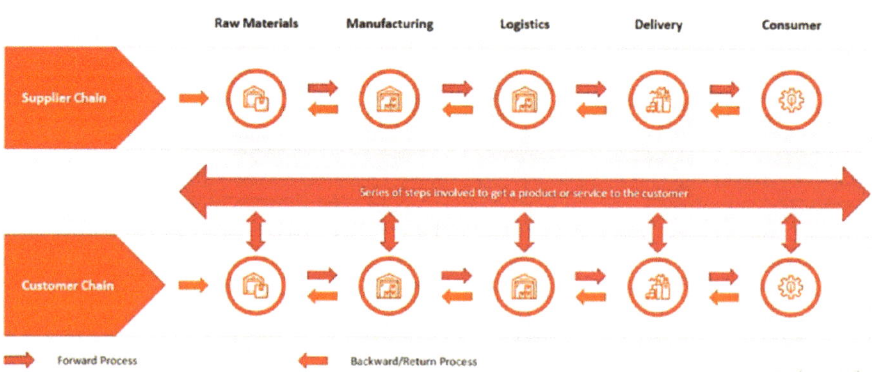

FIGURE 3.2 Supply chain.

Source: PowerSlides https://powerslides.com/wp-content/uploads/2020/08/Supply-Chain-Diagram-Template-1.jpg

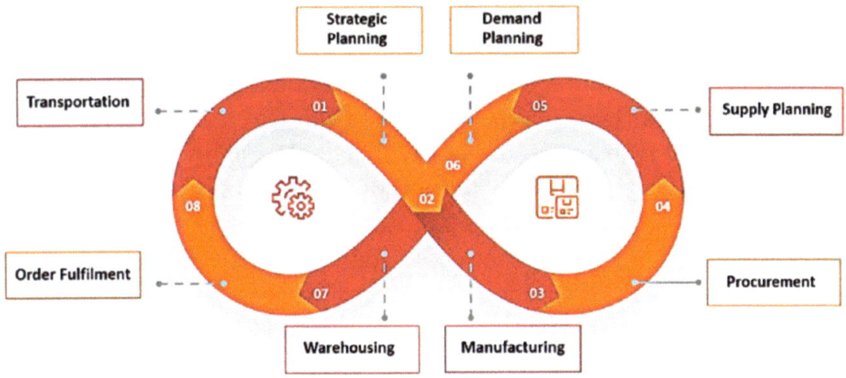

FIGURE 3.3 Supply chain.

Source: PowerSlides https://powerslides.com/wp-content/uploads/2020/08/Supply-Chain-Diagram-Template-4.jpg

3.2.3 BC-BASED SCM

BC-based SCs, in contrast to traditional SCs, will immediately reflect any modifications made in the data transaction records. The term "BC" is used to describe a system that shares database information among all stakeholders in a network (Crosby et al., 2016). There is real-time, comprehensive transaction data available to all parties involved. In the past, all of the information concerning a given transaction was kept in one single location and only made available to those directly involved in that transaction. There are four main players in BC-based SCs, including two that aren't present in traditional SCs. Providers of individualized identification numbers for participants in a network. Groups that establish norms and regulations, such as Fairtrade for environmentally friendly SCs or the policies and technical specifications for BC technology. Certifying bodies, or agencies, that validate the credentials of potential members in a SC. System actors (such as producers, sellers, and buyers) need to be verified by an independent auditor or certifier (Steiner and Baker, 2015). In contrast to Bitcoin and other financial BC applications, which may be open to anybody, SC networks built on BC technology may require a closed, private, and permissioned BC with restricted access and players. However, a more inclusive range of collaborations is not impossible. The automation of governance standards and the increased trustworthiness and transparency of the BC are designed to improve the efficiency with which goods and data may move along the SC. As a result of this change, the economy may move from one based on mass-produced, low-quality goods to one based on individualized service. Knowledge, communication, and information, rather than the physical properties of materials, will play a larger role in the manufacturing process (Pazaitis et al., 2017). By being able to keep tabs on their purchases, buyers can feel more confident about the things they buy because of their dependable quality (Tian, 2016). A financial-ledger system doesn't store all of the facts of a transaction, but a BC does since it consists of a chronological string of blocks that integrate all three types of flows in the transaction. In addition, the BC is distributed in an encrypted form, with each participant keeping their copy. As a result of these characteristics, the BC can be relied upon to produce an unalterable record of the three types of SC activity. The ownership transfer in the BC-based SC model can be carried out automatically by means of a smart contract. When a change of ownership occurs, the BC-based records can be updated by the relevant certifying bodies and registration authorities. This way, there's no way for anyone along the distribution chain to tamper with any of the records from the moment they were created (Akhtar et al., 2021).

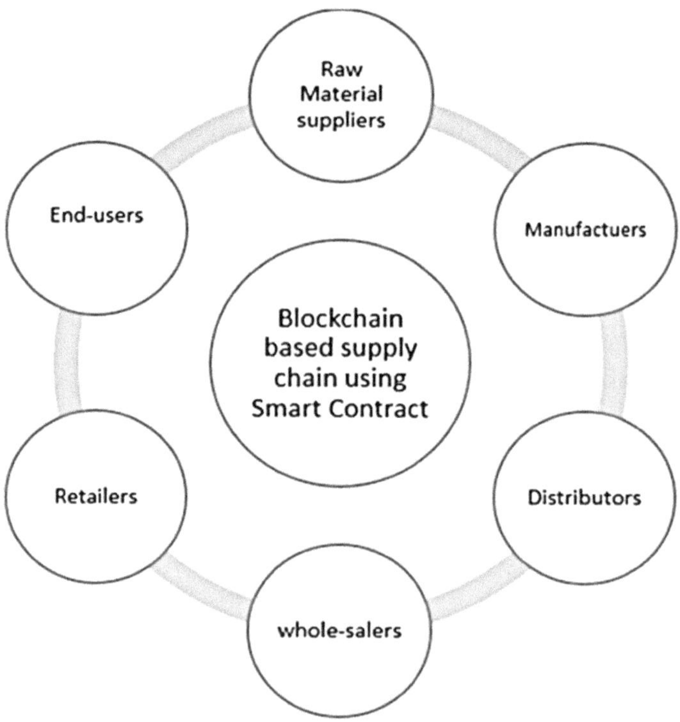

FIGURE 3.4 BC-based SCM.

Source: Reprinted from Anand et al., 2022. https://creativecommons.org/licenses/by/4.0/

3.3 CHARACTERISTICS OF BC

3.3.1 CONSENSUS

To be legally binding, a transaction requires the consent of all involved parties. Without this agreement, no new blocks can be added or updated (Morley, 2021). It also means that when a change is made, everyone involved is aware of it and is fine with it. Each transaction is unanimously deemed valid by all parties in the chain (Morley, 2020). Payment, inventory management, shipping, and more can all benefit from the consensus that BC technology can bring to the SC. Common descriptions of BC refer to it as "one version of the truth" for all products. It's a way to keep track of documents like bills of lading and receipts for cash transactions. Serialization, transport, receipt, and installation are all automatically monitored. These tenets of trust, openness, and audibility form the bedrock of the system.

A BC's consensus facilitates fair and expedited decision-making across the network. The goal of the decision-making process known as "consensus" is to help the network's active nodes conclude as quickly and efficiently as possible so that the network can function normally (Shardeum, 2022). Though they may not trust one another, nodes in a network can put their faith in the algorithm that controls its operations. Without a consensus algorithm, a BC would be useless.

3.3.2 UNANIMOUS

Before a new record may be included in the network, all existing members must verify its accuracy. Public BCs are decentralized, thus it's important that everyone on the network to consent on the same shared state of the BC. One of the most important aspects of BC technology is the consensus reached among all nodes in the network, which results in a single BC holding data (exchanges) that has been validated and is, according to the network, accurate (Shardeum, 2022). If a node wants to add a block to the network, it needs to win approval from the majority of other nodes. There is no easy way for a node to modify or remove its own data from the network. All of the records are revised at once, and the changes spread rapidly through the system. Therefore, no modification can be made without the agreement of the vast majority of the channel's nodes. Adding new blocks of data to a BC relies on consensus, which guarantees that each new block represents the undisputed truth that has been verified by every node in the network (Shardeum, 2022).

3.3.3 FASTER SETTLEMENT

There are many potential failure modes in conventional SC systems, such as the fact that it can take several days to process a transaction once all settlements have been made. However, unlike conventional institutions, BC allows for instantaneous settlement (Joshi, 2022). This convenience added by BC technology is appreciated. Many industries have found uses for it because of its verifiability, trustworthiness, and resistance to manipulation. It's a cornerstone of safer, more efficient, and more productive corporate and government processes (Joshi, 2022). In other words, it cuts out the middleman, which speeds up transactions and improves their efficiency. This fundamental aspect of BC is extremely useful since it allows companies to better monitor their transactions and data. The speed of transactions increases the scope.

3.3.4 PROVENANCE

In reality, traceability back to the source is the single most important factor in the logistics industry. With BC technology, you can track the origin and current location of your goods throughout the SC. Provenance allows anyone working in the SC to swiftly determine when and who had possession of an item (Morley, 2020). Provenance can be tied to any item within a SC, whether it be iron ore, food, money, machinery, or intellectual property.

3.3.5 DISTRIBUTED LEDGER

All details of a deal and its participants can usually be found in a public ledger. There is no escaping the public eye now. Private or federated BCs have a slightly different use case. A large number of people may still discern the truth behind the books in such situations. Because everyone else on the network is responsible for updating the ledger. As a result, the computational load was spread across many machines, leading to a more accurate result. To ensure total openness, each member of the network has access to their copy of the ledger. All network users and their respective transactions can be seen in a public ledger. The increased accuracy is guaranteed by the computers' combined processing power. Distributed ledger is a key component of BCs for several reasons, as outlined by Joshi (2022). Because of how quickly ledger updates propagate in a distributed ledger, monitoring the ledger's activity is a breeze. Every computer in a BC network must take part in updating and validating the distributed ledger. Because the BC relies on a decentralized network of users to record transactions, any changes made to the ledger are immediately reflected. When a user initiates a transaction to add a new block, it must be validated by other nodes in the network before it can be added. A majority of the nodes in the BC system must agree to add a new block to the chain. Nothing in a BC network will give any node preferential treatment. To add a new block to the network, everyone must stick to the established protocol. In the face of fraud or tampering, a distributed ledger reacts admirably. It's simple to keep track of the ledger's activity with so many nodes because the ledger cannot be altered and the data is updated instantly. In this setup, nodes check the ledger for accuracy (Iredale, 2021). When someone wishes to add a new block, others need to check it out and give it the thumbs up before it can be included in the chain. With this, the user is guaranteed an equal opportunity to participate. When it comes to the network, nobody is above the law. Blocks are added by following the standard procedures. Not because you're more powerful does not automatically grant you greater perks. Each participating node is responsible for updating and validating the BC's distributed ledger. By eliminating the intermediaries, the system can respond more quickly. Within minutes, or even seconds, the ledger is updated to reflect any changes that were made.

3.3.6 IMMUTABILITY

Changing the data in a distributed ledger is extremely difficult. Every entry has numerous duplicates, and all of them must be updated at once. The BC is an immutable ledger that cannot be altered once it has been created. The "blocks" in a BC are the building blocks of the system (Joshi, 2022). Reversing the effects of a BC transaction requires a new transaction to be recorded. If you use BC technology in the SC, it will be very impossible to forge any kind of financial transaction, inventory record, warehouse environment, delivery time, etc. (Morley, 2020).

3.3.7 TRACEABILITY

By mapping and visualizing business supply networks, traceability boosts operational efficiency. More and more shoppers want to know where their goods come from. By providing authentic, verifiable, and unchangeable data, BC technology aids businesses in comprehending their SC and connecting with customers.

3.3.8 DECENTRALIZATION

Since there is no centralized authority making choices for the BC network, everyone has a voice in the process. Instead, a collection of nodes creates and maintains the network. In a BC network, every node has a shared, identical copy of the ledger. Joshi (2022) argues that the BC's many benefits might be attributed to the decentralization of its nodes. Since a BC network is automated and invulnerable to human error, it is a very efficient and reliable system. Due to its decentralized design, the BC network experiences fewer outages. Because of the increased cost of attacking the system, successful attacks are more often. Since there isn't a middleman, the system is safer. Due to BC's distributed structure, it's easy to make a public record of every user on the network. This makes it easier to track down the source of each given alteration. Users no longer need to rely on a third party to administer and maintain their properties.

Because it doesn't rely on humans to perform calculations, the BC is particularly resilient to errors. As a result, this system rarely produces unexpected failures due to random causes. Thanks to decentralization, individuals are finally masters of their domains. They are not reliant on outside parties to take care of their property. Everyone is capable of working independently at the same time. Not as prone to failure. It is possible that the problems plaguing frameworks that are overly dependent on explicit labor could be mitigated via decentralization. Critical failures may occur as a result of these vulnerabilities, such as the inability to supply promised administrations or wasteful assistance because of asset tiredness, periodic blackouts, blockages, a lack of suitable motivations for outstanding service, or fraud. BC technology is impervious to harm because of its decentralized nature. This is because it is more difficult and costly for hackers to launch an assault on the system. As a result, it will function for longer before breaking. There isn't any outside interference. The technology's decentralized design means it may function independently of any outside entities, eliminating one potential source of failure. Given that the system is algorithmic in nature, there is no way to be defrauded. BC technology cannot be used for private gain (Iredale, 2021).

3.3.9 TRANSPARENCY

BC technology is being implemented for the sake of absolute transparency. A major reason for this is the increased openness to information that BC technology brings to financial markets. Users of a network can check the balances and see the transactions for certain public addresses by using a tool called a "block explorer" (Shardeum, 2022). Through the use of a block explorer, one can investigate the structure, contents, and other pertinent aspects of a BC. The information included in a block is used as a transaction record in a BC. The most important part is that the chain is not dominated by any single entity (Shardeum, 2022). Transparency allows for the collection and dissemination of essential data, such as certificates and claims, thereby fostering trust. When something is added to the BC, impartial attester nodes can verify its legitimacy. Data may be updated and verified in real-time. The distributed nature of modern technology makes it simple to create an accurate profile of every player. The BC adds a physical element to the process as every change can be observed (Iredale, 2021). The system is unique since it may be used anywhere. And cracking it will be an extremely difficult task for hackers.

3.3.10 SECURITY

Since it eliminates the necessity for a governing body, anyone can unilaterally alter the network to serve their own interests. Since BC relies on a decentralized network of nodes, data is constantly replicated across numerous nodes to ensure that the original data is safe in the event that any single node is compromised. A further safeguard for the system is provided by its use of encryption (Shardeum, 2022). Each block in the BC is encrypted separately. Encryption provides an extra safeguard for the BC network as a whole. While there may be no one to stop you from altering or erasing information on the network, this does not mean that anything goes (Joshi, 2022). Since the BC hashes all data cryptographically, each record in the ledger may be uniquely identified on the system. Each block has its own unique hash as well as the hash from the prior block. This feature ensures the blocks are cryptographically connected. It is nearly hard to alter the data without also altering all of the hash IDs. All the blocks in a BC are encrypted separately. Encryption is used throughout the BC network to ensure the safety of all operations. One of the most appealing aspects of BC as it currently exists is that it makes the internet a more secure place for its users (Web 2.0). The BC network validates and updates itself automatically every few minutes, which helps to create a self-reviewing system and is yet another important benefit of BC technology's secure environment. It helps provide a very stable system. Due to being embedded in the network, all data is accessible to anyone. And thus it helps with openness.

3.3.11 TRADABILITY

The capacity to trade goods and services is a distinctive feature of BC that transforms the conventional market model. To "tokenize" an asset means to divide it into digitally represented shares of ownership, which can be done with BC technology. This form of fractional ownership permits tokens to reflect the value of a shareholder's stake in a specific object in the same way that a stock market permits the trading of a company's shares. Users can transfer ownership of an asset without actually having to transfer the underlying physical token.

3.3.12 FINALITY

All of the duplicates of the public ledger reflect the same, accurate picture of events. As a result, there is greater trust in the transaction as a whole. BC technology provides immutability, which helps resolve SCM conflicts and fosters stronger connections among all parties involved.

3.3.13 BENEFITS OF BC IN SCM

The paradigm shift brought about by BC is seen as both a difficult barrier and an advantage. For example, BC has the potential to greatly enhance things like openness, accountability, trust, safety, effectiveness, and economy (Kshetri, 2018). Furthermore, BC technology is seen as a solution for SCM track and trace difficulties (Lu and Xu, 2017) and for creating closer and more trustworthy relationships not only between businesses and their suppliers but throughout the entire SCM (Aste et al., 2017; Wang et al., 2019). One could argue that the introduction of a cryptocurrency-shared ledger (a script that can trigger a transaction) could greatly improve the efficiency and decentralization of SCM. However, when integrated with other emerging technologies (such as big data analytics, the Internet of Things, and cyber-physical systems), BC has the potential to have far-reaching, disruptive effects across all industries (Laaper, 2023). The BC is a decentralized, immutable digital log of transactions that is protected from modification by cryptography (Pilkington, 2016). The three most crucial characteristics of a BC are highlighted here: decentralization, verification, and immutability (Liu and Li, 2019). The immutability of BC records allows for an open and honest SC. All transactions along the SC are recorded safely, allowing for quick diagnosis of logistical problems and resolution. The same is true when acquiring components or raw materials; doing so helps with accountability, transparency, and reducing the likelihood of illicit conduct (Getsmarter, 2022). Important product and SC data can be collected, stored, and managed with the help of BC technology. In this technical setting, all parties involved in the SC can enjoy openness, transparency, impartiality, dependability, and safety (Abeyratne and Monfared, 2016). By integrating a BC with IoT, equipment like smart sensors and RFID tags may more accurately record the dates and conditions under which products pass through the various points in the SC (temperature, vibration, humidity, and so on). This information is subsequently added to the BC, where it can be monitored in near-real time by means of smart contracts. BC technology's decentralized nature can be useful in developing a transparent payment system that allows all parties participating in a given SC to view payment transactions, hence eliminating fraud and human error. Plus, participants in the SC can make payments to one another in BC-based cryptocurrencies without going via banks, which cuts down on transaction fees and speeds up the payment process.

By digitizing real assets and creating a decentralized immutable record of all transactions, businesses can use BC to improve the transparency and accuracy of end-to-end tracking along the SC, from the point of production to the point of delivery or use by the end user (Laaper, 2023). The improved visibility into the SC benefits both companies and consumers. Integrated payment systems expedite the shipping of goods by shortening the time it takes from placing an order to receiving payment. In addition to these benefits, businesses can save money on legal expenses and penalties for late tax payments, and they can prevent counterfeiting and fraud with the assistance of BC and smart contracts. Radio-frequency identification (RFID) tags employ electromagnetic fields to uniquely identify and track objects, and they are compatible with BC (Getsmarter, 2022). These are commonly used to record data pertaining to a product and to confirm when ownership or possession has changed hands. When an item with an RFID code is delivered and automatically scanned, the smart contract is considered to have been completed (Getsmarter, 2022). Using a shared BC network, manufacturers and retailers may safely document data like a product's nutrient content, country of origin, quality, and whether or not it contains allergies. Plus, when consumers can see where their purchases come from, they can be assured that they are supporting ethical businesses. It can be difficult to coordinate the distribution of commodities, the price of items, and the payment of providers in SCs because of the large number of suppliers, middlemen, and third-party services involved. Typically, businesses have to wait weeks, if not months, to be paid after sending out an invoice. However, if smart contracts built on the BC are established, payments can be sent instantly.

Diamonds and pharmaceutical medications are two examples of high-value commodities where enhanced SC transparency enabled by BC could significantly reduce fraud. With the use of BC technology, businesses may track the flow of raw materials and completed goods through each subcontractor, thereby cutting down on losses due to counterfeiting and gray market transactions and boosting consumer confidence (Laaper, 2023). By eliminating the need for intermediaries in business transactions, BC improves the efficiency of supply networks around the world. It also allows for better data sharing and collaboration among different parties involved in the finance and logistics industries (Getsmarter, 2022). In the context of the logistics industry, "traceability" means the ability to track where goods have been and where they are currently stored. It entails keeping tabs on goods as they make their way from suppliers to retailers to end users across a number of different countries and regions (Singh, 2022). Information gathering via BT is possible. Organizational skills and performance can be enhanced with the use of shared information gathered from across different enterprises.

In addition, contract manufacturing outsourcing allows organizations to keep more of a tight rein on production. With BC, everyone in a SC can see the same data, which might cut down on miscommunications and mistransfers (Laaper, 2023). As a result, more time and resources may be devoted to delivering products and services of higher quality at lower costs (Singh, 2022). One of the most important advantages of BC-driven SC improvements is traceability. Since BC is made up of distributed, open-source ledgers that store data that may be replicated by its users, transactions can be processed instantly. It includes factors like consumers' opinions, interactions, and satisfaction with eco-friendly goods and services (Treiblmaier, 2019). BT is used by all parties involved in satisfying end-user requirements. Each part functions independently to meet the needs of its own set of customers. Customer loyalty, customer retention, and customer relationship management are just a few of the goals that many groups have when it comes to their clientele. The success of your company's customers may depend on these individual goals (Kamble et al., 2019). BT is a tool for reaching high levels of client satisfaction. As an illustration, BC has the potential to boost both client pleasure and loyalty (Kouhizedeh and Sarkis, 2018).

In addition to lowering costs and risks, automating procedures and increasing openness and credibility in SCM are all possible thanks to BC technology. SCM is facilitated by the ability to track a wide variety of data, including but not limited to prices, dates, locations, quality, certification, and many more. The use of BC technology can enhance SC visibility and efficiency, reduce counterfeit and grey market losses, and strengthen SC traceability. In conclusion, BC can facilitate an efficient audit of SC data, which in turn can improve administrative operations and decrease expenses (Laaper, 2023). By centralizing all essential data in one place, a distributed ledger can drastically reduce the time it takes to complete processes like manually checking for compliance or credit, which can presently take weeks.

3.4 DISCUSSIONS

BT has been heralded as a way to combat challenges including product counterfeiting and the lack of visibility into subsupplier operations in multitier supply networks (Francisco and Swanson, 2018; Toyoda et al., 2017; Kshetri, 2018). Digital ledger BC technology offers transparent, honest, and immutable records of the provenance of physical assets (Sultan et al., 2018), which enhances the reliability of logistics data and ensures that all transactions are legitimate. The fight against counterfeiting, environmental damage, faulty goods, etc., can all benefit from the adoption of BC technology because of its ability to track a product's history. Parties working together on a unified platform could significantly cut down on inefficiencies like wasted time, extra money, and mistakes caused by human error. Fewer people involved in the SC means less opportunity for fraud. The technology has a number of advantages, including reduced expenditures (Kshetri, 2019), improved longevity (Saberi et al., 2019), and increased profitability. Because BC databases are distributed, authenticity may be determined even if no single entity can lay claim to the SC's data. This makes BC technology promising for providing extremely secure and immutable access to SC data (Kim and Laskowski, 2016). When fraud does occur, however, thorough records help companies identify the perpetrator. Despite the inflated expectations, the use of BT in SCs and logistics is expected to continue growing around the world (Bauer et al., 2020). In addition to providing a network using BT with visibility, transparency, traceability, and security, BC Technology (BT) also boasts a distributed ledger that can store data, digital and smart contracts, and asymmetric encryption (Dutta et al., 2020; Katsaliaki et al., 2021). The majority of studies (Aste et al., 2017; Wang et al., 2019) have concluded that incorporating BC technology into SCM is an effective way to reduce operational costs, increase efficiency, and enhance SC security and transparency. A lot of researchers (Abeyratne and Monfared, 2016; Kakulapati, 2018; Kache and Seuring, 2017) agree that BC helps SC stakeholders keep track of crucial data like pricing, dates, locations, quality, certification, and more. Better SCM is possible thanks to BC technology, which increases SC visibility and efficiency and reduces counterfeit and grey market losses.

3.5 IMPLICATIONS

Organizations can gain a competitive edge and strengthen their market position by adopting BC technology before their rivals. However, before deciding whether or not to implement BC, managers should look closely at the specifics of their products, services, and supply networks. Organizations need to invest in human capital knowledge to create, deploy, and fully leverage applications of this technology. As a result of BC technology, platforms to promote may now easily and securely share and verify crucial bits of data. In contrast, they can do so without appointing an intermediary and navigating the intricate negotiations and power maneuvers inherent in establishing the norms before disclosing truly crucial business information. To make the most of BC's potential benefits, businesses must equip their human resources departments with the knowledge they need to design, build, and launch BC-based solutions. Companies' adoption of BC and its integration with other technologies, as well as their use of the data generated by BC applications, will all play a role in determining whether or not the technology's promise is fully realized. Having a viable strategy for adopting BC technology throughout the SC, with the backing of a technology provider and the buy-in of key actors, is also essential. There are two ways in which BC technology can assist here. To begin with, it may confirm the authenticity of a product's or material's provenance, or place of origin, and relay that information to customers so they can make an informed purchase decision. Second, because of BC's immutability and tamper-resistance, consumers will be able to more easily track the origins of their purchased goods and services from raw ingredients to final delivery. If a business wants to use BC in the SC, it needs a system that can handle the load and scale as the business grows. In light of BC's growing maturity, SC innovation will probably investigate methods to implement the technology into operations where it makes the most sense. BC platforms that can provide confidence and efficiency to many different types of transactions are necessary for the transformation of the SC industry.

3.6 FUTURE OF BC

Customers' demands for transparency in product origin and compliance with manufacturing ethics are driving interest in BC-based SCs. As BT develops traction, businesses would do well to maintain tabs on the competitors within their sector that have begun exploring its potential. Network effect is very helpful for BC; if a critical mass is reached in a SC, it is easier for others to join in and reap the benefits. When deciding when to construct a BC prototype, businesses could look to other stakeholders in their SC including competitors. Use cases involving BC technology in SC governance may help alleviate some of the issues that have plagued conventional supply networks, such as the requirement to produce copious amounts of paperwork. In addition, organizations' digitalization of physical assets and a decentralized, immutable record of all transactions can make it feasible to track products from the manufacturing unit to the delivery destination, making the SC more open and visible. Because of the need for specialized knowledge, widespread adoption of BC technology throughout the SC has been slow. Because BT is so new, it is regulated differently in several countries, which might disrupt existing SCs. While this is true, it is also conceivable that BC-based solutions will gradually replace traditional SC processes and networks.

3.7 CONCLUSION

It's getting harder and more complicated to manage supply networks. Paper bills of lading are just one example of a manual process that contributes to inefficiencies in the logistics industry. If computer systems within an organization don't talk to each other, or if the computer systems used by the various players in the SC don't talk to each other, chaos ensues. To address the challenges presented by intricate SCs, BC technology can be of great assistance. Utilizing BC technology will boost productivity, reveal inconsistencies in the SC, and finally stop fraud. The SC industry is fraught with difficulties in the areas of quality, cost, and speed. BC technology makes it simple to meet these criteria when applied to logistics. BC has the potential to eliminate such problems as double spending, miscommunication, and duplication of agreements. With the support of BC, the entire SC ecosystem can advance and become more transparent to businesses and customers. Many people, from the factory to the store to the customer, stand to gain from this. As the SC moves more quickly, expenses go down. There is no limit to the amount of users who can access and transact with BC technology. Traceability, transparency, and accountability in the distribution of products and commodities are all made possible through the use of public, private, and hybrid BC systems. Logistics firms can use this innovation to streamline their operations and reduce SC costs. BC has been discussed as a potential solution for global SCM by companies. BC technology is being implemented for the sake of absolute transparency.

KEYWORDS

- **BC**
- **technology**
- **supply chain**
- **logistics**
- **warehouse**

REFERENCES

Abeyratne, S. A.; R. P. Monfared. BC Ready Manufacturing Supply Chain Using Distributed Ledger. *Int. J. Res. Eng. Technol.* **2016,** *5* (9), 1–10.

Akhtar, P.; Azima, N.; Ghafar, A.; Din, S. U. Barricades in the Adoption of Block-Chain Technology in Supply Chain Management: Challenges and Benefits. *Transnational Market. J.* **2021,** *9* (1). https://doi.org/10.33182/tmj.v9i1.1021

Aste, T.; Tasca, P.; Di Matteo, T. BC Technologies: The Foreseeable Impact on Society and Industry. *Computer* **2017,** *50* (9), 18–28. https://doi.org/10.1109/ MC.2017.3571064.
Casey, M.; Wong, P. Global Supply Chains Are About to Get Better, Thanks to BC. *Harv. Bus. Rev.* **2017,** *13*.
Crosby, M.; Nachiappan Pattanayak, P.; Verma, S.; Kalyanaraman, V. BC Technology: Beyond Bitcoin. *Appl. Innova. Rev.* **2016,** (2). https://scet.berkeley.edu/wp-content/uploads/BCPaper.pdf (accessed on 4 Feb 2021).
Delfis, B. GEODIS Unveils Its 2017 Supply Chain Worldwide Survey, 2017. https://geodis.com/fr//sites/default/files/2018-08/20170511_%20pr%20geodis%20white%20paper%20eng2431288865035225216.pdf. (accessed on 6 March 2022).
Dutta, P.; Choi, T. M.; Somani, S.; Butala, R. BC Technology in Supply Chain Operations: Applications, Challenges and Research Opportunities. *Transp. Res. Part E: Logist. Transp. Rev.* **2020a,** *142*, 102067. https://doi.org/10.1016/j.tre.2020.102067
Fernandez, T. E. BC Technology in Supply Chain Management. *BC Technol. Supply Chain Manag.: Logist. Eng*. 2022. DOI: 10.5772/intechopen.105761
Getsmarter. How BC Will Radically Improve the Supply Chain, 2022. https://www.getsmarter.com/blog/market-trends/how-BC-will-radically-improve-the-supply-chain/
Giri, G.; Manohar, H. L. Factors Influencing the Acceptance of Private and Public BC Based Collaboration Among Supply Chain Practitioners: A Parallel Mediation Model. *Supply Chain Manag.: Int. J.* **2021**. https://doi.org/10.1108/SCM-02-2021-0057
Ismagilova, E.; Hughes, L.; Dwivedi, Y. K.; Raman, K. R. Smart Cities: Advances in Research—An Information Systems Perspective. *Int. J. Inf. Manag.* **2019,** *47*, 88–100. DOI: 10.1016/j.ijinfomgt.2019.01.004.
Joshi, T. Features of BC, 24 May 2022. https://www.geeksforgeeks.org/features-of-BC/
Kakulapati, M. Role of BC In Supply Chain Management, 20 June 2018. https://tdan.com/role-of-BC-in-supply-chain-management/23321
Kache, F.; Seuring, S. Challenges and Opportunities of Digital Information at the Intersection of Big Data Analytics and Supply Chain Management. *Int. J. Oper. Prod. Manag.* **2017,** *37* (1), 10–36.
Katsaliaki, K.; Galetsi, P.; Kumar, S. Supply Chain Disruptions and Resilience: A Major Review and Future Research Agenda. *Ann. Oper. Res*. **2021**. https://doi.org/10.1007/s10479-020-03912-1
Kshetri, N. 1 BC's Roles in Meeting Key Supply Chain Management Objectives. *Int. J. Inf. Manag.* **2018,** *39*, 80–89. https://doi.org/10.1016/j.ijinfomgt.2017.12.005.
Kamble, S.; Gunasekaran, A.; Arha, H. Understanding the BC Technology Adoption in Supply Chains-Indian Context. *Int. J. Prod. Res.* **2019,** *57* (7), 2009–2033.
Kouhizadeh, M.; Sarkis, J. BC Practices, Potentials, and Perspectives in Greening Supply Chains. *Sustainability* **2018,** *10* (10), 3652.
Kim, H. M.; Laskowski, M. Towards an Ontology-Driven BC Design for Supply Chain Provenance. Working Paper, Cornell University Library, New York, 28 August, 2016.
Kshetri, N. BC's Roles in Meeting Key Supply Chain Management Objectives. *Int. J. Inf. Manag.* **2018,** *39*, 80–89.
Laaper, S. Using BC to Drive Supply Chain Transparency: Future Trends in Supply Chain. *Deliotte* **2023**. https://www2.deloitte.com/us/en/pages/operations/articles/BC-supply-chain-innovation.html
Liu, Z.; Li, Z. A BC-Based Framework of Cross-Border E-Commerce Supply Chain. *Int. J. Inf. Manag*. **2019**. https://doi.org/10.1016/j. ijinfomgt.2019.102059.

Lu, Q.; Xu, X. Adaptable BC-Based Systems: A Case Study for Product Traceability. *IEEE Softw.* **2017,** *34* (6), 21–27. https://doi.org/10.1109/MS.2017. 4121227.

Morley, M. Top 5 Use Cases of BC in the Supply Chain in 2021, 12 Feb 2020. https://blogs.opentext.com/BC-in-the-supply-chain/

Pazaitis, A.; De Filippi, P.; Kostakis, V. BC and Value Systems in the Sharing Economy: The Illustrative Case of Backfeed. *Technol. Forecast. Soc. Change* **2017,** *125*, 105–115.

Pilkington, M. BC Technology: Principles and Applications. In Olleros, F.X., Zhegu, M., Eds.; *Research Handbook on Digital Transformations*; Edward Elgar: Northampton, 2016. https://papers.ssrn.com/sol3/papers.cfm?abstract_id=2662660

Provenance. BC: The Solution for Transparency in Product Supply Chains, 2015. www.provenance.org/whitepaper (accessed January 21, 2019).

Shardeum. 11 Key BC Features You Need to Know in 2023, 2022. https://shardeum.org/blog/what-are-the-features-of-BC/

Singh, O. How BC Technology Is Used in Supply Chain Management? 26 Nov 2022. https://cointelegraph.com/explained/how-BC-technology-is-used-in-supply-chain-management

Saberi, S.; Kouhizadeh, M.; Sarkis, J.; Shen, L. BC Technology and Its Relationships to Sustainable Supply Chain Management. *Int. J. Prod. Res.* **2019,** *57* (7), 2117–2135. https://doi.org/10.1080/00207543.2018.1533261

Steiner, J.; Baker, J. BC: The Solution for Transparency in Product Supply Chains, 2015. https://www.provenance.org/ whitepaper

Treiblmaier, H. Combining BC Technology and the Physical Internet to Achieve Triple Bottom Line Sustainability: A Comprehensive Research Agenda for Modern Logistics and Supply Chain Management. *Logistics* **2019,** *3* (1), 10.

Tian, F. An Agri-food Supply Chain Traceability System for China Based on RFID & BC Technology. In: *13th International Conference on Service Systems and Service Management (ICSSSM)*, 2016.

Wamba, S. F.; Queiroz, M. M. BC in the Operations and Supply Chain Management: Benefits, Challenges and Future Research Opportunities. *Int. J. Inf. Manag.* **2020,** 102064. DOI: 10.1016/j.ijinfomgt.2019.102064

Wang, L.; Luo Robert, X.; Lee, F. Unveiling the Interplay Between BC and Loyalty Program Participation: A Qualitative Approach Based on Bubichain. *Int. J. Inf. Manag.* **2019,** *49*, 397–410. https://doi.org/10.1016/j.ijinfomgt.2019.08.001.

CHAPTER 4

Robots on Supply Chain Management

ABDUL GANIW HUSSEIN[1], BILKISU MAIJAMAA[2], and MOHAMMED MAJEED[3]

[1]*Department of Logistics and Procurement Management, Tamale Technical University, Tamale, Ghana*

[2]*Department of Statistics, Faculty of Natural and Applied Sciences, Nasarawa State University, Keffi, Nigeria*

[3]*Department of Marketing, Tamale Technical University, Tamale, Ghana*

ABSTRACT

To maintain a competitive edge and boost output and efficiency in the supply chain, businesses are using a variety of cutting-edge technologies. Robots are invaluable for order fulfillment because they can do routine activities that need little to no intelligence. For this reason, this chapter's focus is on the advantages of robots in SCM and how they can be implemented. By assisting businesses in lowering costs, ensuring stability, increasing productivity, reducing mistakes, reducing inventory checks, and optimizing picking, sorting, and storage times, robots are reshaping the future of supply chains. Robotic process automation (RPA) is used in supply chain administration to automate menial jobs, thereby reducing manual effort and increasing efficiency. In response to rising demand, robotics in the supply chain can help expand production and speed up the scaling process. Worker safety is also improved, thanks to robotics, as dangerous tasks like collecting products from high storage places can be outsourced. As a result of RPA reducing human error and speeding up delivery times, customers will be more satisfied. From what has been discussed and what has been published, it is clear that the use of robots can have significant implications for the future of SCM.

New Age Technology in Supply Chain Management: Digital Transformation Tools in Perspective.
Mohammed Majeed (Ed.)

4.1 INTRODUCTION

From an economic point of view, the word "supply chain" is somewhat generic. According to the laws of economics, it is a system in which products and services circulate throughout a network (Min et al., 2019). In reaction to the epidemic in 2020, the distribution network has been under extreme stress ever since, and the current crises in Ukraine and Europe have only added to that stress. At the same time, consumer demand keeps on rising. Many of the causes of the supply chain crisis are being addressed with the use of supply chain technology. With rising competition and pricing constraints, businesses must spend heavily on the automation of purchasing and supply chain management or risk falling behind the competition (Christian et al., 2021). These developments strengthen the system and provide more advantages, like quicker product delivery, lower costs, and less waste and pollution (Newton, 2022). The ideas behind robotic systems have been a source of fascination for science fiction writers and filmmakers for decades. These predictions are starting to come true, as sales of service and industrial robots are expected to skyrocket in the near future (International Federation of Robotics, 2017). Future supply chains will be defined in part by autonomous robots because of their ability to reduce long-term costs, provide labor and utilization stability, boost worker productivity, lower error rates, cut down on inventory checks, shorten the time it takes to pick, sort, and store items, and increase access to areas that are difficult or dangerous to reach (Deloitte, 2023).

The global supply chain is being profoundly affected by the recent proliferation of production and technological breakthroughs. More than 1.9 million robots are already deployed in manufacturing and warehousing around the world. Artificial intelligence is also replacing humans in quality control, and IoT devices and drones keep an eye on production and upkeep (Getsmarter, 2022). By implementing new technologies like RPA, beef supply chains may increase their productivity and speed up their assembly line to better satisfy consumer expectations (E-Fatima et al., 2022). The efficient use of robots increases productivity and competitiveness as a result of the substantial cost reductions and time savings they provide (Viale and Zouari, 2020). However, not a lot of study has been done in this area. As a result, this chapter's focus is on the positive contributions robots can make to SCM. This chapter provides an overview of the current state of robotics in SCM and logistics and a forecast for how this trend in robotic technology will affect the future of our supply chains. The study adds to scientific knowledge by identifying potential benefits of the adoption of robots and makes contributions in practical areas by allowing decision-makers to adopt robust in a way.

4.2 LITERATURE

4.2.1 ROBOTS

Since the first industrial robot was invented in 1961 and the first robotic arm was developed in 1973, companies have steadily integrated various robots into their processes. These robots are cost-effectively designed to improve process security and output. It is expected that robots can raise the number of picking operations per hour from 100 for humans to between 300 and 500 (Bilozor, 2019). Over time, robots have progressed from simple machines to sophisticated ones with multiple uses (Savela et al., 2018). An autonomous robot is a machine that can make decisions and carry them out on its own (e.g. absence of human control or influence). People's familiarity with robots in their everyday lives has grown thanks to technological advancements in recent years (Gnambs and Appel, 2019). Robotics has gained considerable traction, and its effects can be seen across many sectors. The lack of available workers is one of the major issues facing the logistics sector today, according to Bonkenburg (2016). Finding enough qualified people to convey products from manufacturers to consumers is a challenge for businesses all around the world. In particular, two conflicting reasons are making this challenging: the first is a rise in demand for logistics employees, spurred on by the e-commerce revolution and the rise in parcel shipments; the second is a fall in the available workforce as a result of declining population levels in the West.

4.2.2 TYPES OF ROBOTS BY ROLE

4.2.2.1 DRONES

Drone planes, often known as "aerial robots," are designed to operate with minimal human oversight. Ideally, drones would transport items from warehouses to customers without any human intervention (Newton, 2022). A drone is a type of flying robot that can carry a small payload, move items from one location to another, and access hard-to-reach places (both physically, such as remote villages, and virtually, such as higher shelves or loftier regions of a warehouse) (Borras, 2020). Drones range in strength from somewhat weak to extremely potent, with autonomy provided by antennae and batteries.

From ground-based RPA tools to aerial vehicles with high-powered picture and data capture capabilities, there is a wide range of robots available on the market. Artificial intelligence is being increasingly included into the programming of autonomous robots so that they can perceive and learn from their environments (Banker, 2020). Delivery vehicles face challenges such as congestion, detours, several stops, and a lack of available drivers. Since there are no obstacles like roads or traffic in the air, a drone can fly directly to its target (Newton, 2022).

A drone equipped with radio frequency identification technology can be used to track goods throughout a warehouse, allowing for more precise management of the flow of units and stock. When compared to a human, a drone equipped with an RFID technology can read thousands of labels in a short amount of time (Borras, 2020). There is a complete control and connectivity between the robot and the manager because this data is transmitted instantly to the necessary device. The use of autonomous vehicles and drones for the delivery of both bulky items and smaller purchases to individual clients, as in e-commerce, will grow in popularity. A controller can monitor the vehicle's signals, track it in real-time, and ensure the rider's happiness from afar (Borras, 2020).

4.2.2.2 MILE DELIVERY ROBOT

The final leg of a B2C supply chain, the last-mile delivery, is often the most expensive and time-consuming. Autonomous cars are becoming increasingly important as businesses strive to streamline their delivery processes. Autonomous delivery robots are being tested by a growing number of organizations in urban and university settings. The need for autonomous systems is increasing along with the development of the requisite technologies (Banker, 2020). So, the concept of using autonomous cars for home delivery has also been explored. After an autonomous vehicle delivers a delivery to a customer's home, the recipient enters a code to access the vehicle's cargo area and take possession of the shipment.

4.2.2.3 ROBOT VEHICLES

To get around without a human driver or a remote control, you can use robotic vehicles. They can navigate through a warehouse reading QR codes and RFID signals to determine where to go and what to pick up next (Borras,

2020). Robotic cars are becoming increasingly autonomous and trustworthy because of advancements in machine learning; they are often used as a helpful adjunct to human workers in warehouses. Collaborative robots (cobots) get their name from the fact that workers instruct them on which transportation or classification jobs to carry out.

4.2.2.4 SHOP-FLOOR ROBOTS

Robots of this type are useful for stocking shelves. Although there are many companies competing in this market, Bossa Nova Robots has received the most attention due to Walmart's announcement that hundreds of their locations will begin deploying these robots (Banker, 2020). Previous iterations of these AMRs included in-store inventory cameras.

4.2.2.5 MOBILE ROBOTS/ROBOTS ON WHEELS

Autonomous mobile robots (AMR) are mobile robots that can be trained to carry out certain activities with minimal to no human input. RPA tools and flying vehicles with high-powered image and data capture capabilities are just two examples of how widely ranging these tools may be in terms of size, capability, mobility, dexterity, artificial intelligence, and price. Autonomous robots are increasingly being equipped with artificial intelligence so that they can understand their environments and act accordingly. Autonomous robots are no longer the stuff of science fiction; they are already bringing innovation to the supply chain and delivering significant value, such as the following: increasing the speed and accuracy of routine operations, especially in warehousing and manufacturing; increasing efficiency through working side-by-side with humans; and decreasing the risk of employee injury in hazardous environments. Warehouses and factories often employ autonomous mobile robots to expedite and enhance the quality of mundane tasks. Supply chain improvements can be made with the help of robotics solutions, which will lower long-term costs, provide stable labor and utilization, lower error rates, cut down on inventory checks, and speed up the picking, sorting, and storing processes (Borras, 2020). Adaptive mobile robots (AMRs) travel the globe while making judgments in a timely manner. They take in data about their environment with the use of sensors and cameras. They can use the onboard processing equipment to assess the information and make educated decisions, such as when to move out of the way of an arriving worker, which package to select, or which area to disinfect.

4.2.3 ARTIFICIAL INTELLIGENCE AND AUTOMATED PROCESSES

Artificial intelligence and automated processes are greatly assisting the manufacturing and supply sectors in their efforts to become more environmentally responsible. When it comes to materials and time, automation can help reduce waste by minimizing the amount of wasted effort caused by humans. Since robotic cells can reliably and frequently perform the same operation, the manufacturing process is streamlined and improved in terms of precision. In addition to boosting output and lowering expenses, the decrease in accidents also helps businesses save money and produce higher-quality goods more quickly (Newton, 2022). Whether it is for monitoring quality or keeping tabs on productivity, AI has a utility. With the use of sensors and cameras, AI can swiftly scan products as they move through the manufacturing process, identifying and eliminating any problematic items. Utilizing software, businesses may track down their wasteful usage of any and all resources, from raw materials to electrical power. Artificial intelligence can be used to improve digital twins, simulations, modeling, and data analysis to further streamline the supply chain.

4.2.3.1 ADDITIVE MANUFACTURING

While not all production chains can accommodate 3D printing, those that can see significant benefits from the technology. Additive manufacturing is another name for this technology, and it has far more applications than people think. With 3D printing, you just use what you need, so there is less of a chance of excess materials being thrown away. Another way in which a 3D printer helps maximize efficiency is by automating the manufacturing process. These days, machines can print with just about any material imaginable, from plastic to metal to concrete, and they can do it in surprisingly quick time (Newton, 2022). Supply chain sustainability can also be enhanced by reducing wasteful practices in the usage of available resources. Both the generation of garbage and the methods employed to get rid of it are significant causes of atmospheric carbon dioxide. With the use of additive manufacturing, factories can cut down on waste throughout the production process (Newton, 2022).

4.2.3.2 AUTOMATED GUIDED VEHICLES (AGVS)

AGVs are robots used to transport goods around a warehouse. Products can be transferred between different sections of a facility or from a chosen products area to a packaging room. Depending on the type, the robot may be able to transport the cargo in a particular way or perform other tasks. Some models can tow trailers, others can carry loads, while still others can pick up and transfer pallets. Built-in forklifts allow some to lower or raise loads from a height. With the help of built-in markers or high-tech Light Detection and Ranging (LiDAR), AGVs can navigate the warehouse and perform the functions of lifters and pick carts. This method allows robotic warehouse workers to get information by observing reflections off of a moving laser array.

4.2.3.3 TRANSPORTATION

Though transportation automation has ways to go before it can fully automate the supply chain, this is an exciting prospect despite the enormous technical obstacles it faces. SC robots are primarily mobile robots used to automate the movement of goods, though their deployment can vary. Whatever their use, having a high availability rate is the key to making money with them. With more and more businesses realizing the benefits of logistics robots, the sector is primed for explosive expansion. Automated driving systems, complementary delivery mechanisms, and path-finding software all fall under this category of mechanization (Sherrer, 2022). With the advent of self-driving trucks, the lack of long-distance truck drivers would be alleviated, and with the introduction of delivery drones, the use of trucks and vans would be reduced to the absolute minimum. Optimizing delivery routes and auto maintenance schedules are two areas where transportation automation can have the greatest impact in the short term.

4.2.3.4 AUTOMATED ARM AND MACHINERY

These are the most obvious examples of retail robots: manipulator arms that can pick up items, seal boxes, and transfer goods across shelves (Borras, 2020). It is not hard to discover this kind of equipment in many businesses, particularly those related to the automobile industry, as it has been the most popular up until this point. What sets these robots apart from traditional machinery is their ability to take on more complex tasks, apply analytics simultaneously, and provide assistance to employees performing repetitive activities like order management or pallet stacking. The purpose of articulated robots (sometimes called robotic arms) is to do similar tasks as a human arm. These often have two or more rotary joints, sometimes even more. This is because the range of motion increases with each new joint or axis, making them perfect for tasks like arc welding, material handling, machine tending, and packaging. These arms are versatile enough to be attached to a mobile robot or used in a goods-to-person (GTP) setting. They can be fixed in place to deal with recurring tasks like loading empty boxes onto a conveyor system. It can also be used to supplement a unit load sorter with individual items and arrange them into shipping lanes. Picking stations, putting barriers, induction stations for unit sorters, and shipping docks are just some of the places where robotic warehouse technology can cut down on labor needs. Increased precision in pick-and-place operations is also a notable feature.

4.2.3.5 WAREHOUSE/STOCKROOM ROBOTS

Tools like warehouse robots are used to streamline the movement of inventory and boost output. Such technologies can operate completely independently or in tandem with humans to carry out a variety of duties, including transporting goods from one location to another, packing orders, and stocking shelves. From $4.7 billion in 2021, the global market for warehouse robotics is projected to grow to $9.1 billion by 2026, according to a new industry analysis. Companies are learning that they cannot rely only on their present personnel to remain competitive in the face of rising consumer demand and the need for fast, precise order fulfillment (iGPS, 2022). Warehouses are an essential part of the supply chain that can either completely halt production or speed up the process. The operational reliability with which cobots carry out the duties that can be automated gives the logistics and warehousing business a competitive advantage over its competitors in the long run. Because of this, businesses of all sizes will have more available human resources to devote to value-added tasks like data analysis, strategic planning, quality control and assurance, and decision-making. Further, automated software for warehouse management can lessen or completely do away with monotonous tasks. Human workers can find things more quickly with the help of pick-to-light systems. In Amazon's fulfillment centers, robot-guided cars are used to fetch orders without any human intervention (Sherrer, 2022). Maximizing efficiency in warehouses and distribution centers is what warehouse robots are all about. Now more than ever, warehouses need to be quick and efficient, therefore, businesses are looking for ways to automate their logistics processes.

Using robotics has increased the productivity of warehouses around the world, which in turn helps keep the supply chain flowing at breakneck speeds. Warehouse robots come in many forms, from autonomous mobile robots (AMR) to rack-climbing pick-and-put-away robots to cobots (Newton, 2022). Cobots in the warehouse allow logistic organizations to increase picking and palletizing speeds while decreasing worker injuries. It is inevitable that human employees will make mistakes occasionally, but there are ways to minimize the damage they do. On one hand, cobots save time and effort. Cobots with built-in capabilities to ensure precision and accuracy provide an additional layer of quality control by assisting users in the execution of a variety of tasks. Warehouse management is already being affected in numerous ways by automation in the supply chain. Orders can be received and confirmed automatically by SCM software, and shipments can be consolidated and less wasteful by using box algorithms to recommend the optimal box size (Sherrer, 2022).

4.2.3.6 ROBOTS IN SCM

The incorporation of robotics and AI in supply chain management and transportation is one of the most promising but under-discussed developments in the industry. The introduction of this application brings a substantial shift in corporate practices, which will benefit some while hurting others. Manufacturers and firms will need to learn more about robotics and advanced analytics before this situation becomes commonplace. Autonomous robots have typically been used for mundane activities due to their sophisticated programming, high initial cost, and inability to quickly adapt to changing circumstances (Deloitee, 2023). Autonomous robots are becoming more and more advanced, cutting setup times, requiring less human oversight, and increasingly working side-by-side with their human counterparts. As autonomous robots improve to the point that they can work around the clock with more consistent levels of quality and productivity, the benefits for the supply chain of the future grow (Deloitee, 2023). Robots can be employed in the logistics and supply chain to keep an eye on stock, keep tabs on shipments, and keep in touch with clients and vendors in response to triggers set in advance. Robot allows for the potential automation of a wide range of applications in supply chain management, retail operations, and inventory administration. Robotics can streamline logistics by automating transport management and providing precise tracking of shipments in motion. Based on the statistical data set, robots can also provide useful information about carriers and insurance providers. Automation of formerly manual processes reduces the likelihood of errors and defects in supply chain management through the use of RPA. RPA tools and methods are programmable computer programs that run on a cloud-based server and may be activated or deactivated on the fly. Companies now hire and train people to use robots for creative problem-solving and brainstorming rather than performing repetitive, routine chores (Khan et al., 2022). The application of robotics to industrial distribution entails the employment of robots and machines equipped with intelligent systems to automate errands such as storage, transportation, distribution, and product retrieval.

4.2.4 BENEFITS OF ROBOTS IN SUPPLY CHAIN MANAGEMENT

Companies in the modern era of e-commerce have to constantly innovate in order to keep up with the changing needs of their customers. Due to the importance of prompt shipping dates to customer satisfaction, forward-thinking companies are increasingly relying on robotics and other forms of cutting-edge automation technology to streamline their order-filling processes and reduce turnaround times. Distribution network innovation and value creation are mostly propelled by driverless robots' ability to cut operational costs and boost profits (Deloitee, 2023). Robots improve production and efficiency by decreasing the occurrence of mistakes, redos, and accidents. To better protect workers in hazardous conditions. Carry out low-value, routine chores so that people can work together on more important, non-automatable jobs. Maximize earnings by boosting order accuracy, shipping speed, and patron contentment (Deloitee, 2023). Technology strengthens supply chains by streamlining and modernizing manufacturing, resource management, and other back-end operations. As was previously noted, shipping and warehousing firms that adopt cobots can anticipate increased output, reduced cycle times, and streamlined operations. The result is that employees may focus on the most important, challenging jobs that directly affect income. After all, cobots are dependable workers who can get the job done no matter the weather, hastening the time it takes to get a return on the initial investment. With the help of robotic technologies, warehouses may increase output without sacrificing quality. When this is implemented, warehouse workers will be able to process far more inventory each day. When working in tandem with humans, robots can improve precision and hasten the pace of repetitive tasks (Bilozor, 2019).

When robots take care of the monotonous, time-consuming chores involved with order fulfillment, humans are free to focus on more valuable endeavors, such as quality assurance and expansion of the business (River System, 2023). Robotic order fulfillment can speed up the completion of mundane tasks by improving pick rates and utilizing optimized pick routes. In order to increase efficiency, robots can move about between picking cycles on their own. Adopting new technologies and making full use of the most up-to-date options are essential building blocks of any effective system. Many of these tools make labor easier, safer, and more efficient while also decreasing the number of injuries that occur. As a result, everyone—from factory workers and customers to investors and the environment—will benefit from a stronger, more reliable supply chain (Newton, 2022). Since each company uses its own system for managing its operations, client information is constantly being updated in several locations and must be synchronized to provide consistent quality of service. For example, the supply chain procedure mandates that customers' ordering rights be temporarily revoked until the account manager is notified. Robots can automate these manual processes that affect multiple databases. For example, when a user submits a service request using a mobile app, an intelligent virtual assistant communicates with the user before sending the request on to the system. Together with RPA robots, intelligent document processing solutions may read information from a wide range of service request documents and then store, organize, and retrieve that information as needed (Khan et al., 2022).

Using robots in manufacturing boosts product quality. As with any manual process, there is a significant opportunity for mistakes to creep into the product management process when done manually (e.g. putting an item in the wrong location or preparing an order without the corresponding product). Fully autonomous robots perform tasks in warehouses and distribution centers. Because they are following the WMS's directions, they are quite precise and never make any mistakes (Mecalux, 2021). If a customer wants to return an item for repair or replacement, a mobile app for third-party service and reverse logistics partners can increase awareness of location, time of arrival, and time to finish work. It is possible that robots could soon be able to track customers' orders in real-time and confirm their purchases with instantaneous emails (Mecalux, 2021). Incorporating such technology allows firms to reallocate their customer care personnel's efforts toward more fruitful endeavors like fostering stronger bonds with their clientele. With the labor market tightening and posing additional staffing issues in supply chain and order fulfillment operations, robots are becoming an intriguing alternative. By increasing productivity and supplementing human efforts, cobots assist mitigate the effects of a lack of human workers (River System, 2023). Productivity and effectiveness are both increased by the use of robots. Using robots in the warehouse increases productivity and decreases wait times. For instance, operators can stay put at pick stations while stacker cranes and conveyors carry the supplies they need to fill orders (Mecalux, 2021). This eliminates the need for them to physically search for the products they need throughout the warehouse. Machines in a warehouse may be trusted with big loads, relieving the strain on human laborers. With this benefit, there is less potential for harmful mishaps on the job, which is good for everyone's health and safety. Errors are less likely to occur during ordinary warehouse operations when robots are used, in part because of an obvious improvement in the conveyance of information inside the warehouse (Bilozor, 2019).

Further, robots never need rest or a break. They are capable of working nonstop, day or night, without sacrificing accuracy over time. This allows warehouses to achieve economies of scale that would be impossible with human labor alone, as more orders may be filled in a shorter amount of time. Employees are more valuable when they are able to shift their attention from routine duties to strategic ones (Deloitee, 2023). Robots prioritize worker safety by limiting their exposure to risky environments. Robotic order fulfillment has several advantages, but one of the most notable is a decrease in employees' amount of time spent moving around the building. Human operators can devote more time to tasks that directly affect customer satisfaction if they spend less time walking the length of the warehouse. With robots, warehouse workers can spend less time traveling between picking operations, as the robots do the traveling for them. Since there will be fewer people going in and out of the building, the aisles will be less crowded (River System, 2023). The use of artificial intelligence and machine learning by some mobile robots enables them to optimize pick routes in real-time, speeding up the fulfillment process for the majority of orders. Strengthened the company's reputation by demonstrating its commitment to cutting-edge methods and cutting-edge technology. Machine learning through exponential data collection and analysis. Providing customer service is only one of several retail tasks that may be automated with the help of software robots. The addition of robots typically results in increased security. When goods are handled, the danger of injury increases, especially when the weights are large, when workers are in awkward positions, or when routine tasks require a lot of motion. Robots are able to do a wide range of jobs without human error, thereby reducing the possibility of harm being caused (Mecalux, 2021).

Productivity gains are a key advantage of using robots in the warehouse. Since the demand from customers is at an all-time high, it is crucial that distribution facilities maximize their effectiveness. Adapting the supply chain to a new period of declining supply and increasing demand is a complex task that can be greatly aided by automation technology, such as robotics. Every advancement made at distribution centers and logistics hubs has a ripple effect across the supply chain (iGPS, 2022). Robotic warehouses are only one example of the new technologies being implemented to improve productivity and speed up the delivery of goods to customers. To stay competitive while the supply chain continues to face its current obstacles, businesses are looking into any and all ways to improve efficiency. Most robots work in tandem with humans. Robots improve operator productivity by making mundane activities easier to do (Mecalux, 2021). Machines like these can move massive amounts of stuff with ease, freeing up human hands for more valuable tasks. Scheduling is simplified because of robots. Time off is necessary for traditional employees to recharge their batteries. The robots, however, do not require rest periods. They have the stamina to last the whole shift. There will be fewer mistakes made thanks to the use of robots. Errors are practically eliminated thanks to the deployment of robots in the warehouse. This system cuts down on not only mistakes but also the time needed to travel to various locations within the warehouse. This is why there has been an increase in the emphasis placed on quality assurance. For safety purposes, robots can use sensors that have been designed to detect and avoid obstacles. An employee's health and safety are protected from any threats thanks to this perk. Pallet racks that collapse, tripping and falls, and ladders that fall from high places are the most common causes of injury in warehouses. Workers who are able to climb, pick up, package, and otherwise move around the warehouse without risk are no longer at risk thanks to warehouse robots.

Robotic order fulfillment has several advantages, but one of the most notable is a decrease in employees' amount of time spent moving around the building. To better serve customers, warehouse workers should spend less time walking from one end to the other (Tailor, 2020). Robots in the warehouse cut down on the time it takes workers to complete orders by shortening the distance they have to travel between pickups (River System,

2023). Due to the number of people involved, the transportation chain occasionally experiences difficulties in communicating. There is a chance that the accountable manager will not be able to speak with the selected employee. Automated tools such as chatbots and auto-responders can be used to address this issue. Robotic tools can regularly notify the proper authorities with status reports via email or push notifications. In the same vein, chatbots can be used to respond to a customer's inquiries concerning their order, its shipment, any potential delays, or anything else associated with the order process (Khan et al., 2022). By eliminating human error from the process, robots may greatly improve the precision of SCM activities. If the robot has been properly programmed and its functionality has been tested and validated, it will carry out the work with consistent assurance. To the user, any change to the variable that prevents the process from completing successfully is a clear sign of an error and an indication that the process did not go as planned (River System, 2023).

Employees' time is better spent on creative and critical thinking projects than on mundane, repetitive work. However, robots have been developed to perform mundane tasks with long-term accuracy. The monotonous work of product packaging and distribution, for instance, can be done by automated packaging systems. As more and more people buy from online retailers, consumers' expectations shift. Customers who shop via omnichannel and online channels have access to improved pricing, product variety, shipping alternatives, and overall shopping experiences because of the use of social media. Fulfillment skills, such as the employment of warehouse robots, are crucial to a company's ability to maintain customer satisfaction. Robots in warehouses can boost output without sacrificing quality. Warehouse robots can be quite useful if they help increase output in the supply chain. When used in tandem, they can improve precision, speed up regular procedures, and address a variety of staff issues. These robots already improve our lives by helping us become more accurate, precise, and strong while also removing risky, repetitive, tiresome, or uninteresting duties. Even though the global labor force is aging, robots help us get more done every day (Bonkenburg, 2016).

4.3 IMPLICATION

From the perspective of supply chain management, this chapter surveyed the existing literature on robot applications. Managers should keep an eye on the development of autonomous robots to see if they may be useful in the supply chain. Especially as consumer perceptions and quantities of deliveries, shipping, and requests reach record levels for conventional procedures, autonomous robotics present new options to enhance operations through increased productivity, reduced risk, decreased cost, and enhanced data collecting. Since there has not been a lot of theoretical work done on how autonomous robots might be adopted in supply chains, this study fills a gap in the literature (Hofmann et al., 2019). It explains why and how autonomous robots can be used in the logistics and supply chain industry. Supply chain managers should be approached by companies marketing these technologies to show them the value of these innovations and explain why supply chain operators should start using them. In order to meet current and future demands, manufacturers of such autonomous robots should collaborate closely with decision-makers to gain a thorough understanding of the difficulties associated with today's supply chains (e.g. consumers' demands for rapid delivery, rising costs, and rising service levels). Because there has not been a lot of studies done on the topic of autonomous robots in the supply chain and logistics industry, case study research to prove their worth is an exciting prospect for the future of this profession. This is useful since it provides more information about where logistics robots are now being used and how their use might be expanded. In addition, future studies can investigate how emerging technology in general can aid in resolving issues in the supply chain.

4.4 THE FUTURE OF ROBOTS

Increased use of autonomous robots is anticipated during the next five years, especially in supply chain activities involving low-value, high-risk tasks. There is already a significant presence of autonomous robots in many industries, such as production, final assembly, and storage. To free up human resources for more strategic, less hazardous, and higher-value tasks in the supply chain of the future, autonomous robots are expected to continue proliferating in these sectors.

Manufacturers and logistics firms are under increasing pressure to reduce their environmental effects as consumers become more cognizant of the consequences of their product choices. Because warehouse robots eliminate room for error, they can drastically cut down on the amount of waste produced by a fulfillment center. When robots are employed to pick and package orders, for instance, there is less of a chance that the order will need to be repacked or that a customer will ask for a replacement, thereby minimizing the amount of packing and fuel that is needlessly thrown away. As technology improves and robots gain more human-like capabilities, they will become increasingly common in the supply chain of the future. By way of illustration, advancements in haptic sensors (those linked to the sensation of touch) will enable robots to grip objects ranging from fragile eggshells to multi-surfaced metal assembly parts without requiring any alterations to the underlying programming or robotic components.

The setup times for autonomous robots are getting shorter, they need less human oversight, and they can now function in tandem with their human counterparts. As autonomous robots improve to the point that they can work autonomously around the clock with more consistent levels of quality and efficiency, the advantages grow. These robots undertake activities that people either cannot, should not, or do not want to do. As warehouse robotics continue to advance, there is a widespread belief that these occupations will become obsolete. As more businesses adopt robotics, however, researchers and business leaders are discovering that the technology improves workers' quality of life by fostering a more flexible work environment and a higher level of worker safety. These robots are meant to aid with routine tasks, but they will not be able to do everything by themselves.

Since the need for robots that can work independently of humans is rising, there will be less rigidity in the supply chain from beginning to end. Many businesses today use autonomous robots for specific tasks in the supply chain, often employing pilot programs to test out new robots and confirm efficiency advantages. Some experts predict that robots that produce other robots will become commonplace in the manufacturing industry as innovative businesses continue to emerge.

4.5 CONCLUSION

From the perspective of supply chain management, this chapter surveyed the existing literature on robot applications. Operations in warehouse management and supply chain management include things like transporting items, receiving them, storing them, sorting them, packing them, and sending them out to customers. Typically, most tasks at such hubs have required the assistance of human laborers. The easiest approach to get around the inefficiencies of doing such work by hand is to have robots do it and related work. Fortunately, AMRs provide promising avenues for the automation of a number of these laborious, time-consuming tasks. They improve the effectiveness of many tasks related to distribution centers by, for example, speeding up the transit of items, facilitating the most economical picking routes, shortening the time it takes for pickers to complete a certain task, etc. Order picking and inventory management are only two areas where autonomous mobile robots and drones are being put to use in warehouses. In the meantime, autonomous truck road tests continue, and platooning technology has several promising applications. Autonomous delivery bots and automobiles are already in use in cities and on college campuses for last-mile deliveries. Using SC-based robotics, the warehousing and transporting of items along the supply chain can be carried out automatically. Intra-logistics, the method by which they are utilized to organize and transfer products, is most common in warehouses and storage facilities, but they have a wide range of potential applications. Since logistics robots have significantly higher rates of uptime than human workers, businesses that use them see significant increases in output and income. The infrastructure and interest are already in place, but there are still several regulatory hurdles that must be overcome before the supply chain can rely more heavily on autonomous trucks. Organizations can use robots in SCM to improve process performance, efficiency, scalability, audibility, security, convenience, and compliance, among other goals. Though the process of integrating robots can be complex, businesses should weigh the benefits against any potential drawbacks. Based on the two examples offered, it is clear that robots can be used to do some of the more mundane and repetitive jobs in SCM. Robots make SC operations quick, adaptable, potent, and cheap. From what has been discussed and what has been written, it is clear that robots may contribute significantly to the growth and improvement of SCM.

KEYWORDS

- **benefits**
- **robots**
- **technology**
- **robotics**
- **supply chain management**

REFERENCES

Banker, S. Robots and the Autonomous Supply Chain. *Forbes* 2020. https://www.forbes.com/sites/stevebanker/2020/04/02/robots-and-the-autonomous-supply-chain/?sh=7a821eaa787a

Borras, I. Robotics in Logistics: How Distribution Is Changing, 15 Oct 2020. https://blog.saleslayer.com/robotics-in-logistics#what

Bonkenburg, T. Robotics in Logistics. DHL Customer Solutions & Innovation, 2016. https://www.thehive-network.com/wp-content/uploads/2017/03/DHL_RoboticsInLogistics.pdf

Christian, F.; Franziska, A.; Rainer, L. Robotic Process Automation in Purchasing and Supply Management: A Multiple Case Study on Potentials, Barriers, and Implementation. *J. Purchas. Supply Manag.* **2021**.

Deloitte. Using Autonomous Robots to Drive Supply Chain Innovation: Future Trends in Supply Chain, 2023. https://www2.deloitte.com/us/en/pages/manufacturing/articles/autonomous-robots-supply-chain-innovation.html

Getsmarter. How Blockchain Will Radically Improve the Supply Chain, 2022. https://www.getsmarter.com/blog/market-trends/how-blockchain-will-radically-improve-the-supply-chain/

Hofmann, E.; Sternberg, H.; Chen, H.; Pflaum, A.; Prockl, G. Supply Chain Management and Industry 4.0: Conducting Research in the Digital Age. *Int. J. Phys. Distrib. Logist. Manag.* **2019,** *9* (10), 945–955.

International Federation of Robotics World Robotics Industrial Robots 2017; IFR: Frankfurt, Germany, 2017.

iGPS. How Warehouse Robotics are Changing the Supply Chain, 23 Feb 2022. https://igps.net/blog/2022/02/23/how-warehouse-robotics-are-changing-the-supply-chain/

Khan, S.; Tailor, R. K.; Uygun, H.; Gujrati, R. Application of Robotic Process Automation (RPA) for Supply Chain Management, Smart Transportation and Logistics. *Int. J. Health Sci.* **2022,** *6* (S3), 11051–11063. https://doi.org/10.53730/ijhs.v6nS3.8554

Mecalux. Warehouse Robots: Technology Automates Logistics, 27 Sept 2021. https://www.mecalux.com/blog/warehouse-robots

Min, S.; Zacharia, Z. G.; Smith, C. D. Defining Supply Chain Management: In the Past, Present, and Future. *J. Bus. Logist.* **2019,** *40*, 44–55.

Newton, E. 6 Ways Technology Makes the Supply Chain More Efficient, 25 Feb 2022. https://supplychainbeyond.com/6-ways-technology-makes-the-supply-chain-more-efficient/

River System. 6 Benefits of Robotic Order Fulfillment, 2023. https://6river.com/benefits-of-robotic-order-fulfillment/#:text=Reduces%20labor%20demands,augmenting%20the%20work%20of%20humans.

Slashgear. 2014. http://cdn.slashgear.com/wp-content/uploads/2014/11/K5-2.0-Green.jpg.jpg

Sherrer, K. Supply Chain Automation: Robotics & AI in the Supply Chain, 15 Aug 2022. https://www.cioinsight.com/big-data/supply-chain-automation/

Tailor, R. K. Application of Robotic Process Automation in Shopping Malls in India. *Int. J. Adv. Res. Comm. Manag. Soc. Sci.* **2020,** 234–238.

Viale, L.; Zouari, D. Impact of Digitalization on Procurement: The Case of Robotic Process Automation. *Supply Chain Forum: Int. J.* **2020,** 185–195. https://www.cigen.com.au/cigenblog/8-real-world-cases-rpa-transportationlogistics

CHAPTER 5

Assessing the Effect of Information Technology on Supply Chain Management in SMEs

MOHAMMED MAJEED[1] and JAYADATTA S.[2]

[1]*Marketing Department, Tamale Technical University, Tamale, Ghana*

[2]*KLE's Institute of Management Studies and Research (IMSR), Hubballi, Karnataka, India*

ABSTRACT

The objective of this research was to ascertain the advantages of information technology (IT) in enhancing the performance of supply chain operations. This chapter further aimed to examine different IT applications used in supply chain operations. The research conducted was a quantitative study, consisting of a sample size of 38 participants from small and medium-sized manufacturing enterprises located in the Tamale-Northern area of Ghana. The data collected was analyzed using SPSS-AMOS software in the current study. The study's findings indicate that the hurdles to supply chain management (SCM) in road building include many key factors. These include a lack of commitment from senior management, poor technical skills, insufficient utilization of IT, supplier resistance to change, and a lack of encouragement from the organization. Barcoding, Material Resources Planning, and Distribution Requirement Planning have a substantial influence on the effectiveness of SCM. Nevertheless, the impact of Enterprise Resource Planning (ERP) on supply chain performance in manufacturing small and medium enterprises (SMEs) located in Tamale, NR-Ghana was found to be beneficial, but statistically negligible. Therefore, the information and communication technology

New Age Technology in Supply Chain Management: Digital Transformation Tools in Perspective.
Mohammed Majeed (Ed.)

(ICT) tools that have the greatest influence on SMEs are barcoding, material resources planning, and distribution need planning. These technologies have a substantial effect on the performance of SCM.

5.1 INTRODUCTION

5.1.1 BACKGROUND OF THE STUDY

Since the 1980s, companies have implemented and cultivated supply chains in order to reduce management burdens and manufacturing expenses (Ataseven and Nail, 2017). The high failure rate of SMEs in Ghana may be attributed to the ineffective implementation of business practices by managers, as highlighted by Ogunyomi and Bruning (2016). According to Awal (2018), the failure rate of SMEs in Ghana was estimated to be over 75% in the year 2018. The organization has augmented its manufacturing capacity, improved product quality, and enhanced its New Product Development (NPD) efforts via the use of outsourcing. The majority of research has been undertaken within the realm of operational performance in the field of SCM. Nevertheless, there is a dearth of substantial research in the field of strategic performance. The use of IT is often regarded as an essential need for the efficient management of contemporary intricate supply chains. The rapid expansion of IT within supply chain networks has brought about a substantial shift from traditional paper-based communication to electronic communication. However, this transition has also introduced a significant concern in the form of cybercrime, specifically the risk of unauthorized or illegal access to computer systems or networks through physical or virtual intrusion (Khan, 2014).

The supply chain (SC) idea, which originated in the 1990s as a strategic management tool, has evolved into a significant catalyst for improving overall organizational performance (Maestrini et al., 2017; Ataseven and Nail, 2017). The strategic component of the SC has been the subject of investigation in several research studies. These studies have empirically examined the relationships between numerous contextual variables of SCM and the design of small and medium-sized enterprises (SMEs), as well as their impact on both operational and financial performance (Qi et al., 2017). However, there is a lack of research that thoroughly investigates the influence of social media and enterprise systems (SMES) information features on either the operational or financial performance of SCs. This area of study is still in its early stages and requires more development (Burritt and Scaltegger, 2014).

The existence of this gap has led to the identification of supply chain integration (SCI) and knowledge exchange as the primary factors that contribute to the successful design and implementation of SMES information in improving manufacturers' supply chain performance (Kwon et al., 2016). Furthermore, the current body of research on SCI and performance has mostly been influenced by the industrial dynamics and logistics literature. This literature has largely concentrated on organizations that produce discrete components and consumer products (Wang et al., 2011; Qi et al., 2017). There is a scarcity of research examining the influence of information features of SMES on SCM choices inside service-oriented organizations, particularly in the context of healthcare institutions (Anderson and Dekker, 2015).

The proliferation of the internet and the continuous progress in ICT have resulted in enhanced efficiency in the delivery of real-time information, prompt accessibility, as well as the sharing and exchange of data and information. These advancements have also led to improvements in coordination and interactions, logistics, and other aspects of SCM (Manochehri et al., 2012). The design and cost of SCM have been impacted by these improvements, leading to changes in the interaction between supply chain players, including suppliers, vendors, workers, and consumers (Elango, 2018). SCM performs a diverse range of tasks across numerous businesses and sectors. In the manufacturing sector, the SC operation starts with the initiation of a product order. Subsequently, the product is carried out by a logistics firm and ultimately received by the client. This process may be referred to as a network of end-to-end business-to-business (B2B) activities.

Numerous scholars and practitioners alike have acknowledged the use of ICT in the realm of SCM. The discipline of ICT has played a significant role in facilitating the internationalization of production and distribution networks across diverse economic sectors. In the dynamic economic climate, several firms engage in multiple SCs. In order to enhance market competitiveness and achieve comparative advantage, the use of ICT tools has been acknowledged as crucial in leading global supply chains. According to Kable (2014), a worldwide study indicated a 40% rise in ICT expenditures, including hardware, software, communication, and IT services, as reported by 168 manufacturers in the year 2013.

ICT tools are extensively utilized in various aspects of SCM. These include order placement, inventory management, shipment tracking, exchanging information and conducting transactions with vendors, e-payment information exchange with suppliers, as well as utilizing mobile connectivity and cloud-based services (De Marchi et al., 2017). Manufacturers in several developing countries are using ICT solutions inside their supply chain operations to augment their operational agility, effectiveness, and economic productivity.

5.1.2 PROBLEM STATEMENT

Generally, SMEs tend to lag behind in the use of ICT and analytics. The adoption of ICT analytics in SMEs remains limited, as shown by a study conducted by SAS in 2013. Another area of interest is the examination of the adoption rates of ICT in various nations, as explored by Coleman et al. in 2016. According to research by Dresner Advisory Service in 2017, it has been projected that the market for business intelligence (BI) and analytics in SMEs would see a significant surge. Additionally, Coleman et al. (2016) have anticipated a growth rate of 42% in the worldwide adoption of analytics among SMEs from 2013 to 2018.

However, it should be noted that this figure remains rather modest in comparison to the overall number of SMEs present in the worldwide market. Furthermore, due to substantial obstacles in the implementation of data analytics, a majority of SMEs would be categorized as having low levels of digitalization and limited use of data-driven strategies. According to Arunachalam et al. (2017), the use of analytics and ICT has the potential to create a digital gap between SMEs and bigger organizations in the future. According to a recent analysis by Dresner Advisory Service (2017), the adoption of certain practices is mostly driven by the need for revenue development and the pursuit of competitive advantages. Nevertheless, there is a dearth of scholarly literature examining the extent to which analytics adoption occurs in SMEs and the underlying factors driving such adoptions, particularly within the realm of SCM. Previous research has examined the variables that influence the adoption of ICT, although these studies have mostly concentrated on bigger firms (Chen et al., 2015; Verma and Bhattacharyya, 2017). The primary conclusions derived from this research indicate a favorable correlation between the implementation of ICT and the perceived advantages associated with ICT instruments.

Additional variables, such as the presence of competitive pressure from rival firms and the specific sector in which a company operates, serve as moderating influences on the uptake and effective use of analytics inside organizations. However, there are notable distinctions in SCM between

SMEs and bigger corporations. These disparities stem from variations in their respective strategies, resulting in divergent competitive pressures. Given this context, it becomes imperative to do research focused on the utilization of analytics within SMEs. Given the significance of analytics and ICT in the context of BI investment for SCM, it is essential to assess the present condition of BI implementation inside SMEs. According to Hatta et al. (2015), despite the observed increase in demand for ICT among SMEs, these enterprises continue to lag behind in their adoption and development of ICT. The existing literature mostly centers on the acquisition of information, with a majority of articles focusing on the development of frameworks and models for creating concepts. Additionally, these papers also address the obstacles faced by SMEs in the field of BI, as mentioned by Llave (2017). However, there is a dearth of research that offers empirical examinations of these conceptual studies. Consequently, it is imperative for future investigations in this domain to include empirical studies on the adoption of ICT or conduct case studies. These endeavors will provide valuable insights and suggestions for the future endeavors of SMEs.

The use of ICT tools has been more prevalent in the management of global SCs inside large-scale manufacturing establishments, such as supermarkets and hypermarkets. This adoption of ICT tools serves the purpose of reducing operating expenses and enhancing the value provided by manufacturers (Ataseven and Nail, 2017). The use of ICT has had a significant impact on the automation of SC activities in the food and manufacturing industries. Moreover, this technology is now advancing in the context of large-scale manufacturing businesses. Nevertheless, the use of ICT in the small-scale manufacturing sector is now in its nascent phase (Heeks et al., 2015). Despite the various advantages associated with the deployment and utilization of ICT tools, manufacturers have shown a sluggishness in their acceptance of such tools for the purpose of leading and managing SCs.

SCM has significant importance in Ghana, particularly due to the advent of globalization, which has facilitated the integration of the local economy with the worldwide market (Ataseven and Nail, 2017). Nevertheless, the small-scale industries, which hold a dominating position in Ghana, have yet to fully comprehend the relevance and advantages of SCM (Gurumurthy et al., 2013). The use of ICT in the industrial industry exhibits a notable disparity. Hence, it is essential to conduct a thorough examination of the influence of ICT on SCM. Additionally, it is crucial to explore the potential for ICT utilization within the small-scale manufacturing sector, as it may assist manufacturers in enhancing SC performance, operational efficiency, and the development of competitive SCs.

This may also provide valuable insights for small and medium-sized manufacturing enterprises (SMEs) seeking to comprehend the potential benefits of ICT tools in optimizing SC operations on a smaller scale. The study results will provide fresh insights into the existing body of literature on the effects of ICT on small-scale enterprises. Previous studies have mostly concentrated on the influence of ICT on large-scale manufacturing models. Therefore, the objective of this study is to examine the influence of ICT on SCM within the industrial sector, specifically focusing on small-scale businesses in Ghana.

5.1.3 RESEARCH OBJECTIVES

5.1.3.1 MAIN OBJECTIVE

The objective of this research is to examine the effects of ICT on SCM within the small-scale manufacturing industry in Ghana.

5.1.3.2 SPECIFIC OBJECTIVES

In order to accomplish the aim of this study, the following research objectives will be concentrated on by the researcher for this study:

1. To find out the various ICT tools that affect SCM implementation in SMEs in Tamale.
2. To find out the importance of ICT implementation of SCM in SMEs in Tamale.
3. To find out the challenges facing SCM ICT applications in SMEs in Tamale.

5.1.4 SIGNIFICANCE OF THE STUDY

As stated by Crawford et al. (2016), it is crucial to clearly express the importance of a study in order to effectively communicate the practical implications, influence policy modifications, and stimulate more research. This study was anticipated to have significance for many stakeholders, including organizations, society, and the researcher, in the subsequent manners. The study's results have suggested that more research should be undertaken in the future by subsequent researchers. The study has helped the researcher in gaining valuable insights in the field of inquiry. The research has unveiled the influence of IT on organizational operations, particularly in the context of SMEs. The completion and accomplishment of this study would allow the researcher to fulfill the necessary criteria for obtaining an Advanced Diploma in Logistics and Transport (CILT) degree from CILT International, via Tamale Technical University (TaTU). This study aims to examine the issues faced by organizations in overcoming operational obstacles via the use of IT in their SCM practices. Additionally, potential solutions will be proposed specifically for SMEs. Assist in formulating and presenting efficacious approaches suitable for the integration of ICT within the context of SCM. This resource may serve as supplementary material for researchers investigating procurement, suppliers, professionals, and other relevant topics pertaining to the influence of IT on SCM.

The results of this research might potentially provide valuable insights for professional practitioners by shedding light on distinct encounters and viewpoints on ICT and SCM, as well as the difficulties faced within the consumer products manufacturing sector in Ghana.

5.2 LITERATURE REVIEW

5.2.1 SC

The SC refers to a complex network of organizations that engage in various processes and activities, both upstream and downstream, to create value in the form of goods and services for the end customer or consumer (Lyson and Farrington, 2006). A SC refers to a complex interconnected system including manufacturers, distributors, transporters, storage facilities, and suppliers. This network collaboratively engages in various stages of production, delivery, and ultimately, the sale of a product to the end customer. According to Sharma (2010), the term "SC" encompasses the comprehensive network of interconnected and interdependent enterprises that together serve a common client or consumer.

The SC is composed of various entities, including vendors responsible for supplying raw materials, procedures for converting these materials into products, warehouses for storage, distribution centers for delivery to manufacturers, and manufacturers who ultimately bring the product to the end user. These value chains within the SC are crucial, as they enable producers to meet customer demands in terms of product availability, timing, location, and pricing. Procedures are interconnected only via the SCs, and whatever level of enhancement at the conclusion of a process cannot compensate for shortcomings in the SC that hinder the procedure's capacity to be finalized. A SC refers to a comprehensive network including organizational structures, people, operational processes, data exchange, and material assets that together facilitate the efficient movement of a product or service from its source to the end consumer. The actions within the SC include the conversion of natural resources, raw materials, and components into a final product, which is then transported to the ultimate consumer. The primary goal of the SC is to optimize the total value creation process. The value generated by a SC may be defined as the discrepancy between the perceived worth of the final product to the customer and the level of effort exerted by the SC in fulfilling the customer's demand.

5.2.2 SCM

The notion of SCM, which encompasses the flow of resources throughout an organization, is not a novel idea. The inception of the SCM idea can be traced back to the early 1980s when consultants specializing in resources and asset management first used it to conceptualize the interconnectedness of internal and external functions and logistics, with the aim of achieving coherence (Asgari et al., 2016). According to Ellram and Cooper (2014), the first depiction of SCM mostly focused on the management of material and information movement. The field of SCM involves the operational and tactical activities inside an organization that are aimed at systematically and strategically coordinating all stakeholders both within and outside the logistics channel. This coordination is done with the goal of achieving effective performance and benefiting all parties involved (Mentzer et al., 2015). SCM has been conceptualized by different writers as a process, discipline, philosophy, governance structure, and function (Ellram and Cooper, 2014; Mentzer et al., 2015). The process-oriented perspective of SCM is crucial in comprehending and improving organizational effectiveness in the domains of cross-functional, inter-organizational, collaborative, and sustainability endeavors (Ellram and Cooper, 2014).

The procedures of SCM include the effective administration of several aspects, including customer interaction, supplier relationship, customer service, demand management, order fulfillment, production flow, product development, commercialization, and returns (Lambert and Enz, 2017).

Reefke and Sundaram (2017) conducted a comprehensive analysis of the SC literature and identified many key activities inside the SC. These activities include planning for design, manufacturing, distribution, supply, forward and reverse logistics and are carried out at different levels of the SC, namely strategic, tactical, and operational. The implementation of strategies and oversight of operations, as well as the integration and supervision of activities across different functions and organizational boundaries, and the fostering of collaborative partnerships for long-term mutual benefits, are also fundamental aspects of SC operations (Reefke and Sundaram, 2017).

The aforementioned processes and activities include the comprehensive management of connections and the synchronization of functions within SCs. The management of SCs plays a pivotal role in facilitating the flow and transfer of commodities and energy throughout society (Chardine-Baumann and Botta-Genoulaz, 2014). Therefore, the task of minimizing costs in order to facilitate the movement of products, services, resources, and information is a significant problem (Sitek and Wikarek, 2015). This difficulty arises from the need to coordinate and collaborate across several firms and industries in order to achieve optimal performance in SC operations. According to Jadhav et al. (2018), the integration of collaboration within an organization's SC perspective is a fundamental element in achieving sustainable performance.

The phenomenon of globalization, along with the intricate dynamics of SC operations, has influenced the development of novel management viewpoints aimed at enhancing efficiency and achieving a competitive advantage for enterprises. Consequently, performance assessment systems have become pertinent in this context (Asgari et al., 2016; Avittathur and Jayaram, 2016). According to Balfaqih et al. (2016), the use of measuring systems enables the evaluation of relevant variables within a suitable timeframe, hence facilitating efficient decision-making processes. Various variables may comprise a range of responsibilities and procedures inside partner enterprises operating in the SC (Maestrini et al., 2016). The contemporary approach to SC planning has evolved beyond a sole focus on cost efficiency, and now emphasizes the integration of economic and social considerations in order to address the concerns expressed by many stakeholders (Boukherroub et al., 2015; Zhang et al., 2014). The use of SCM allows organizations to incorporate sustainability concepts into their operational and decision-making processes, making it a crucial component of their business goals (Halldórsson, 2019). The significance of this route is in its comprehensive approach to considering SC operations for the purpose of effective performance evaluation and decision-making, as noted by Balfaqih et al. (2016).

5.2.3 SMES

According to Weeratunge, Bene, Siriwardane, and Charles (2014), small-scale sectors are crucial to the growth of any economy because of the value they provide to the provision of services and the enhancement of national competitiveness via their contributions to industrial output and international trade. Each nation's government takes the necessary precautions to guarantee these efforts are fruitful. Even yet, small-scale and cottage enterprises must contend with internal and external rivalry.

Sannino and Engeström (2017) argue that there is little differentiation between microeconomies and cottage enterprises. Despite the fact that it has been uncovered that cottage business is run entirely by family members, the small-scale industry does employ employees and laborers. Size is used by Singh, Garg, and Deshmukh (2010) to categorize the various small-scale industries. Industrial units with a limited size of operation are represented by the small-scale sectors.

Harris, Riley, and Hand (2017) describe convenience stores, delicatessens, greengrocers, health food stores, and general stores as examples of small-scale formats in manufacturers' production units. Small-scale industries are mentioned in the research by Singh et al. (2010) because they typically demand less initial investment than large-scale industrial facilities. The writers also claim that starting a small business is simple for young people. From the above, we may infer that small-scale sectors signify businesses of a smaller size that need less initial investment and that new-generation individual entrepreneurs will find it simpler to launch a small-scale unit. When discussing the importance of small-scale industry, Rao (2015) emphasizes the role it plays in a country's exports.

However, Sahu (2017) claims that the small-scale industry in developing nations helps drive regional and national economic growth. Many emerging nations, as Rao (2015) explains, possess the requisite capital infrastructure and other resources to launch expansive manufacturing. This shows how crucial the small-scale sector is to the development of the social and economic infrastructure of the world's poorest nations. According to Singh et al. (2010), small-scale businesses make better use of human resources. Sahu (2017), on the other hand, claims that the growth of small-scale industry in developing nations has been helpful in addressing regional issues of poverty, local development, and inequality. Harris, Riley, and Hand (2017) add that the small business sector is associated with stronger employer–employee relationships, leading to more positive working conditions overall. When discussing the difficulties faced by the progressive state in meeting the needs of the small-scale sector, Alam and Noor (2009) take a different tack, emphasizing the importance of developing a robust physical and technical infrastructure for transport and new technologies.

5.2.4 SMES IN GHANA

The following are some of the ways that SMEs are defined in Ghana. According to the National Board for Small-Scale Industries, SMEs are defined as companies with annual sales of $200,000 to $5 million (Branttie, 2017). According to the Venture Capital Trust Fund Act 2004, Act 680, an SME is any business that employs 100 or more people but has assets of less than $1 million (Daily Graphic, 2006). Based on the number of employees they had, companies were divided into three groups in an RPEDG manufacturing survey study: (a) micro-enterprises with fewer than five workers, (b) small businesses with five to 29 workers, and (c) medium businesses with 30 to 99 workers (Teal, 2002). Micro, small, and medium businesses are all categorized in accordance with their staff count. The paper from the Regional Project on Enterprise Development in Ghana's manufacturing sector (Bandari, 2020) provides the definition of SMEs used here. SMEs are crucial to Ghana's economic growth and development. However, Kamunge, Njeru, and Tirimba (2014) found that 40% of SMEs in Africa fail during the first five years of operation. SMEs account for over 90% of businesses and 50% of employment.

It has been shown that (Amoako, 2013) sales and profits increased; expenses were kept under budget; employees showed dedication; and meetings began and ended on time (Yazdanfar and Ahman, 2015). It is been known for a long time that SMEs are crucial to help developing nations reach their economic targets (Bandari, 2020). One reason so many SMEs in Ghana fail is that their managers do not properly implement HRM practices (Ogunyomi and Bruning, 2016). In 2018, almost 75% of small and medium-sized businesses in Ghana failed (Awal, 2018).

5.2.5 IT

ICT is, according to Majchrzak, Markus, and Wareham (2016), a vital component of every growing organization. The importance of ICT in helping businesses achieve their goals has grown. ICT are those that facilitate conversation and provide access to data (Bloom et al., 2014). Throughout the organization, ICT is utilized for a variety of purposes, including but not limited to planning, transaction processing, and decision-making. ICT may be described as the components and infrastructure that are necessary to enable contemporary computing (as outlined by Dwivedi, Shareef, Simintiras, and Weerakkody, 2016). People and businesses alike benefit from being able to engage with the online world because of advancements in ICT. ICT is described as an outgrowth of IT that employs communication technologies by Donnellan, Sheridan, and Curry (2011). IT and information and communications technology have grown synonymous in recent years (Bloom et al., 2014). According to Kushwaha (2011), ICT is an information system instrument that facilitates cooperation and coordination between businesses and marketplaces to create a buyer-seller dynamic.

Internet, computer networks, mobile phones, and wireless networks together comprise the backbone of ICT, which allows for the rapid dissemination of information and its prompt retrieval in order to boost productivity. The authors note that ICT is a crossroads where several technologies meet to allow for instantaneous information access. This crossroads is formed by hardware, software, IT services, networking, and communication. Based on the above, we may conclude that ICT is primarily concerned with the use of communication technologies and applications to provide digital access to and exchange of information for both internal and external communication. The wirelessly connected mobile world and the internet-enabled sphere are both included in ICT.

According to Ilomäki, Paavola, Lakkala, and Kantosalo (2016), one of ICT's primary roles is to provide its customers with the features they need in order to carry out their businesses' daily operations successfully. Thus, it can be shown that information systems are often the carrier of features. As can be seen above, the corporate entities, customers, partners, firm personnel, and other parties are not the sole users of functionality; some other system also plays a role. Improvements in the realm of ICT have also boosted productivity and bottom lines in the logistics, transportation, and industrial service industries. The requirement and utilization of ICT solutions in SCM to deal with time problems, communication breakdown, real-time information demands, and rapid customer delivery has been emphasized by the rising market competitiveness in order to get an advantage over competitors (Kushwaha, 2011).

Gualandris and Kalchschmidt (2014) argue that businesses that are able to think beyond the box are better able to meet the demands of their customers.

The creation of renewable, energy-efficient, and healthful products is one example of the kind of innovation that might benefit society and the environment (Marshall et al., 2015a).

Firms in the SC may benefit all stakeholders by being more creative since this helps them create more sustainable SC practices (Silvestre, 2015). Culture, openness to information, and new ideas may all contribute to an organization's long-term viability if given the proper attention. For optimal efficiency, the SC's sustainability practices should be driven by an innovative and creative corporate culture (Ahmad et al., 2016; Shuen et al., 2014). Reverse logistics may be avoided by the use of eco-efficiency, socio-efficiency, miniaturization, lean manufacturing, renewable resources, and biodegradable manufacture (Schaltegger and Burritt, 2014).

5.2.6 FACTORS INFLUENCING ICT USE IN SMALL-SCALE SECTOR

Manufacturers are using ICT in the form of mobile technologies to track shipments in real-time and keep tabs on delivery systems, according to research by Tan et al., 2012. Behera et al. (2015) note, however, that many manufacturers are adopting cutting-edge ICT tools in order to stay competitive in the market. The integration cost of adopting new technology and the risk involved in making the switch from legacy systems to cutting-edge systems are also cited as factors affecting the adoption of ICT by small enterprises. According to Hashim (2007), small businesses have a dilemma when it comes to adopting cutting-edge technologies because of the disparity between the high costs of doing so and the potential payoffs. On the other hand, Apulu, Latham, and Moreton (2011) note that small-scale firms' poor trust in ICT solutions is driven by concerns about security and privacy.

SMEs are realizing that technology is playing an enabling role in the SC industry's rapid growth. IT has the potential to streamline operations and save money for the business. When it comes to managing IT, the manufacturing sector has its own unique set of problems. Because the manufacturing business is so customer-focused, many manufacturers find it difficult to process the vast volumes of data generated by their customers. Olatunji (2015), on the other hand, argues that manufacturers need to improve communication and tracking across their various systems in order to better integrate those systems from start to finish, from production to consumption. According to Ongori's (2009) illustration, electronic product labeling and radio frequency identification have made the whole SC smarter. To keep tabs on stock, manufacturers need to make real-time data available. Furthermore, the firm is in a better position to secure its shipments thanks to radio frequency identification tagging, which enables items to be monitored from the factory all the way through the SC.

While external threats to payment security are being addressed by PCI Security Compliance, the internal security infrastructure and procedures of manufacturers are also being addressed. To accept credit card payments, a company must ensure it complies with PCI Security Standards. Manufacturers risk losing the ability to accept credit card payments if they collect or maintain credit card information that is subsequently hacked. Other outcomes may include legal action, insurance claims, closed accounts, and monetary penalties from authorities. Manufacturers who make use of IT outsourcing will reap the benefits of expert guidance and cost savings (Ongori, 2009). In order to reduce overhead and boost service quality, many manufacturers are now using IT outsourcing.

5.2.7 ICT IN SCM

Christopher (2016) argues that improved communication between suppliers, manufacturers, and companies may lead to a more efficient SC. When it comes to data sharing, information interchange, and information processing in real-time to increase communication among external SC partners and organizational members, it is safe to say that ICT role has revolutionized the conventional SC. In a similar vein, Wang, Rodrigues, and Evans (2015) argue that ICT has greatly aided manufacturers' organizations in terms of obtaining, processing, and exchanging transactional information, which in turn has led to better cooperation, coordination, and communication in leading SC business operations from supplier to manufacturing units to distribution centers to wholesalers/manufacturers to customers.

Researchers Mangiaracina, Melacini, and Perego (2012) looked at the impact of ICT on SMEs in the sector of manufacturing. The authors found that ICT has been a primary factor in SCI, opening up fresh possibilities for fostering better interactions with both suppliers and consumers. Christopher (2016) argues that the flexibility and adaptability afforded by ICT technologies are what ultimately boost the SC's efficiency and efficacy. In terms of SCM, it is safe to say that customization aids in integrating planning processes across all operations.

However, Wang et al. (2015) show that opportunities exist for manufacturing manufacturers sector in the United Kingdom thanks to ICT technologies that cut carbon emissions from road freight transit. According to Tan et al. (2012), ICT on SCM is a concept involving the sharing of information between stakeholders of the manufacturers industry chain, that is, manufacturers, manufacturer, and distributor, to achieve high efficiencies and also reduce the cost of the products sold by reducing lead times and inventory cost, and improve the quality of the products to be delivered. Rapid progress has been made in the use of ICT in logistics and SCM throughout the years. Many businesses now use ICT in a broad variety of departments and functions. It has opened up new channels of communication between businesses and their suppliers and consumers, as well as inside businesses themselves. According to studies (Tan et al., 2012), the use of ICT is quickly increasing in SCM.

Due to rising levels of competition, businesses of all sizes are adopting new methods to boost SC efficiency through deeper integration, with ICT serving as a crucial enabler of this process through its facilitation of data sharing and mitigation of operational inefficiencies. The Bullwhip effect is a prime example of the inconsistencies and uncertainties that may be reduced with the use of ICT in SCM, which is the focus of the research. This necessitates a heightened emphasis on data exchange, the foundation for SC automation. To better optimize the company's SC operations, research is applied to projects like vendor-managed inventory (VMI) and collaborative planning, forecasting, and replenishment (CPFR) (Singh et al., 2010), which are described as initiatives that call for automation in the transport of physical materials and the exchange of information between businesses. While establishing technology's significance, several studies have emphasized the need to incorporate technology into the company's culture and restructure its operations in order to gain a competitive edge (Oyebiyi et al., 2017).

Optimal inventory levels, cheaper transportation, and simplified procurement processes are just some of the ways that the current research characterizes the positive benefits of ICT on the SC (Majchrzak et al., 2016). Studies agree that SCM's pricing, quality, and lead time all change if ICT is introduced. Businesses have restructured to take advantage of IT and are re-establishing the way work is done inside their organizations. This is good news for customers because it means they have more options for purchasing high-quality goods at affordable costs. Although SCM has been around as long as commerce itself, improvements in ICT have led to more efficient, quicker, and cheaper supply chains in the present day. SC operations have been completely transformed by information engineering, which integrates cutting-edge IT with more efficient means of manufacturing, inventory management, distribution, and purchasing.

5.2.8 ICT TOOLS FOR SCM IMPLEMENTATION

To boost organizational (or individual) efficiency and effectiveness, ICT technologies play a supporting role in human resource operations (Cohen et al., 2002). As a result, ICT tools aid in speeding up the execution of tasks, bolstering autonomous decision-making processes, and enabling distributive operations (Huang and Nof, 1999) to increase logistics efficiency (Jack et al., 2006). As Bharadwaj (2000) points out, improved business practices may be adopted to fulfill customer service standards if ICT tools are used to increase transparency. Here are a few examples of cutting-edge communication tools that can help businesses stay ahead of the competition by improving their customer service and cutting down on delays.

5.2.8.1 BARCODING

According to Lysons and Farrington (2006), a barcode is a machine-readable representation of data. Information on barcodes used to be recorded in the widths and spacing of written parallel lines, but today there are many alternative patterns available. Optical scanners, often known as barcode readers or scanners, can read barcodes. Barcodes are often employed in automated data capture systems because they facilitate more precise and rapid data input into computers. Barcoding streamlines the distribution of goods and data within an organization. Automatic warehouse applications such as receiving, put away packing and shipping, package tracking, access control, and lot tracking are just some of the many ways barcoding can be put to use in a warehouse (Lysons and Farrington, 2006).

5.2.8.2 ERP

ERP is an integrated business management system powered by modularized software applications that span the whole enterprise. Unlike Material Resource Planning (MRP), which is only useful for factories, ERP can be implemented by any business and gives managers across all departments insight into what is and is not happening in the company at any given time (Lysons and Farrington, 2006). Most ERP systems are built on a set of modules that may function alone or in tandem with one another. The ERP system is made up of many modules that handle different aspects of business operations. Accounting data, such as accounts receivable and payable, payroll, and other financial and management accounting data are monitored by the finance module, as stated by Leenders and Fearon (1993). Inventory and warehouse management, as well as transportation, are often treated as sub-modules inside the logistics module.

ERP allows for more precise inventory counts with fewer audits, cutting down on the requirement for frequent physical counts. Setting up takes less time when people and machines are well-coordinated and when downtime is kept to a minimum via regular maintenance. ERP software promotes high-quality output with robust manufacturing subcomponents by proactively identifying quality concerns and furnishing the data necessary to boost output while decreasing waste and rework (Jack and Samuel, 2006).

5.2.8.3 MRP

This method is a computer-based information system that helps with the precise planning of production; it is mainly demand-based and tailored for assembly activities. The purpose of MRP is to ensure that components are accessible for use in the next phase of production or shipment before they are needed. Purchasing and control departments may use this to ensure that the proper materials are delivered to production and distribution facilities at the right time (Lysons and Farrington, 2006). SCM software also facilitates analysis of decision-making ramifications, allowing for on-the-fly adaptation to factors like rush orders and coordination of production with purchasing, marketing, and human resources regarding, for example, the timing of supply deliveries, using sales forecasts to determine master budgets, and planning recruitment or run-downs of personnel.

5.2.8.4 DISTRIBUTION REQUIREMENTS PLANNING (DRP)

Scheduling method DRP regulates stock levels by adapting the concepts of MRP for use with distribution stock. It is also possible to see it as a technique for managing stock restocking inside a company. Both production-focused businesses like automakers selling via a network of dealers and retailers at the local, regional, and national levels, as well as pure retail operations like grocery stores, may benefit from DRP (William, 2009).

5.2.9 RESEARCH MODEL

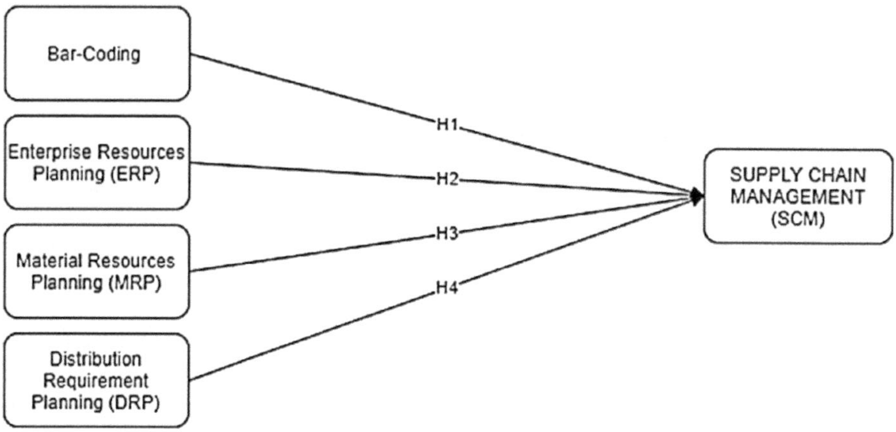

FIGURE 5.1 Conceptual framework.

5.2.10 HYPOTHESIS

H_1: There is a significant positive relationship between barcoding and SCM performance.

H_2: There is a significant positive relationship between ERP and SCM performance.

H_3: There is a significant positive relationship between MRP and SCM performance.

H_4: There is a significant positive relationship between DRP and SCM performance.

5.2.11 BENEFITS OF ICT IN SCM

Using ICT technologies in SCM in manufacturing and even manufacturing has several advantages. Supply chain efficiency may be increased with the use of ICT solutions, as stated by De Marchi et al. (2017). The authors also claim that ICT updates the static, inflexible, and unreliable conventional SCM by facilitating real-time, trustworthy information interchange and sharing. The use of cloud computing, mobile, and wireless technologies in the industrial industry has facilitated more accuracy, efficiency, and openness in SCM. Improvements in SCM, logistics costs, lead time (LT), and customer loyalty as a result of long-term connection and trust building were listed as the benefits of using an ICT solution in manufacturing outlets by Mangiaracina et al. (2012). Lu and Swatman (2009) found that the Australian grocery manufacturing industry benefited from ICT solutions such as increased data gathering capabilities, SC planning integration with producers, and greater information availability through mobile technology. Due to the many advantages offered by ICT in areas such as managing store operations, inventory, and stock, marketing, etc., its usage in grocery stores, shops, and supermarkets has been ubiquitous in recent years. ICT has advantages over conventional, non-computerized methods of advertising, according to research by Nurmi, Salovaara, Forsblom, Bohnert, and Floreen (2014).

According to research by Donner and Escobari (2010), the usage of emails has benefited manufacturers in rapid communication with suppliers in a cost-effective way, which is one of the benefits of ICT in the small-scale food industry. According to Sin Tan, Choy Chong, Lin, and Cyril Eze (2010), manufacturers may reach their target audience and connect with them through mobile phone applications at a low-cost thanks to internet advertising. In contrast, research by Nurmi et al. (2014) found that implementing ICT into the grocery industry has the added bonus of improving decision-making. According to Novotny, David, and Csafor (2015), ICT technologies gather, process, and disseminate real-time information, allowing manufacturers to make rapid and effective choices to manage day-to-day company operations. Sin Tan et al. (2010) also point out the importance of using ICT tools to spot business opportunities and dangers early on, allowing manufacturers to act swiftly and effectively.

Another way in which ICT has helped the food industry is by allowing manufacturers to respond more quickly to consumer questions, concerns, and compliments via the use of ICT solutions (Nurmi et al., 2014). With the use of ICT, businesses can easily collect data about their customers, such as their demographics, spending habits, and service preferences. Manufacturers may benefit from increasing consumer knowledge by capitalizing on possibilities to offer more items. Lopez-Nicolas and Soto-Acosta (2010) note that satisfying the company's informational demands is another way that ICT may be used to improve the efficacy and efficiency of organizational learning. However, the research by Kurnia et al., (2015) highlights the advantages of ICT, highlighting how ICT tools and solutions aid in lowering costs and raising revenues via increased productivity and decreased human error. One advantage of ICT is that it helps businesses in the grocery industry do better financially.

5.2.12 CHALLENGES IN IMPLEMENTING IT ON SC

5.2.12.1 LEGAL AND REGULATORY BARRIERS

Most African nations have challenges in technology development and growth due to legal and regulatory hurdles (Manuere et al., 2012). Due to the high turnover rate of governments and the associated uncertainty of policy, small company owners are hesitant to make ICT investments (Manuere et al., 2012). In addition, the government and industry groups seldom back small enterprises with a strong enough legal framework to enforce IT regulations. According to Olusola and Oluwaseun (2013), legal and regulatory difficulties are a significant barrier to IT deployment for small firms in developing nations. In order to justify IT expenditures, Riaeche (2015) said that, although developing nations must acquire IT and have proper laws in place, company leaders and workers must comprehend the advantages of IT in the corporate growth process.

According to Edoho (2013), the fundamental foundations for using ICT for development in Africa are incomplete and lack coordination. According to Edoho, weak institutional and regulatory capabilities in poor nations make it unlikely that they will embrace the 2-G or 3-G models of ICT in the next decade. It is the responsibility of governments and other stakeholders to ensure that ICT platforms and frameworks meet the needs of all companies, from sole proprietorships to multinational conglomerates (Kamunge et al., 2014).

5.2.12.2 HUMAN RESOURCE DEFICIT

According to the research conducted by Obeng and Boachie (2018), it was suggested that the human intellectual resource, which encompasses factors such as training, experience, intelligence, and skills of individuals, plays a pivotal role as an internal organizational resource. This resource is considered to be the primary catalyst for achieving profitability, facilitating the development and delivery of new products, optimizing the utilization of innovative technology, and catering to diverse customer preferences. According to Navimipour et al. (2015), the use of human resource capabilities, including strength, expertise, knowledge, and skills, has the potential to contribute to the achievement of organizational success. According to the findings of Jimenez et al. (2015), it can be argued that the pursuit of tertiary education has a positive impact on formal entrepreneurship. This assertion is based on many factors, including heightened self-confidence, reduced perception of risk, and improved human capital. Research has shown that individuals who attain a higher degree of education are more inclined to start their own entrepreneurial endeavors in comparison to those with lower levels of education (Byrd et al., 2013; Jimenez et al., 2015). Furthermore, scholars in the field of business have proposed a direct connection between human capital and the achievement of economic enterprises. Tsekouras, Kanellou, and Rai (2013) conducted an observation indicating that small enterprises have a disadvantage in the realm of management skills training, which is essential for their competitiveness in an economy driven by information and knowledge. The expertise in ICT has a significant impact on the processes and advancement of information management. This involves several aspects such as the generation and transfer of data, as well as the coding and preservation of information systems (Al-Halaly and Alnajjaar, 2016; Hawajreh and Sharabati, 2012).

The limited proficiency in ICT has had a notable impact on the acceptance and utilization of technological advancements among small company proprietors (Mng'ong'ose and Victor, 2018). According to Martina et al. (2013), the primary factor driving the adoption of ICT is excitement. According to Martina et al. (year), it was suggested that insufficient skills and knowledge among both management and departmental personnel contribute to the emergence of additional obstacles to the deployment of ICT, as well as internal employee resistance toward adopting ICT. ICT allows corporate executives to provide a framework that facilitates the effective acquisition, retention, and application of information (Bogdanović, 2014). According to Lasch, Robert, and Le Roy (2013), the concept of human capital is often recognized as a significant driver of competitive advantage. Given that ICT is mostly reliant on knowledge and expertise, a substantial proportion of the population possessing limited educational attainment and skills would have a detrimental impact on the effectiveness of ICT.

5.2.12.3 CAPITAL INVESTMENT

According to Kiveu and Ofafa (2013), a significant barrier to IT adoption for small enterprises is a lack of financial and capital commitment. According to research by Cunningham, Cunningham, and Ekenberg (2016), company owners in poor countries have limited resources to put toward the purchase of ICT tools and equipment. Many company owners can only afford to cover the most fundamental costs (Cunningham et al., 2016). Small business owners have it tough when it comes to securing bank loans to fund SCM, as observed by Osano and Languitone (2016). Osano and Languitone argued further that these difficulties posed a considerable SCM problem, especially for smaller enterprises.

5.3 RESEARCH METHODOLOGY

5.3.1 RESEARCH DESIGN

The three most popular types of study designs are exploratory, descriptive, and explanatory. Based on the general concepts of theoretical saturation, the constant comparison technique of analysis, and theoretical saturation, grounded theory is generated via exploratory research (Glaser and Straus, 1967). Similarly, the purpose of an exploratory research design is to learn as much as possible about a topic. Flexibility and adaptability are two further benefits of exploratory research (Saunders et al., 2009). The purpose of descriptive research, on the other hand, is to provide a detailed picture of a topic of study. According to Saunders et al. (2009), descriptive studies may be seen as either an expanded exploratory or an explanatory study. Explanatory research is the last strategy. The goal of an explanatory design research is to investigate a problem or issue and determine if there is a connection between two or more independent factors (Ibid). Nonetheless, this study was mostly descriptive in nature.

5.3.2 RESEARCH STRATEGY

This study made use of a quantitative methodology. Focusing on numerical representations of data and using statistical processes in data analysis are hallmarks of the quantitative research approach (Dietz and Kalof, 2009). Despite the preliminary and unpredictable character of the findings, statistical techniques as the major drivers of quantitative analysis aid in enhancing decision-making (Frankfort-Nachmias and Leon-Guerrero, 2015). Denzin and Lincoln (2013) and Babbi (2017) argue that the quantitative approach, which emphasizes causation and measurements, is less thorough and nuanced. Through conversation, qualitative research may shed light on participants' backgrounds and worldviews (Merriam and Tisdell, 2016; Yin, 2016). Therefore, the qualitative technique was not suitable for this research since it aimed to give an in-depth explanation of the sustainability issue in the everyday surroundings of the participants.

5.3.3 POPULATION

Most urbanized and industrialized regions of Ghana are home to several thriving SMEs. The Northern Region of Ghana has had its share of growth in a variety of industries, and the researcher has given considerable thought to interviewing small-scale businesses in Tamale. However, the focus of this research is on the small-scale sector in the southern region of the Northern Hemisphere. Most of the Northern Region's industrially developed regions also have thriving small business communities. The city of Tamale, in Ghana's Northern Region, was taken into account because of the rapid expansion of its small-scale industrial sector in recent years.

5.3.4 SAMPLING AND SAMPLE SIZE

Sampling is the process of choosing individuals to take part in a study or experiment. The study accounted for the respondents' demographics (in particular, where they were located), as well as the research topic, aims, methodology, and consequences. Purposeful sampling was utilized to zero down on the most relevant respondents. To get answers that are both representative of the population of interest and compelling, the researcher used purposive sampling to select civil engineers and quantity surveyors from the ten regional offices of the SMEs in the Northern Region. In addition, non-probability sampling strategies are appropriate when the population size is uncertain or when individual members of the population cannot be uniquely recognized (Yin, 2018). In addition, Burns and Grove (2003) stress that this kind of sampling allows the researcher to pick and choose which respondents will give the most in-depth information regarding the topic under study. In all, 38 people were found to be in possession of accurate data. This results in a sample size of 38.

5.3.5 DATA COLLECTION AND INSTRUMENTATION

Depending on the goals of the research, choosing the right people to engage in the study is crucial (Creswell and Poth, 2018). Access to participants was taken into account as part of the study's design in light of the inclusion and exclusion criteria I outlined in the section on participant selection reasoning. I used my social connections in the area to meet with site gatekeepers and get approval for sending out invitations to potential study participants among the SC members.

The study relied on primary sources for its data. To learn more about people's thoughts on the implementation of ICT in SMEs, a questionnaire was designed. The items were categorized in accordance with the study's aims. The information was gathered with the use of a standardized, closed-ended questionnaire. The questions on the survey were straightforward and simple to answer. The arrangement was both aesthetically pleasing and straightforward, making it a pleasure to read and digest. Respondents were given questionnaires to fill out, and the researcher collected them after the allotted time for responses had passed. In order to ensure that the data obtained is consistent and reliable, questionnaires were employed. The researcher's depiction of problems is less likely to be skewed as a result. A self-administered questionnaire was used to compile the data. One extreme to the other on the five-point Likert scale was chosen.

5.3.6 DATA ANALYSIS

In order to draw conclusions from a large amount of numerical data, statistical techniques are used in quantitative data analysis. As was mentioned before, questionnaires were distributed in the field to gather information from factory employees in the Tamale-Northern area. Data reduction was performed after data collection to choose, organize, refine, concentrate, and summarize data for further study. The acquired information was formatted such that it might be used in further studies. The questionnaire results were revised for completeness, uniformity, and correctness. Primary data was analyzed using SPSS version 24 and Amos to analyze a survey that relied on questionnaires. The data was analyzed using descriptive statistics, a t-test on a single data set, and a factor analysis. Quantitative data was then given meaning and consequences via quantitative explanations. These allowed for reasonable inferences and suggestions based on the study results.

5.4 DATA ANALYSIS AND INTERPRETATION

5.4.1 IMPORTANCE OF ICT-BASED SCM IMPLEMENTATION

Respondents rated the importance of using SCM during road building, and the results are shown in Figure 5.1. According to the data, over 52% of those surveyed thought that using SCM during road building was crucial. The vast majority of respondents (approximately 91%) ranked the adoption of SCM as either "important" (39%) or "very important" (52%), respectively. Only 3% of respondents said that execution was not at all essential, and only 6% said that it was only somewhat important. SCM's use in the road building industry was rated as unimportant, on average.

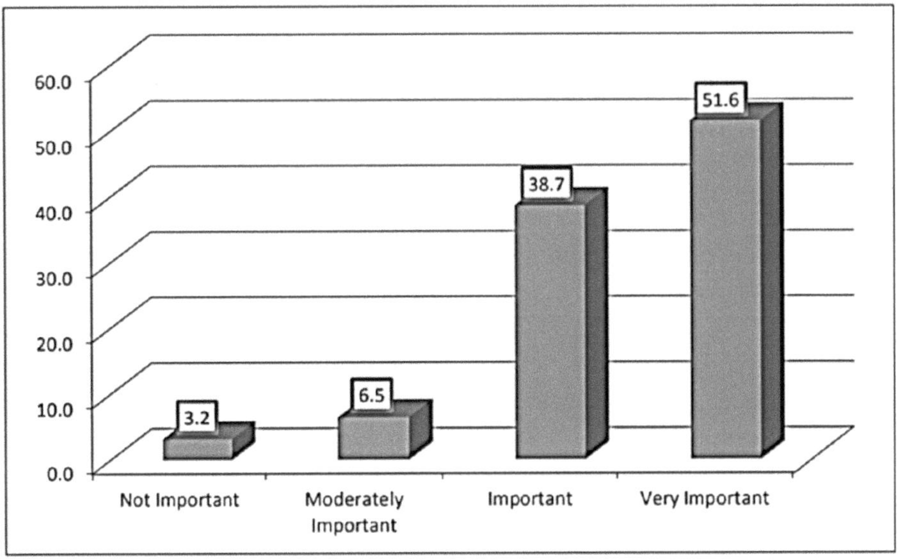

FIGURE 5.2 Importance of ICT-based SCM implementation.

Source: Field survey, 2021

5.4.2 DESCRIPTIVE STATISTICS

Descriptive statistics were used to ascertain the manner in which respondents scaled each variable, with the aim of identifying the commonly utilized SC tactics in road building. A chi-square statistical analysis was conducted to assess the significance of scaling. The descriptive statistics in Table 5.2 display the mean and standard deviation as the primary focus.

TABLE 4.1 ICT Tools on SCM Descriptive Statistics.

Factor	No.	Mean	SD
Bar-coding (B-C)	38	4.22	0.992
Enterprise Resources Planning (ERP)	38	3.81	0.749
Material Resources Planning (MRP)	38	3.65	0.709
Distribution Requirement Planning (DRP)	38	4.64	0.911
Supply Chain Management (SCM)	38	3.45	0.995

Source: Field survey, 2021

Table 5.1 displays the average values and standard deviations of the variables related to ICT-based SCM techniques in the SME sector. The DRP method exhibited the highest mean value in SCM, with a mean of 4.34 and a standard deviation of 0.911. This low standard deviation indicates the importance of DRP in the context of SMEs' ICT-enabled SCM. Subsequently, bar codes were observed to possess a mean value of 4.22 and a standard deviation of 0.992. There were three variables whose mean values ranged from 3.45 to 3.81. The aforementioned strategies included enduring partnerships, the process of choosing suppliers, and the management of the SC. The mean values of the other techniques were found to be more than 3.0. There was a notable disparity seen among the various groups of each variable. The observed trend indicated a positive tendency, as the majority of respondents ranked the variables as often or very frequent, while only a small number of respondents assessed them as moderate, less frequent, or not frequent. The only characteristic that exhibited no statistically significant variation between evaluations was long-term partnerships.

TABLE 4.2 Challenges of ICT-SCM Implementation

Factor	No.	Mean	SD
Resistance to technology advancement adoption	38	3.86	0.735
Lack of organization encouragement	38	4.00	0.731
Lack of communication between supply chain partners	38	4.22	0.853
Insufficient information technology	38	3.94	0.854
Inadequate technical capabilities	38	3.94	0.964
Supplier reluctance to change	38	3.77	0.956
Lack of top management commitment	38	3.65	0.877

Respondents were asked to rate the severity of twenty obstacles to ICT-SCM on a scale from 1 to 5, where 1 meant "not severe" and 5 meant "very severe," in an effort to expose the obstacles of ICT-SCM. As can be seen in Table 5.2, the mean values for the difficulties encountered in managing the ICT SC by SMEs are rather high. There were seven scaled variables, and their means varied from 3.65 to 4.22. Lack of organization encouragement had the highest mean value (4.22), indicating the greatest severity of all the variables. There were also high mean values for characteristics including not enough IT, not enough top-level management commitment, not enough technical chops, not enough IT, and not enough supplier openness to change. There was no discernible pattern in the absence of support from upper management and the absence of adequate IT. Both factors were found to scale between moderately severe and extremely severe.

TABLE 4.3 Loadings and Validity/Reliability

Factor	Item	Loadings	α	CR	AVE
Bar-coding (B-C)	B-C1	0.655	0.870	0.805	0.755
	B-C2	0.774	0.805	0.784	0.565
	B-C3	0.722	0.784	0.854	0.784
	B-C4	0.841	0.870	0.944	0.644
Enterprise Resources Planning (ERP)	ERP 1	0.854	0.805	0.805	0.605
	ERP 2	0.744	0.784	0.784	0.784
	ERP 3	0.753	0.854	0.854	0.742
	ERP 4	0.712	0.744	0.944	0.505
Material Resources Planning (MRP)	MRP 1	0.854	0.753	0.805	0.784
	MRP 2	0.645	0.912	0.784	0.575
	MRP 3	0.874	0.805	0.805	0.784
	MRP 4	0.751	0.784	0.784	0.654
	MRP 5	0.674	0.860	0.870	0.744
Distribution Requirement Planning (DRP)	DRP 1	0.870	0.854	0.805	0.575
	DRP 2	0.805	0.944	0.784	0.784
	DRP 3	0.784	0.805	0.854	0.854
Supply Chain Management (SCM)	SCM 1	0.812	0.784	0.744	0.744
	SCM 2	0.780	0.854	0.805	0.505
	SCM 3	0.920	0.784	0.984	0.784
	SCM 4	0.880	0.871	0.870	0.754
	SCM 5	0.760	0.855	0.815	0.544

Source: Field survey, 2021

5.4.3 MEASUREMENT MODEL AND FACTOR LOADING

The measurement framework illustrates the connection between each item and its underlying variable. The evaluation of the measurement structure is conducted through assessments of convergent and discriminant validity. The findings from tests of reliability, internal consistency, and validity are also displayed. The analysis of the measurement model's results can be found in Table 5.3. To determine the convergent validity of constructs, the average variance extracted (AVE) metric is employed. A value of AVE equal to or exceeding 0.5 is considered satisfactory for confirming the convergent validity of constructs (Fornell and Larcker, 1981). For gauging the internal consistency of constructs, Cronbach's α and composite reliability (CR) are the two parameters employed. The internal consistency should ideally fall within the range of 0.70 to 0.95 (Hair et al., 2014). Table 5.3 indicates that all values surpass the acceptable threshold, thus affirming the presence of convergent validity and internal consistency. Discriminant validity signifies that distinct constructs exhibit dissimilarity and share substantial variance with their respective variables rather than with variables from other constructs (Geotz et al., 2010; Hulland, 1999). This evaluation involves comparing the square root of AVE with the correlation among latent variables, with the square root of AVE expected to exceed the latent variable correlation (Chin, 1998). Table 5.3 displays values that surpass the established thresholds, indicating the attainment of satisfactory discriminant validity. Consequently, the measurement model demonstrates both reliability and validity.

TABLE 4.4 Discriminant Validity

Constructs	B-C	DRP	MRP	DRP	SCM
Bar-coding (B-C)	**0.708**	-	-	-	-
Enterprise Resources Planning (ERP)	0.181	**0.718**	-	-	-
Material Resources Planning (MRP)	0.066	0.369	**0.726**	-	-
Distribution Requirement Planning (DRP)	0.222	0.157	0.144	**0.759**	-
Supply Chain Management (SCM)	0.365	0.269	0.442	0.343	**0.710**

Source: Field survey, 2021

For the purpose of making the measurement applicable on a broader scale, it becomes necessary to establish predictive validity or criterion-related validity. This involves the comparison of second-order factor models with one or multiple external variables, known or presumed to assess the particular attribute. Criterion-related validity entails forecasting against an external criterion and entails evaluating a measuring instrument's alignment with a specific outcome or measure, either presently or in the future (Kerlinger, 1986).

Within this study, the criterion chosen to evaluate predictive validity is the dependent variable, also referred to as the endogenous latent variable. To assess the preliminary statistical validity (predictive validity) of the four hypotheses outlined in Chapter 4, the Pearson correlation was employed, which does not establish causal connections. Each construct was denoted by a composite score derived from averaging the scores of all items within a specific construct. For instance, the sub-construct's score was determined by averaging its constituent items' scores, and subsequently, the higher-order construct's composite score was calculated by averaging the sub-construct scores it comprised. The outcomes are detailed in Table 5.4. The results from the table clearly indicate that all correlations hold statistical significance at the 0.01 level.

TABLE 4.5 Path Coefficient and Hypothesis Analysis

Hyphothesis	Paths	β	t-statistics	Sig.	Decision
H_1	B-C→SCM	0.182	1.918	0.001	Accepted
H_2	ERP→SCM	0.077	0.575	0.066	Rejected
H_3	MRP→SCM	0.305	2.962	0.003	Accepted
H_4	DRP→SCM	0.222	0.963	0.040	Accepted

Path coefficient (β) = 1-1; p-value<0.05

Source: Field survey, 2021

Soleimani et al. (2017) indicate that when assessing construct validity, the utilization of structural equation modeling (SEM) is considered more advantageous compared to alternative statistical methods like multiple regression analysis. Thus, the employment of IBM SPSS and AMOS was deemed suitable for this research endeavor due to their alignment with exploratory studies and potential contributions to the existing literature (Gefen et al., 2011; Henseler et al., 2009). The research employed the Analysis of Moment Structures (AMOS) software, utilizing a bootstrapping technique involving 5000 resamples. This method was applied to scrutinize hypotheses and ascertain the significance levels of route coefficients (Chin, 1998).

With the exception of the ERP to SCM route, all pathways demonstrated statistical significance. It is noteworthy that the study's hypotheses yielded positive outcomes, evident through the favorable Path coefficient values (β). The affirmation of H1 is derived from the identification of a statistically significant advantageous relationship between the utilization of barcoding technology and SCM performance ($\beta=0.182$; $t=1.918$ and $p=0.001$).

Hypothesis 2, which proposes a substantial positive correlation between ERP and SCM performance, is contradicted by the statistical analysis results ($\beta=0.077$; $t=0.575$ and $p=0.066$). Conversely, Hypothesis 3 establishes a statistically significant positive correlation between MRP and SCM performance, as substantiated by the calculated coefficient ($\beta=0.305$), associated t-value ($t=2.962$), and p-value ($p=0.003$).

Furthermore, Hypothesis 4 gains support from the study, revealing a statistically significant positive connection between DRP and SCM performance (β=0.222; t=0.963 and p=0.040). These summarized findings are encapsulated in Table 5.5.

5.5 SUMMARY OF FINDINGS

H1, which asserts that a considerable favorable connection exists between barcoding and the enhancement of SCM performance, is affirmed (β=0.182; t= 1.918 and p=0.001). H2: A notable constructive correlation between ERP and SCM performance is refuted (β=0.077; t=0.575 and p=0.066). H3: A significant positive association between MRP and SCM performance is validated (β=0.305; t= 2.962 and p=0.003). H4: An important affirmative link between DRP and SCM performance is acknowledged (β=0.222; t= 0.963 and p=0.040).

This study identifies barriers within the realm of SCM in road construction, encompassing the absence of commitment from upper management; insufficient technical competencies; inadequate utilization of IT; supplier resistance toward change; and absence of encouragement within the organizational framework.

5.6 CONCLUSION

A well-coordinated and efficient SC cannot exist without the information that drives every business. Therefore, it must be up-to-date, accurate, vetted, focused on the scope, and intelligently controlled by analytics. By providing a bird's eye view of inventory (demands patterns, carrying costs), transportation (customer location, shipment sizes), facility (location, capacity, smart grid), and use design for recycling and reusing materials, reducing waste, and minimizing defects, ICT tools aid in SC activities, proper planning, and management strategic decisions. Lysons and Farrington (2006) found that using an ICT tool (ERP, CRM) improved SC performance overall. Companies need to be aware of the dynamic nature of the business and the competitive landscapes in which they operate. When an organization fails to keep pace with its rivals, it risks going out of business. In order to maximize earnings, the SC must strike a balance between meeting the demands of its customers and keeping its operating expenses in check. A company's strategic objectives of customer pleasure and profitability via cost management may be effectively pursued with the help of ICT solutions. Recently, businesses have turned to ICT instruments to guarantee productive

SC operations. More and more businesses are adopting technical innovations like DRP, ERP, MRP, Barcodes, and RFID to get a competitive advantage in their material management.

SC activities are aided by ICT technologies. Workload, lengthy LT, responsiveness, consistent quality, and efficiency are just a few of the issues that plague businesses that do not use ICT technologies in their SC. Every company, particularly those in manufacturing, understands the importance of ICT tools to SC success. Distribution and transport networks are highly coordinated, making it simpler for these businesses to keep accurate records of inventory and raw materials.

5.7 RECOMMENDATION

Findings reveal that small manufacturing companies may benefit from a training program that emphasizes the use of ICT to better manage SC activities and functions. It is also recommended to work with technology companies in order to learn about the price, advantages, and training needs of emerging ICT technologies. Therefore, it is recommended to improve knowledge and upgraded the skills of the employees in the manufacturing sector to adapt to new communication technologies, which can increase use of ICT in supply chain operations management, and thereby increase the positive impact of ICT on SCM.

Researchers need to have a more futuristic view of ICT tools given their potentially transformative effect on SC performance. Logistics and industrial businesses may benefit the most from using ICT tools as a mean to gradually improve SC performance. Building reliable theoretical models and tools is an important area for future study. Learn why and how ERP may help your business, how to overcome deployment obstacles, and how to keep the system working smoothly.

It is also recommended that funds be set aside to support the growth and improvement of the company's technological infrastructure and the implementation of new ICT. The development and upkeep of an ICT system in a manufacturing organization are made easier when small-scale enterprises with limited budgets are provided with enough funding and resources. The advantages of an ICT investment should exceed the expenses of obtaining and implementing the system, therefore, small-scale manufacturing enterprises are urged to plan carefully when adopting new ICT technologies for their SC practices in line with business needs.

KEYWORDS

- **benefits**
- **robots**
- **technology**
- **robotics**
- **supply chain management**

REFERENCES

Al-Halaly, M. A. M. S.; Alnajjar, F. J. S. Knowledge Management Processes and Their Impact on Organizational Performance, the Adoption-Balanced Scorecard: The Moderating Role of Quality Assurance Standards—An Applied Study on Private Jordanian Universities. *Int. J. Bus. Manag.* **2016,** *11*, 70–86. DOI: 10.5539/ijbm.v11n6p70

Alharbi, T. S. J.; Olsson, L. E.; Ekman, I.; Carlström, E. The Impact of Organizational Culture on the Outcome of Hospital Care: After the Implementation of Person-Centered Care. *Scand. J. Public Health* **2014,** *42*, 104–110. DOI: 10.1177/1403494813500593

Al-Nuaimi, E.; Al-Neyadi, H.; Mohamed, N.; Al-Jaroodi, J. Applications of ICT to Smart Cities. *J. Internet Serv. Appl.* **2015,** *6*. DOI: 10.1186/s13174–015-0041-5

Al-Shoul, M.; Rababah, O.; Al Shoul, M.; Ghenemat, S.; Al-Saqqa, S. Challenges Affecting the Implementation of E-Government in Jordan. *J. Softw. Eng. Appl.* **2014,** *7*, 1111–1127. DOI: 10.4236/jsea.2014.713098

Bharadwaj, A. A Resource-Based Perspective on Information Technology Capability and Firm Performance: An Empirical Investigation. *MIS Quart.* **2000,** *24*.

Bhattacharjya, J.; Ellison, A.; Tripathi, S. An Exploration of Logistics-Related Customer Service Provision on Twitter: The Case of e-Manufacturers. *Int. J. Phys. Distrib. Logist. Manag.* **2016,** *46*, 659–680.

Bogdanović, M. Learning in Serbia and Modern Information and Communication Technology. *J. Comput. Sci. Appl.* **2014,** *2*, 9–13. DOI: 10.12691/jcsa-2- 1–3

Bottani, E.; Rizzi, A. Economical Assessment of the Impact of RFID Technology and EPC System on the Fast-Moving Consumer Goods SC. *Int. J. Prod. Econ.* **2008,** *5* (2), 56–67.

Byrd, K.; Ross, L. W.; Glackin, C. E. W. A Preliminary Causal Analysis of Small Business Access to Credit During Economic Expansion and Contraction. *J. Appl. Finance Bank.* **2013,** *3*, 77–84.

Chen, C. P. L.; Zhang, C. Y. Data-Intensive Applications, Challenges, Techniques and Technologies: A Survey on Big Data. *Inf. Sci.* **2014,** *275*, 314–347.

Chen, D. Q.; Preston, D. S.; Swink, M. How the Use of Big Data Analytics Affects Value Creation in Supply Chain Management. *J. Manag. Inf. Syst.* **2015,** *32* (4), 4–39.

Cohen, G.; Salomon, I.; Nijkamp, P. Information-Communication Technology (ICT) and Transport: Does Knowledge Underpin Policy? *Telecommun. Policy* **2002,** *26*.

De Marchi, V.; Di Maria, E.; Gereffi, G., Eds. *Local Clusters in Global Value Chains: Linking Actors and Territories Through Manufacturing and Innovation*; Routledge, 2017.

Effy, O.; Jones, A. *Management Information Systems*, 5th edn.; Cabrian Printers, 2008.

Fine, C. H. *Clockspeed: Winning Industry Control in the Age of Temporary Advantage*; Perseus Books, 1998.

Haag, S.; Cummings, M. *Management Information Systems: For the Information Age*, 8th ed.; McGraw-Hill Inc: New York, 2010.

Hassan, H.; Ogundipe, A. ICT Adoption by Micro and Small-Scale Enterprises in Nigeria: A Case Study of the Federal Capital Territory, Abuja. 2017; pp 1–25. DOI: 10.2139/ssrn.2951901

Haun, J. N.; Margeaux, C.; Hathaway, W.; Antinori, N.; Melillo, C.; Cotner, B.; McMahon-Grenz, J. Virtual Medical Modality Implementation Strategies for Patient Aligned Care Teams to Promote Veteran Centered Care: A Community-Based Participatory Research Protocol. *J. Virtual Med. Modality Rev.* **2018,** *7*, 1–14. DOI: 10.2196/preprints.1126

Hawajreh, K. M.; Sharabati, A. A. The Impact of Information Technology on Knowledge Management Practices. *Int. J. Bus. Human. Technol.* **2012,** *2*, 102–107. Retrieved from www.ijbhtnet.com

Helo, P.; Anussornnitisarn, P.; Phusavat, K. Expectations and Reality in ERP Implementation: Consultant and Solution Provider Perspective. *Ind. Manag. Data Syst.* **2008,** *108* (8).

Huang, C. Y.; Nof, S. Enterprise Agility: A View from the PRISM Lab. *Int. J. Agile Manag. Syst.* **1999,** 1.

Jiménez, A.; Palmero-Cámara, C.; González-Santos, M. J.; González-Bernal, J.; Jiménez-Eguizába, J. A. The Impact of Educational Levels on Formal and Informal Entrepreneurship. *Bus. Res. Quart.* **2015,** *18*, 204–212. DOI: 10.1016/j.brq.2015.02.002

Jiménez, A.; Palmero-Cámara, C.; González-Santos, M. J.; González-Bernal, J.; Jiménez-Eguizába, J. A. The Impact of Educational Levels on Formal and Informal Entrepreneurship. *Bus. Res. Quart.* **2015,** *18*, 204–212. DOI: 10.1016/j.brq.2015.02.002

Johnson, B. Ethical Issues in Shadowing Research. *Qualit. Res. Organ. Manag.: Int. Jo.* **2014,** *9*, 21–40. DOI: 10.1108/QROM-09–2012–1099

Larson, D.; Chang, V. A Review and Future Direction of Agile, Business Intelligence, Analytics and Data Science. *Int. J. Inf. Manag.* **2016,** *36*, 700–710. DOI: 10.1016/j.ijinfomgt.2016.04.013

Lasch, F.; Robert F.; Le Roy F. Regional Determinants of ICT New Firm Formation. *Small Bus. Econ.* **2013,** *40*, 671–686. www://ssrn.com/abstract=2281104

Leenders, R. M.; Fearon, E. H. *Purchasing and Materials Management*, 13th ed.; Irwin: Chicago, 1993.

Llave, M. R. Business Intelligence and Analytics in Small and Medium Enterprises: A Systematic Literature Review. *Procedia Comput. Sci.* **2017,** *121*, 194–205.

Lysons, K.; Farrington, *Purchasing and Supply Chain Management*, 6th ed.; Prentice- Hall: London.

Martina, F. M.; Ciovicab, L.; Cristescua, P. Implications of Human Capital in the Development of SMEs Through the ICT Adoption. *Procedia Econ. Finance* **2013,** *6*, 748–753. DOI: 10.1016/S2212-5671(13)00198-6

Meredith, J. R.; Mantel, S. J., Jr. *Project Management—A Managerial Approach*, 6th ed.; John Wiley & Sons, Inc, 2006.

Mng'ong'ose, W. A.; Victor, M. Challenges Facing Adoption of ICT in Rural Areas of Tanzania. *Int. J. Econ. Bus. Manag. Res.* **2018,** *2*, 343–359. ijebmr.com/uploads2018/

Navimipour, N. J.; Rahmani, A. M.; Navin, A. H.; Hosseinzadeh, M. Expert Cloud: A Cloud-Based Framework to Share the Knowledge and Skills of Human Resources. *Comput. Hum. Behav.* **2015,** *46*, 57–74. DOI: 10.1016/j.chb.2015.01.001

Obeng, A. Y.; Boachie, E. The Impact of IT-Technological Innovation on the Productivity of a Bank's Employee. *Cogent Bus. Manag.* **2018,** *5*, 1–19. DOI: 10.1080/23311975.2018.1470449

Odongo, K.; Kalu, O. Does Infrastructure Really Explain Economic Growth in Sub-Saharan Africa? *Rev. Dev. Finance* **2016,** *6*, 105–125. DOI: 10.1016/j.rdf.2016.12.001

Post, P.; Anderson, D. L. *Management Information System: Solving Business challenges with Information Technology*, 2nd ed.; McGraw-Hill: New York, 2000.

SAS. Big Data Analytics Adoption and Employment Trends, 2012–2017. https://www.thetechpartnership.com/globalassets/pdfs/research2013/bigdataanalytics_rep ort_nov2013.pdf (accessed on 21 Mar 2018).

Tran, K. Q. K. E-Business Adoption in Micro Business in NSW, Australia: Does the Government Tick the Right Boxes? A Qualitative Multiple Case Study. (Doctoral dissertation). Southern Cross University, 2015. https://pdfs.semanticscholar.org.pdf

Tsekouras, G.; Kanellou, D.; Rai, N. Redefining Learning Networks Through ICT Capabilities: Representations, Behaviors and Intermediation Strategies. *Technol. Anal. Strat. Manag.* **2013,** *25*, 257–279. DOI: 10.1080/09537325.2013.764985

Varma, T. N.; Khan, D. A. Information Technology in Supply Chain Management. *J. Supply Chain Manag. Syst.* **2014,** *3* (3), 35–46.

Verma, S.; Bhattacharyya, S. S. Perceived Strategic Value-based Adoption of Big Data Analytics in Emerging Economy. *J. Enterprise Inf. Manag.* **2017,** *30* (3), 354–382.

Wamba, S. F.; Akter, S. *Big Data Analytics for Supply Chain Management: A Literature Review and Research Agenda*; Lecture Notes in Business Information Processing. Springer International Publishing: Cham.

Waziri, A.; Ali, K. N.; Aliagha, G. U. The Influence of Transformational Leadership Style on ICT Adoption in the Ghanaian Construction Industry. *Asian Soc. Sci.* **2015,** *11*, 123–133. DOI: 10.5539/ass.v11n18p123

William. S. *Operations Management*, 10th ed.; McGraw-Hill/Irwin, 2009.

Yazici, H. J. The Role of Communication in Organizational Change: An Empirical Investigation. *Inf. Manag.* **2002,** *39*, 539–52.

CHAPTER 6

Internet of Things (IoT) on Supply Chain Management in the Hotel Sector

MUSTAPHA ABDUL AZIZ, ADAM OSMAN OSCAR, and ABUKARI INUSAH

Department of Logistics and Procurement Management, Tamale Technical University, Tamale, Ghana

ABSTRACT

Internet of Things (IoT) is one of the most promising new developments for hoteliers. It is crucial that hotel owners, managers, and other business executives make use of it, but many still have questions about what it is and how it might assist them. In this piece, we will learn more about the IoT and how it can help the hospitality industry. Hotels, resorts, cruise liners, sportsbooks, eateries, and other leisure sector firms may find that the IoT drastically alters the ways in which they collect data, interact with customers, and automate tasks. IoT is used to describe the interconnection of mechanical items that have sensors, actuators, and other devices built into them to gather and relay data in real time. It is concluded that a new era of hospitality has come to stay; hence, the combination of IoT with other technologies such as consumer mobility and data analytics has better avenue for growth, speed, and ease.

6.1 INTRODUCTION

For a long time, the hotel sector has been notoriously slow to accept new technologies (Pizam, 2017). Nonetheless, developments in social, local, and mobile marketing have been sparked by rising visitor desire for online interactions via digital touchpoints, and this has a marginal effect on the guest experience. Digitally connected "non-phone" gadgets, commonly known

New Age Technology in Supply Chain Management: Digital Transformation Tools in Perspective. Mohammed Majeed (Ed.)

as the Internet of Things (IoT), interact autonomously between themselves through established wireless communication protocols in the period after the rise of the smartphone (Oskam and Boswijk, 2016). The IoT is transforming every part of a factory. There is an abundance of IoT options for any market niche. The hospitality sector is a type of catering that strives to make its clients happy by giving them first-rate care. Businesses and manufacturers with an eye on innovation will reap huge rewards from using IoT principles in the hospitality sector.

With more and more people using smart devices, hotels are investigating how they might use IoT and other similar systems to provide a better experience for their patrons (Buhalis and Leung, 2018; Wu and Cheng, 2018). This bodes well for the sector's prospects of achieving hitherto unheard-of levels of operational efficiency. These technologies have become indispensable because of the profound impact they have had on business administration and customer service (Infante-Moro et al., 2021). The same thing has happened in the hotel industry. Trends in hotel administration and service delivery are being influenced by the IoT (Europa Press, 2020). When it comes to supply chain management (SCM), the IoT promises unprecedented transparency through its vision of a global infrastructure of networked physical items (Tu et al., 2018). Consequently, studies focusing on the design and deployment of IoT system techniques to boost hotel profits should be conducted in other regions or settings. Furthermore, an additional quantitative study could investigate the connection between IoT system tactics and hotel profit with the goal of generalizing the research findings. If hotel owners desire to maximize the technical potential of IoT devices used for reasons other than financial gain, they may find new studies on the method used to establish the technological and instructional design of IoT systems for hotels to be valuable. The IoT bridges the gap between traditional, in-person interaction and more convenient, on-the-go participation, which is crucial to the development and deployment of smart settings (Gretzel et al., 2018). By fusing the virtual with the real, it facilitates communication between individuals, organizations, and their respective systems and products (cyber-physical systems). Over the past decade, IoT devices have seen widespread adoption across all sectors of industry as a means to boost operational efficiency and save expenses (Breidbach et al., 2018; Jones, 2008). The number of IoT devices is projected to reach 22.3 billion by 2024 (Cerwall, 2019) and permeate all industries. There are several ways in which the hotel sector could profit from this development. Supply chains will be able to respond to changes in real time with the help of IoT because the time it takes to collect data will be drastically reduced (Ellis et al., 2015). The IoT will also allow for remote administration of supply chain activities, enhanced cooperation with partners, and the provision of more accurate information for more informed decision making.

Despite the many benefits that the IoT is said to have, it has not yet been generally adopted by the business world for use in logistics and SCM. The adoption of logistics innovations across a supply chain is a new and complex subject that has to be studied (Tu, 2018). The aim of this article is to do a desktop review of the areas and benefits of IoT that affect logistics and SCM. This article reviews the available literature on the subject of the IoT and its effects in the field of SCM. We looked at the definition of IoT, the primary IoT technologies required for its implementation in a supply chain environment, and some of the most relevant SCM uses of IoT.

6.2 CONTRIBUTION

This chapter is groundbreaking because it is one of the first to analyze hotels' plans to implement IoT technologies in supply chain and logistics management. The review helps shed light on the motivations of decision-makers within businesses for the first time. The study shows how IoT and hospitality merge, a convergence that has been largely neglected until now, by synthesizing IoT applications in hospitality and bringing to light their relationship with other technology. This discovery paves the way for further academic investigation and widespread adoption of IoT in the hospitality industry. This analysis surveys the state of IoT studies and projects in the hospitality industry. It helps expand comprehension of current tendencies and opportunities. Instead of narrowing in on just one facet of the topic, we took a more all-encompassing approach. The reader is provided with theoretical backing in addition to the technical elements, challenges, and concerns.

6.3 LITERATURE

6.3.1 INTERNET OF THINGS (IOT)

The IoT was first implemented in 1998, and Kevin Ashton, while employed at Procter & Gamble, is credited with coining the phrase "IoT" in 1999. (Car et al., 2019). Ashton was working in supply chain optimization at the time, and he hoped that the new and innovative technology of radio frequency identification (RFID) would catch the eye of upper management. The IoT is a network of physical objects (things) that can be remotely located, sensed, and/or operated through the exchange of data and information in real time. This network consists of things that can be uniquely identified and connected (termed Internet-connected constituents) with the ability for virtual representation and virtual accessibility (Ng and Wakenshaw, 2017). The IoT is best described as a system of digital devices and machines linked together through the internet to improve service quality and cut costs in the hospitality sector. Connecting all digital gadgets to the internet to make them "smart" is the basic idea behind the IoT. Agriculture, logistics, healthcare, sports, manufacturing, travel, and tourism are just some of the fields that have found real-world uses for the IoT. However, the IoT is more than simply a novelty in the hospitality business (Mistry, 2022).

6.3.2 IOT AND SCM

According to the research, the IoT as an extension of information and communications technology (ICT) (Borgia, 2014) also has the extended ability to help with real-time information flow, which in turn facilitates inter- and intrafirm communication and further integrates supply chains. Like the Internet links computers worldwide together, an IoT platform could link products, machines, and people together in unison, streamlining and unifying an organization's internal and external operations (Li and Li, 2017). IoT devices can authenticate products and shipments using global positioning system (GPS) and other technologies, making them invaluable in the supply chain.

It has long been acknowledged that there are significant benefits to integrating suppliers with ICT. Additionally, according to organizational capability theory, ICT as a core capability can significantly affect supplier integration (Huo, 2012). Even though ICT has not been shown to have any direct correlation with performance, studies have shown that it can have an indirect effect on performance via its favorable impact on SCI (Kim, 2017). The IoT is a key enabler for all three dimensions of SCI (supplier, internal, and customer integration) as shown by studies from a multi-perspective perspective (Vanpoucke et al. 2017; Zhang et al. They reason that because IoT is an evolution of ICT, it can improve the ability to integrate suppliers, employees, and customers. Devices connected to the IoT have completely altered the logistics industry (SCM). Locating items, learning how they are being stored, and anticipating when they will arrive at a given location are all simplified. Naser (2019) investigates the impact of IoT implementation on supply chain operations and business outcomes. The analysis of the results shows that the increased supply chain transparency, automatic data capture, and information sharing are all made possible by the IoT. The IoT integration technology has shown to have a positive effect on the overall cost, efficiency, distribution, and adaptability of the supply chain, and to boost the sustainable performance of retail businesses in terms of performance, social, and environmental outcomes.

6.3.3 HOSPITALITY IOT

For the hospitality industry, the IoT holds the potential to realize a fully customized experience for each guest at the lowest possible operational cost. Hotels may get off to a great start on their digital transformation path by taking use of the IoT (Turton, 2019). IoT devices are employed in a wide variety of contexts within the hospitality sector. Improved customer insights and experiences (Ng and Wakenshaw, 2017), asset and facility management (Sklyar and Kharchenko, 2018), safety and security (Rigoli, 2017), and decision making through data analytics (Aluri, 2015) all contribute to higher revenues and lower expenses, giving businesses an IT competitive advantage (Ng and Wakenshaw, 2017). According to Pizam (2017), companies such as Disney, Marriott, and Royal Caribbean Cruises have investigated the potential of IoT systems in their supply chains to enhance their guests' experiences.

6.4 AREAS OF IOT IN THE HOSPITALITY SECTOR

6.4.1 HYPERCUSTOMIZED HOTEL ROOMS

In the hospitality industry, hyperpersonalization has been the primary focus of IoT implementation thus far. For instance, Hilton and Marriott have both tried out variants of the "connected room" concept, in which guests can operate various room elements using their smartphones or a complimentary tablet computer (Revfine, 2023). When visitors check-in, they will immediately receive a welcome message detailing the hotel's amenities, perks, and events for the duration of their stay. In the same way, hotel workers may use IoT devices such as smartwatches to improve communication and get real-time updates on things such as guests' needs and the state of their rooms (eHotelier, 2022). In this hotel, customers may use their own mobile devices to do anything from unlocking their rooms to controlling the temperature and lighting to requesting room service. Additionally, hotels can reduce the amount of time and effort required to engage with their customers by installing a virtual assistant into each guest's TV or providing voice command devices, such as Amazon Alexa, in the room (Turton, 2019). This might give visitors a centralized location to manage heating, ventilation, and air conditioning (HVAC) settings or even let them set a temperature and have the system automatically maintain that level throughout the area. In most cases, it will also let them manage the TV, and certain gadgets may even recognize their name.

6.4.2 LOCATION-BASED DATA

Hotels and other hospitality businesses may now reach guests at the precise moment when their messages are most relevant to them thanks to advancements in Bluetooth, GPS, and beacon technologies. Because of advancements in Bluetooth, GPS, and Beacon technology, the hospitality sector may now take use of new channels for disseminating location-specific details to guests. Hotels can significantly improve their information delivery with the use of IoTized GPS management or real-time tracking of customers. Hotels can use this data to target local consumers with timely short messaging service (SMS) messages. In addition, this is a novel and customized approach to a customer's first encounter with your brand-new services and amenities. Products can still be tracked using IoT sensors even when they are stored in a warehouse. This allows for more precise product identification and management, and it can make it much simpler to track down specific items in a massive warehouse.

6.4.3 PREDICTIVE MAINTENANCE AND REPAIRS

IoT provide maintenance and repairs that are planned ahead of time. IoT might be put to use in the hospitality sector by giving hotel employees real-time data on the condition of various machines and equipment and by raising alarms if the data suggests any indicators of impending failure or abnormal operation. Chatbots with IoT and voice assistants are two examples of how the IoT can be used to improve the customer service experience. Several major hotel chains, such as Marriott and Best Western, have been early adopters of these techniques, which have helped them provide superior guest service. The main advantage of this is that it gives you time to make repairs or replace parts before the gadget or appliance completely breaks down. This can be especially helpful in the case of essential hotel appliances that must be operational at all times; repairs can be made before a catastrophic failure.

6.4.4 SMART HOTELS

Guests can feel more at home and have a more customized experience when they use their smartphones to adjust the room's temperature, lighting, television settings, door locks, and other features. In addition to the safety and energy savings provided by smart locks, this also assures the security of the building.

6.4.5 ACCESS CARDS TECHNOLOGY

The IoT enables new opportunities for hotels, such as sending digital or electronic key cards straight to guests' mobile phones, while before only physical key cards or actual keys were used to gain access to guest rooms. The door lock can then be unlocked using this method, eliminating the requirement for a key. This technology has tremendous promise. To expedite the check-in process, hotels can use internet communication technology to transmit the electronic key to a guest's phone an hour before the check-in time, synchronize the door with the check-in desk, and then let them enter the room without ever having to interact with a human.

6.4.6 CONTINUING DEVELOPMENTS IN THE WORLD OF DIGITAL TECHNOLOGY

It's hardly surprising that as digital technology develops, new uses for it will emerge in the hotel and tourism sector. In the articles that follow, we will discuss some of the most interesting developments in the use of digital technology in the hospitality sector.

6.4.7 VOICE-ACTIVATED SUPPORT

Finally, hotel chains such as Best Western, Marriott, and Wynn have been pioneers in voice-controlled customer service, and this is an area that is expected to grow significantly over the next five years as gadgets such as Amazon Echo become more generally accepted in the house. Its primary value to individuals in the hotel sector lies in the quality of the service they are able to provide their clients. Customers can use voice-controlled room assistants to do things such as order room service, reserve a seat at the hotel restaurant, and schedule spa appointments without leaving their rooms.

6.4.8 BENEFITS OF IOT IN HOSPITALITY

Because the IoT has numerous significant benefits that are especially pertinent to hotels, many in the hospitality industry have already used the technology. They range from helping businesses save money on energy bills to improving the quality of service provided to customers.

IoT systems in hotels' warehouses record real-time product information, and hotels permit suppliers to reorder supplies in response to inventory levels using this information (Mengyuan et al., 2022). Furthermore, the supplier can modify the nature and quantity of the products it provides to the hotel in response to user usage data received by the IoT system, thereby better meeting market demand. To improve the hotel's operational effectiveness and customize the transportation and supplies, IoT equipment can be utilized to swiftly and efficiently monitor the logistics and commodities data using sensors and RFID technology. IoT enhances logistics processes. In 2021 and 2022, the supply chain crisis was a major topic of discussion (eHotelier, 2022). While previously businesses were particularly exposed to supply chain flaws, with the advent of the IoT, this is no longer the case. Companies now have more tools than ever before to efficiently manage their supply chains due to the IoT sensors they deployed. For instance, these sensors can be used to monitor the temperature of perishable goods, pinpoint their location, and log the times and dates of shipment and delivery (eHotelier, 2022). This means you would not have to worry about having too much or too little stock because you will always have access to the data you need. Food and chemicals, for example, require perfectly stable storage environments. Specialist Environments can be tracked by IoT sensors, including things such as temperature, humidity, air quality, and lighting levels. If specific conditions are not met, these gadgets may sound an alert. There will be less spoilage and better visibility into product quality throughout the supply chain as a result of this. Particularly in last-mile logistics, where the obligation typically falls on trucks, paperwork is a significant source of dissatisfaction among workers. Businesses can save time and resources by using smart logistics solutions to automate the most tedious and time-consuming paperwork procedures, such as checking the bond of a trucker's freight broker or processing a bill of lading (Ashcroft, 2022).

By streamlining interactions between supply chain participants, IoT has revolutionized logistics. Managers can check in on shipments and drivers to make sure everything is running smoothly from the warehouse to the customer's front door, including ensuring that products are stored properly and that deliveries aren't delayed (Digiteum, 2021). Managers who have access to location, productivity, and environmental data in real time may also keep their end customers in the loop, allowing them to provide better, more individualized service. The IoT facilitates numerous interconnected platforms that are designed for workers. Warehouse workers can save time with the use of tools such as smart glasses which provide instructions in a seamless manner. Additionally, IoT collects data that relates to efficiency, which raises the level of consciousness in the management of both resources and personnel. Managers of the supply chain can now rest assured that everyone participating in the delivery process is performing to their full potential thanks to the tools at their disposal (Digiteum, 2021). As a result, operations may be simplified. A hotel that makes use of the IoT could have sensors installed to detect a leaking pipe, faulty wiring, or broken lightbulb, and then alert the appropriate staff members via mobile notification or email. A ticketing system could also help a hotelier keep track of a leaking pipe by ensuring that it is followed up. After that, workers can fix the issue immediately and close the ticket (Mitchell, 2022). Improve stock management with real-time data thanks to IoT's increased connectivity (IoT). In the absence of such transparency, inventory management must rely on educated guesswork. Another source of inventory chaos is the manual data collection process. Sensors improve inventory accuracy to one hundred percent. With sensors enabled by the IoT attached to each shipment, it is now possible to track the temperature and humidity of packages in transit across a vast and intricate supply chain. The manager can track a cargo from its origin at the farm to its final destination at the distribution center thanks to the availability of real-time location data. When a shipment is expected to arrive early (or late) (Abdel-Basset et al., 2018), The use of smart objects will increase logistical transparency by making all transport data (transport condition, destination, etc.) available to all parties in the supply chain. Better tracking and product preservation will be possible as a result of this. Automation of the warehouse is made possible by AI. Supply chain automation will continue to gain traction, especially in warehouses, many of which are starting to look like they belong in a science fiction movie. Businesses that are automating more and more warehouse processes will need access to timely, accurate data (Ashcroft, 2022).

It has a significant effect on customer satisfaction and reduces the cost of returns. IoT monitors will alert management to the problem in advance, allowing them time to make preparations (Dukach, 2018). On a macro scale, complete data on when and where shipments tend to be damaged or delayed in transit enables data-driven optimization across the supply chain by identifying and eliminating root cause issues. Management of the supply chain that occurs in real time, as opposed to the traditional model in which demand information is passed to only one partner. But the advent of RFID tags has made it possible to keep track of manufacturing and expiration dates, as well as warranty periods, for more efficient SCM. Measures for protecting against cyber-threats are improved by the IoT. Every visitor worries about being safe, and the IoT gives you more and better ways to ensure their safety than ever before (Mitchell, 2022). For instance, the need for lost or stolen door keys is negated by the use of electronic key cards. In addition, a high level of security can be achieved by issuing each guest a unique smart key that contains a biometric scanner, such as a fingerprint reader. When a guest checks out, or if a smart key is lost or stolen, it can be disabled immediately and remotely (eHotelier, 2022). With the information provided by IoT, retail and supply chain managers are able to accurately predict how many units of each product they will need to stock. High precision in asset tracking, shipping, and navigation for drivers is just one more way that the IoT mitigates the effects of human mistakes (Digiteum, 2021).

The overall speed of the supply chain increases significantly with the help of smart route-planning tools and IoT tracking technologies. By using these tools routinely, managers may reduce the time it takes to get answers to questions, make more informed decisions, prevent or at least minimize delays, and speed up the process of finding items wherever they may be in the warehouse (Digiteum, 2021). Retailers may gain valuable insights into their products, customers, and demand by integrating IoT and SCM into their operations. The market can be better understood and products can be more precisely segmented for their intended consumers with the use of data collected at various points in the product life cycle (Digiteum, 2021). With a more integrated supply chain, businesses are better able to provide superior support to their clientele. When managers have access to data via mobile apps, they can accurately predict when packages will be delivered. It is easy to pinpoint where problems are occurring with deliveries and keep tabs on what customers expect. It is crucial that managers have the ability to reschedule service delivery to keep service-level agreements (SLAs) in place (Ashcroft, 2022).

In comparison to closed systems, connected platforms offer greater speed and convenience. By constructing an IoT system on the cloud, businesses guarantee that all participants in the supply chain lifecycle will have access to critical data and be able to resolve issues promptly. In addition, web and mobile tools for various users (workers, managers, operators, and consumers) assist in working with insights, utilizing the data obtained, and constructing plans and scenarios according to user roles and needs (Digiteum, 2021). The logistics and SCM systems of a hotel are accountable for acquiring necessities such as food and drink. Implementing effective methods toward this purpose can make a hotel's services stand out from the competition. As a hotel highlights the challenges of supply chain management, it is vital to have the appropriate information technology, such as IoT (Mitchell, 2022). In a well-designed supply chain, the IoT is a sustainability enabler that can be used to assist businesses adhere to emission restrictions and other regulations governing their operations (Digiteum, 2021). They can now combine environmental activities at scale (renewables, electric vehicles, and energy-efficient places) and receive a very clear picture of how resources such as power and water are used thanks to various IoT sensors for SCM and asset tracking (Digiteum, 2021). For increasingly complicated value chains, which are often fragmented into a number of data silos, IoT offers a bird's eye view of how the supply chains affect the organization. By eliminating these barriers, the IoT equips teams all along the supply chain with the information they need to work together effectively and head off any possible problems or bottlenecks (Ashcroft, 2022).

6.5 DISCUSSION AND IMPLICATIONS

In this chapter, we give business owners and executives several criteria to use when determining whether or not their logistics and supply chains should adopt IoT. Further, this research can help IoT solution providers enhance their products to better meet the challenges associated with IoT adoption. While IoT system technology can aid in decreasing transactional activities, hoteliers should realize that it also frees up time for significant human-only work. The importance of genuine human connection in memory-dependent industries such as hospitality cannot be overstated (Harrington et al., 2019). Hoteliers may put into practice their goal of providing end-to-end guest experiences through innovation by utilizing an IoT system that caters to guests' needs and expectations at every stage of the customer journey, from research to booking to poststay follow-up (Casais et al., 2020).

Pilot IoT projects can help companies considering implementing IoT in their supply chain operations determine whether or not it is feasible to do so. Participants in the qualitative study also shared the view that trust in the IoT system is closely related to the reliability of IoT technology. The IoT will usher in exciting new possibilities for the hospitality industry by making possible cutting-edge tools for delivering individualized service. There will be a rethinking of operational procedures to increase productivity and quickness. As a result, incorporating it will be crucial for success and competitiveness as it will transform expectations and the servicescape. Guests' appetites and the need for extra food can be communicated to the kitchen via autonomous trolleys and carts. These automated assets are tailored to meet the needs of guests upon their arrival at the hotel, from transporting their bags to their rooms to waving farewell as they check out.

Once the guest checks out, the IoT gadget will immediately alert the third-party service procured by the hotel, which will then publish the task on the platform and the hotel cleaning personnel will take the order on the service side. It allows hotels to pool their service employees and cut costs. Predictive maintenance conducted via the IoT ensures the hotel's upkeep and safety. Sensors linked to the enterprise resource planning (ERP) system keep tabs on the hotel's wear-and-tear, sending notifications before failures occur or crucial consumables run out. This facilitates better maintenance planning and lessens the need to stockpile spare parts. Because of the prevalence of cigarette smoke in the hotel, fires might easily break out in guest rooms. Smoke detectors with IoT connectivity are just one component of an intelligent fire protection system that can save lives in the event of a fire. Additionally, they have an alarm system that will notify the hotel staff to take action.

6.6 THE FUTURE OF IOT

One of the best ideas to improve customer service is to use the IoT in the hotel sector. Features such as a robust wireless network, the use of sensors to detect problems and inefficiencies, and the ability to run on advanced analytics to predict repairs are all a part of this. With the use of data analytics and the IoT, hotel management can now automatically respond to guests' preferences when it comes to the type of room they require and the amenities they like to enjoy. Hotels, resorts, cruise ships, casinos, restaurants, and other leisure service providers can be revolutionized by the IoT because of the way it collects data, interacts with people, and automates procedures.

BizIntellia (2022) claims that the IoT is a technology that is greatly enhancing the industrial operational capability of every segment and is especially assisting hospitality organizations in saving money on energy bills and infrastructure upkeep. On top of that, technology updates a user's options and emphasizes leisure as the primary way to enjoy hospitality. It could aid in providing guests with hyperpersonalization and answers to their problems in real time. By integrating the IoT with smart solutions, the hospitality industry can provide its clients with a more convenient and cost-effective way to live. The Statista study predicts that by 2022, there will be 42.62 billion IoT-enabled devices online. This is why many firms, particularly those in the hospitality sector, are coming to see the benefits of using smart technology solutions. This is the single most effective tactic for hotels looking to improve their customer service. IoT applications in hotels are easy to imagine because providing guests with a pleasant and personalized experience is the greatest way to increase repeat business.

6.7 CONCLUSION

New apps and studies are flourishing alongside the expanding IoT There is little doubt that IoT will have a significant effect on the hotel business, and several establishments have already begun exploring the technology and incorporating it into their unique offerings. Improvements in all three areas of the triple bottom line can be expected to result from the widespread adoption of IoT in the hospitality industry and its interaction with Big Data. This opportunity appears to have been fully appreciated on the part of suppliers. Interel, a major player in the hospitality IoT market, has trademarked the name "Hotel of Things" to describe a lodging establishment where guests, staff, and amenities are all empowered by interoperability. As vendor-driven solutions, theoretical models paired with empirical evidence, and practice—based capacity and ability will need to converge seamlessly to deliver on the promise of IoT and its associated technology applications for hospitality, it remains to be seen how far Hotels will be able to take advantage of the IoT.

KEYWORDS

- **IoT**
- **technology**
- **SCM**
- **hospitality**
- **hotels**

REFERENCES

Abdel-Basset, M.; Manogaran, G.; Mohamed, M. Internet of Things (IoT) and Its Impact on Supply Chain: A Framework for Building Smart, Secure and Efficient Systems. *Fut. Gener. Comput. Syst.* **2018,** *86*, 614–628. DOI: 10.1016/j.future.2018.04.051

Ashcroft, S. Top 10: Strategic Benefits of IoT Tech in Supply Chains. https://supplychaindigital.com/digital-supply-chain/top-10-strategic-benefits-of-iot-tech-in-supply-chains

BizIntellia. Applying IoT Concepts in the Hospitality Industry, 2022. https://www.biz4intellia.com/blog/applying-iot-concepts-in-the-hospitality-industry/

Breidbach, C.; Choi, S.; Ellway, B.; Keating, B.W.; Kormusheva, K.; Kowalkowski, C.; Lim, C.; Maglio, P. Operating Without Operations: How Is Technology Changing the Role of the Firm? *J. Serv. Manag.* **2018,** *29* (5), 809–833.

Buhalis, D.; Leung, R. Smart Hospitality-Interconnectivity and Interoperability Towards an Ecosystem. *Int. J. Hosp. Manag.* **2018,** *71*, 41–50. DOI: 10.1016/j.ijhm.2017.11.011

Car, T.; Stifanich, P. L.; Šimunić, M. Internet of Things in Tourism and Hospitality - Opportunity and Challenges. *ToSEE—Tourism Southern Eastern Europe* **2019,** *5*, 163–175.

Casais, B.; Fernandes, J.; Sarmento, M. Tourism Innovation Through Relationship Marketing and Value Co-Creation: A Study on Peer-to-Peer Online Platforms for Sharing Accommodation. *J. Hosp. Tour. Manag.* **2020,** *42*, 51–57. DOI: 1016/j.jhtm.2019.11.010

Cerwall, P. Ericsson Mobility Report. www.ericsson.com/49d1d9/assets/local/mobility-report/documents/2019/ericsson-mobility- report-june-2019.pdf (accessed 15 Dec 2019).

Chen, M.; Jiang. Z.; Xu, Z.; Shi, A.; Gu, M.; Li, Y. Overviews of Internet of Things Applications in China's Hospitality Industry. *Processes* **2022,** *10*, 1256. DOi: 10.3390/ pr10071256.

Digiteum Team. Impact of Internet of Things (IoT) on Supply Chain Management, 22 May 2021. https://www.digiteum.com/iot-supply-chain/

Dukach, D. How the IoT-Powered Supply Chain Provides a New Level of Visibility, 30 Oct 2018. https://hospitalitytech.com/how-iot-powered-supply-chain-provides-new-level-visibility.

eHotelier. How the Internet of Things Can Revolutionize the Hospitality Industry, 27 June 2022. https://insights.ehotelier.com/insights/2022/06/27/how-the-internet-of-things-can-revolutionize-the-hospitality-industry/

Ellis, S.; Morris, H. D.; Santagate. J. IoT-Enabled Analytic Applications Revolutionize Supply Chain Planning and Execution. *Int. Data Corp. (IDC) White Paper*, 2015. www.idc.com.

Europa Press. Hoteliers Are Betting on the Internet of Things to Personalize the Experience. http://www. europapress.es/turismo/hoteles/noticia-hoteleros-apuestan-internet-cosas-personalizar-experiencia-20180322111219.html (accessed on 28 Oct 2020) (In Spanish).

Gretzel, U.; Sigala, M.; Xiang, Z.; Koo, C. Smart Tourism: Foundations and Developments. *Electron. Markets* **2015,** *25* (3), 179–188.

Harrington, R. J.; Hammond, R. K.; Ottenbacher, M. C.; Chathoth, P. K.; Marlowe, B. From Goods-Service Logic to a Memory-Dominant Logic: Business Logic Evolution and Application in Hospitality. *Int. J. Hosp. Manag.* **2019,** *76*, 252–260. DOI: 10.1016/j.ijhm.2018.05.014

Infante-Moro, A.; Infante-Moro, J. C.; Gallardo-Pérez, J. The Acquisition of ICT Skills at the University Level: The Case of the Faculty of Business Studies and Tourism of the University of Huelva. *Pixel-Bit. Rev. Medios Educ.* **2021,** *60*, 29–58.

Mistry, S. How Can IoT in Hospitality Industry Grow Your Hotel Business? *eZee Absolute*, 28 Sept 2022. https://www.ezeeabsolute.com/blog/iot-in-hospitality-industry/

Mitchell, A. Why Should the Hospitality Industry Invest in IoT? *GuestRevu*, 2022. https://blog.guestrevu.com/why-should-the-hospitality-industry-invest-in-iot

Ng, I. C. L.; Wakenshaw, S. Y. L. The Internet-of-Things: Review and Research Directions. *Int. J. Res. Market.* **2017,** *34* (1), 3–21.

Oskam, J. & Boswijk, A. Airbnb: The Future of Networked Hospitality Businesses. *J. Tour. Fut.* **2016,** *2* (1), 22–42.

Pizam, A. The Internet of Things (IoT): The Next Challenge to the Hospitality Industry. *Int. J. Hosp. Manag.* **2017,** *62*, 132–133.

Revfine. How the Internet of Things (IoT) Can Benefit the Hospitality Industry, 2023. https://www.revfine.com/internet-of-things-hospitality-industry/

Rigoli, J. Digi Smart Solutions. www.digi.com/news/press-releases/taco-johnsselects-digi-smart-solutions (accessed 23 Dec 2019).

Sklyar, V. V.; Kharchenko, V. S. RAMS Issues in Hotels Management. ICTERI Workshops **2018**; pp 624–636.

Tu, M. An Exploratory Study of Internet of Things (IoT) Adoption Intention in Logistics and Supply Chain Management. *Int. J. Logist. Manag.* **2018,** *29*, 131–151.

Turton, A. How the Internet of Things (IoT) Is Transforming the Hospitality Industry, 7 Jan 2019. https://blog.trginternational.com/transforming-the-hospitality-industry-with-internet-of-things-iot-tech

Wu, H. C.; Cheng, C. Relationships Between Technology Attachment, Experiential Relationship Quality, Experiential Risk and Experiential Sharing Intentions in a Smart Hotel. *J. Hosp. Tour. Manag.* **2018,** *37*, 42–58. DOI: 10.1016/j.jhtm.2018.09.003

CHAPTER 7

Machine Learning on Supply Chain Management

MOHAMMED MAJEED

Marketing Department, Tamale Technical University, Tamale, Ghana

ABSTRACT

Agile and effective logistics processes are crucial in today's age of information technology and ever-increasingly complicated technological and industrial procedures. Success in the supply chain (SC) is predicated on a number of factors, including reliability, transparency, and adaptability in the face of uncertainty, as well as favorable economic conditions. Technology capable of handling the growing complexity of supply networks is essential for operations that are constantly evolving. The purpose of this chapter was to give readers a bird's eye view of how machine learning (ML) methods are being used in the logistics industry. In this context, after a quick overview of popular ML techniques, the usage of each in overseeing distinct parts of the SC was discussed. This chapter describes supervised learning algorithms that can predict demand, classify images, detect fraud, or even make medical diagnoses based on incoming data. Customers can be categorized and products can be recommended using unsupervised ML techniques. This study aims to provide an overview of ML and the techniques it employs to improve SC efficiency. Several positive effects of ML on supply chain management (SCM) have been documented in the literature. ML helps derive actionable insights, allowing for rapid problem solving and continuous improvement, resulting in lower costs. This is accomplished by optimizing product flow in the SC without requiring supply chain firms to hold much inventory.

New Age Technology in Supply Chain Management: Digital Transformation Tools in Perspective. Mohammed Majeed (Ed.)

7.1 INTRODUCTION

It used to be that supply chain (SC) managers were worried as there was not enough data availability to work with, but in today's complicated and rapidly evolving environment, the opposite problem exists: there's too much. There has been a shift in the character of SCM analysis as a result of the sheer quantity of data produced by every link in the SC (Tirkolaee et al., 2021). The SC is an integral part of most businesses nowadays. Therefore, supply chain management (SCM) business process adoption is critical to a company's performance. After deploying an enterprise resource planning (ERP) system, many businesses then go to top vendors such as systems applications and products in data processing (SAP) and Oracle to provide them with a SCM solution (Jayantakut, 2022). The general manager used to be in charge of compiling and analyzing all of this information for use in the company's bookkeeping and inventory management processes, a time-consuming process that involved either using paper forms or a laborious, manual data entry process. Machine learning (ML) makes it simple to automate these processes, freeing up a business (e.g., restaurant) operators to focus on what they do best: cooking and hosting customers. ML methods are used to train computers to automatically and effectively process massive amounts of data. It is often impossible to use conventional methods to extract useful patterns or information from massive datasets and make sense of the results (Dey, 2016). The availability of so many datasets has increased interest in ML methods. Discovering and extracting knowledge and information from the data is a common use case for ML approaches across many sectors, from medical to the military. Mathematicians and computer scientists have conducted a plethora of investigations, the results of which are a wide variety of ML methods (Bowles, 2015). ML is a branch of AI that permits a computer program or system to learn and improve itself without being explicitly taught how to do so.

Data or observations are utilized in ML to "train" a computer model, which is then used to enhance the technology by analyzing various patterns in the data (along with actual and expected results) (Jayantakut, 2022). Algorithmically based ML models are excellent at analyzing patterns, identifying outliers, and drawing predictive insights from large datasets. Due to its robust features, it is a viable option for resolving some of the most pressing issues in the SC sector. SCM solutions provide adaptable workflows for managing the whole range of activities along the SC, from sourcing raw materials to marketing the final product for sale. As more and more information is collected, stored, and analyzed, datasets have grown in size and complexity. In many cases, processing is inefficient or impossible using common, useful management tools. New methodologies and applications, such as predictive analytics, have been created to handle and evaluate these novel and potentially valuable datasets (Copeland, 2016). Predictive analytics tools include ML as one example. The development of complex ML models, the accessibility of massive datasets ("big data"), and the exploitation of hardware architectures such as GPUs all contribute to the success of this methodology (Abadi et al., 2016; Steinbach, 2018).

Despite the high and growing importance of ML in SCM in both the research and practice domains, very few academics have addressed the necessity to investigate the research tendencies within this area. The back-end logic of most SCM solutions is based on classical algorithms and optimization, not ML techniques. A smart, automated, and self-repairing SC is hoped to be attainable with the application of ML. This means it should be a major focus of firms' efforts. The purpose of the chapter is to look at the aspects of ML affect SCM as well as the benefits of ML on SCM. When the SC task and prevailing aspects of ML use are linked, an overview of ML in SCM can be made. This makes it easier to find areas that companies might want to use and areas that scientists might want to study in the future.

7.2 LITERATURE

7.2.1 MACHINE LEARNING

ML is an artificial intelligence (AI) technique that allows a computer algorithm or program to learn and improve itself without being explicitly programmed. Over time, it learns new information that could help it run more efficiently. ML frequently makes use of statistical evidence or observational data. ML examines these data for patterns, taking into account both the expected and actual outcomes (Singh, 2022). By discovering new patterns in utilization data provided by Internet of Things (IoT) sensors, businesses are prolonging the lifespan of important SC assets such as machinery, engines, transportation, and warehouse equipment. When compared to other sectors, manufacturing generates the most data per year. To understand which elements most affect machinery performance, ML has shown to be beneficial in analyzing data generated by machines (DHL, Artificial Intelligence in Logistics, 2018). The cycle continues, and each iteration improves the technology in some way. Statistical analysis, SC optimization, forecasting, and cost reduction are just some of the ways in which ML may be put to use in the logistics industry. When there is a discrepancy between supply and demand, ML methods immediately react. To optimize routes, cut costs, and shorten processing times, the ML algorithm studies past data in real time. To improve the accuracy of demand forecasting, ML algorithms and the apps that run them can quickly analyze massive, diverse datasets. Predicting the future demand for production is one of the most difficult components of managing a SC. Moving averages and other simple methods of statistical analysis sit alongside complex simulation models (DHL, Artificial Intelligence in Logistics, 2018). It has become clear that ML is superior to other methods at tracking and quantifying time-varying elements.

7.2.2 TYPES OF MACHINE LEARNING

It is grouped into supervised, semi-supervised, and unsupervised ML (Geron, 2017).

7.2.2.1 SUPERVISED MACHINE LEARNING

This form of ML necessitates human intervention in the form of "supervision," when machines are taught to make predictions by studying annotated datasets. Many of the input and output parameters have been predefined in the labeled dataset. Machines are trained with the help of labeled datasets in this method of ML. Using this data, machines may make predictions about future output (Emeritus, 2022). Since the goal variable is already known, supervised learning algorithms simply map the inputs to those they know how to produce. With Supervised Learning, ML models are trained with the help of an expert (Brownlee, 2019). That's why it's called "supervision." To produce the intended outcome, they require direction and extra data. Typically, classification and regression issues are addressed using supervised learning algorithms. The primary goal of super learning methods is to establish a correlation between input and output data. It finds widespread application in fields including spam filtering, threat analysis, and fraud detection. Classification algorithms based on Supervised Learning are used to detect fraudulent financial transactions, clients, etc. This is accomplished by analyzing past data for indicators of potential fraud (Sareen, 2022). Emeritus (2022) lists the following as five of the most common uses of supervised learning: image classification and segmentation; disease identification and medical diagnosis; fraud detection; spam detection; and speech recognition. Regression (both linear and logistic), support vector machine (SVM), k-nearest neighbor (KNN), decision tree (DT), and random forest are all some examples of supervised learning methods. To find solutions for regression issues with a linear relationship between input and output variables, regression methods are typically employed. Market trends, weather forecasts, and other continuous output variables can all benefit from these forecasting methods (Javatpoint, 2022). If you have a classification problem where the answer can be "yes" or "no," "male" or "female," "red" or "blue," etc., then you will want to utilize a classification algorithm to help you out. The dataset's categories are predicted by the categorization algorithms. Spam detection and email filtering are two practical applications of categorization algorithms (Geron, 2017). Speech recognition also makes use of supervised learning methods. Voice data is used to train the algorithm, and then that data can be used for a variety of identifications (passwords, voice commands, etc.) (Brownlee, 2019). Classification and regression are two major problems (Kirste and Schürholz, 2019).

7.2.2.2 SEMI-SUPERVISED MACHINE LEARNING

When there are more unlabeled instances than labeled ones in the training data, the learning process is called semi-supervised. Between the two extremes of Supervised and Unsupervised ML is Semi-supervised learning (Geron, 2017). Semi-supervised learning is introduced to address the limitations of both supervised and unsupervised learning methods. It combines labeled and unlabeled data throughout learning, representing a middle ground across supervised (with labeled training data) and Unsupervised learning (without labeled training data) techniques. Semi-supervised learning models are intended to utilize all of the data at their disposal, not only the labeled data as is the case with supervised learning (Brownlee, 2019). Aspects of semi-supervised learning include many common computer science tasks, such as document categorization, speech recognition, and fraud detection. It is common for semi-supervised learning to make use of hybrid unsupervised and supervised algorithms that have been trained on both types of data (Biba, 2022).

There are elements of both supervised and unsupervised ML in semi-supervised learning. To train its algorithms, it takes advantage of both labeled and unlabeled datasets. Semi-supervised learning takes a middle ground by processing both huge raw datasets and smaller, tagged datasets (Geron, 2017). This approach saves time and money compared to more labor-intensive supervised learning algorithms while giving algorithms a leg up on unsupervised learning algorithms in terms of recognizing relevant patterns and producing accurate predictions (Biba, 2022).

7.2.2.3 UNSUPERVISED MACHINE LEARNING

In contrast to the supervised learning method, here no human intervention is required. Machines are trained on unlabeled and unclassified datasets. They are then able to forecast the outcome with no help from humans (Geron, 2017). To organize large amounts of unstructured data, this technique is frequently employed. Hidden patterns and trends in the input can also be discovered by machines. The model takes in input, uses that data to find patterns and features, and then gives you back the results (Emeritus, 2022). The goal of unsupervised learning is to locate the output by identifying patterns and trends in the data. In this way, the model makes an effort to assign labels to the data by analyzing its many characteristics. Unsupervised learning methods do not rely on human oversight during the training process. They can automatically learn and predict results. Clustering and association problems are best tackled with unsupervised learning. Emeritus (2022) lists the following as common unsupervised learning use cases: network analysis; plagiarism and copyright check; online shopping site recommendation; and financial transaction fraud detection. Both association and clustering fall under the umbrella of unsupervised learning (Brownlee, 2019). When searching for patterns in data, clustering is a useful tool. The items are clustered so that those with the most in common stay together, while those with less in common go on to different clusters. The clustering method might be used, for instance, to categorize clients according to their buying habits (Javatpoint, 2022). An unsupervised learning method, association rule learning explores a dataset in search of potentially useful correlations between previously unrelated variables. This learning algorithm's main goal is to maximize profit by discovering and mapping the interdependencies between different pieces of data. Market basket analysis, web usage mining, continuous production, etc. are some of the most common uses of this technique (Javatpoint, 2022).

7.2.2.4 REINFORCEMENT ML

Problems that fall under the purview of reinforcement learning (RL) are those in which an agent is deployed in an environment and must learn how to function by incorporating the results of previous deployments (Brownlee, 2019).

RL is directly influenced by how people learn in the real world by analyzing facts (Potentia, 2022). It uses a trial-and-error algorithm that constantly refines its performance and adapts to new circumstances. Positive results are "reinforced" (or rewarded), whereas negative results are "punished" (or deterred). Due to its style of working, RL is applied in numerous domains such as Game theory, Operation Research, Information theory, and multiagent systems. Based on the psychological notion of conditioning, RL works by putting the algorithm in a work environment with an interpreter and a reward system. The algorithm's output is passed to the interpreter at each iteration, and the interpreter determines whether or not the result is desirable (Potentia, 2022). The Markov Decision Process (MDP) can be used to formally define a problem in RL. Every time an agent in a Markov decision process (MDP) takes any sort of action, the environment reacts by changing its state. In the event that the program does find a solution, the interpreter will reward the algorithm for its efforts (Geron, 2017). If the result is unfavorable, the algorithm will have to try again and again until it gets it right. The effectiveness of the incentive is typically proportional to the quality of the outcome.

The solution is not an absolute value in typical RL applications, such as determining the shortest path between two points on a map. It is replaced by a percentage-based effectiveness score (Sareen, 2022). The algorithm receives a larger reward in proportion to the value of this percentage. Therefore, the program is taught to provide the optimal response to maximize reward.

7.2.2.5 ML IN SCM

While several parts of SCM are still underutilized, current applications of ML concentrate on a small number of them. Thus, the article's goal is to establish a connection between the SCM activity and contemporary ML technologies. Big data analytics can assist in predicting future trends, which can aid with decision making in numerous SCM areas and create a valuable paradigm for businesses. A self-aware framework where several functioning devices are networked at once can be added to SCs by emerging technologies including the IoT, blockchain, and advanced deep learning (ADL) approaches (Sareen, 2022). Such a self-adaptive intelligent system is really needed by SCM to handle changes in consumer demand. IoT and blockchain technology can help the SC become more transparent and connected, which can help it meet the customers' evolving needs (Tirkolaee et al., 2021). In any location in the world, this can offer a stream of real-time data and information between different SC components. ML will be utilized in SCM for procurement strategies to oversee the complete enterprise and guarantee the successful supply of a product to both single and many suppliers (Puri, 2022). Numerous users, including suppliers, distributors, retailers, and manufacturers, will have a choice with ML. SC and logistics, healthcare, banking, and insurance are just a few of the industries that use ML. It is used to forecast which members of a loyalty program are most likely to leave and what premiums insurers ought to charge for particular policies. By utilizing data from prior experiences, ML algorithms can assist businesses in making more informed business decisions without the need for human participation (i.e., historical data). There are numerous SC application categories where ML can be employed. ML can be used to forecast or predict risks, supply, on-time delivery, and demand. ML can assist in automating a number of routine SC operations' components and assist in identifying or predicting exceptions to typical operations (Sareen, 2022). Planning and designing things such as networks, inventory, schedules, and routes can be done using ML. The autonomous SC vehicles, including trucks, ocean freighters, delivery drones, and forklifts, depend heavily on ML (Sareen, 2022).

7.2.3 AREAS OF SCM ML AFFECT

Puri (2022) claims that ML may be observed throughout the entire SC, in areas including production, inventory control, warehousing, shipping/transportation, and customer support. Let's examine the advantages of ML in managing SCs in more detail.

7.2.3.1 VENDOR SELECTION

Extracting useful features for supplier assessment. ML helps in decreasing computational consumption as a result of fewer characteristics (Tirkolaee et al., 2021).

7.2.3.2 SC PLANNING

One of the most crucial components of a SC management strategy is SC planning or SCP. Consequently, having trustworthy tools is essential for creating effective plans (Badwi, 2022). The decision-making processes in the SC of a company can be greatly improved by implementing ML. The team or business will balance demand and supply while also optimizing the delivery procedures through the analysis of vast datasets and the application of sophisticated algorithms (Haponik, 2021).

7.2.3.3 PRODUCTION

By taking into account various constraints, ML tools will increase the accuracy of production planning and factory scheduling. Additionally, ML tools will enable the limitations to be balanced more effectively than in the past, especially for manufacturers who rely on build-to-order and make-to-stock production workflows (Badwi, 2022). For components and parts used in their most intricately designed goods, manufacturers can employ ML techniques to reduce SC delay, enhancing the precision of production planning and scheduling, efficiently balancing the limitations of the build-to-order and make-to-stock production workflows (Badwi, 2022). ML increases the accuracy of planning and control and factory schedule by accounting for many restrictions and improving for each one. ML is enabling manufacturers who rely on build-to-order and make-to-stock manufacturing workflows to manage the constraints of both more successfully than had been achievable manually in the past (DHL, Artificial Intelligence in Logistics, 2018). ML makes it feasible to spot quality problems in line production early on. For instance, producers can use computer vision to determine whether the final appearance of the products meets the necessary degree of quality. Before the products reach the clients, it is simple to find any flaws in them.

7.2.3.4 TRANSPORTATION

To deliver goods and services to consumers on time, the best route for vehicle transportation must be determined. Routing is typically beyond the capacity of the human brain. The performance of ML tools is great for parameter forecasting and analysis of big, heterogeneous datasets. It is employed to produce better delivery routes. Timely investigation of consumer behavior patterns (Tirkolaee et al., 2021). ML aids in determining a package's location throughout the logistics process. It enables SC experts to monitor the whereabouts of cargo while it is being transported. Additionally, it gives insight into the circumstances of the package's transportation. Retailers may monitor variables such as humidity, vibration, temperature, etc. with the aid of sensors (Tirkolaee et al., 2021).

7.2.3.5 WAREHOUSING

ML's application to SC management has the potential to streamline a wide range of administrative chores, freeing up resources for more important, long-term initiatives. By optimizing logistics, AI will also change the face of warehouse management. For example, it may determine how many pallets need to be moved on a given day, how much machinery is needed, and how many people would be needed to operate the machinery and move the pallets (Badwi, 2022). Such calculations traditionally relied on variables such as operator skill level and SKU (stock-keeping units), but now ML algorithms provide detailed stock movement predictions and administration to fine-tune warehouse operations (Badwi, 2022). (Badwi, 2022). It might help businesses develop an AI-driven SC strategy from the ground up, which is essential for lowering costs, increasing efficiency, and ensuring the model can remain competitive for the long term. Predicting increases and decreases in demand is made much easier with the use of ML's precise inventory management. Warehouse optimization makes use of ML to help with things such as early detection of stock outs and surpluses (Badwi, 2022). By identifying familiar trends, inspecting storage, and checking inventory every now and then throughout a lot of suitable method, this can be crucial in preventing sales losses.

7.2.3.6 INVENTORY

Eliminating unnecessary expenditures and illuminating latent inventory tendencies. Damage inspection in warehouses and homes could be streamlined with automation. The goals of ML-SC inventory management are to reduce expenses, expand product options, and boost service quality for customers. Warehouse data may be quickly analyzed with ML techniques that can compare patterns with minimal input. To better predict future lead times, Tirkolaee et al. (2021) used neural networks. Tracking products with digital tags and allowing for more precise and accurate inventory control, radio frequency identification (RFID) is quickly replacing paper trails and barcode scanners in the organization and control of inventories (Badwi, 2022). RFID scanners do not need direct line-of-sight control to identify products and direct their movement into, out of, and around the warehouse; instead, they need just be pointed in the approximate direction of a product (Badwi, 2022).

7.2.4 SPECULATIONS ON SUPPLY AND DEMAND/SALES

To properly manage a SC, it is essential to accurately predict future demand. Businesses may better prepare for client needs if they have a sense of where that demand is headed. From straightforward trend research to sophisticated ML algorithms, businesses have a lot of options when it comes to predicting future demand. By introducing nonlinear analysis, ML approaches have been utilized to accurately estimate and forecast demand, sales, and inventory, leading to optimization of SC performance. Profit, sales, and efficiency can all be improved with the help of an advanced prediction system (Tirkolaee et al., 2021). Sales and demand forecasting accuracy can be enhanced by ML. Also, ML is helping businesses save money on inventory management by improving the precision with which they predict what they will need to stock. As a result of predictive analytics, businesses can plan ahead and always have available stock of what customers want. This also helps cut expenses by ensuring that excess supplies are not acquired unnecessarily (Unext Editorial Team, 2022). (Unext Editorial Team, 2022). Another benefit is enhanced efficiency. Through the use of predictive analytics, manufacturing schedules, and delivery routes may be optimized, ensuring that goods are delivered on time and without incurring excessive expenditures due to making unneeded stops along the way. In addition, it optimizes stock by considering historical trends such as sales demand swings and product popularity shifts. Improved demand forecasting is only one of the many benefits of using an algorithm powered by ML. Businesses may easily construct the client portfolio and better match possible shopping patterns by monitoring customer behavior trends. Businesses may manage production and distribution across the spectrum of supply shortages and excesses with the help of predictive analytics in the SC.

7.2.5 WORKFORCE PLANNING

Staffing strategies are essential for any successful business in the present day. Human resource management entails a wide range of activities, including but not limited to hiring, firing, training, placement, monitoring, and development of employees. The use of ML technologies can greatly streamline and improve the effectiveness of your labor planning strategy (Haponik, 2021).

7.2.6 FORECASTING

Setting these upper and lower limits such that the actions they imply allow the targeted flow to be realized proactively is the key difficulty for good supervision of material handling by business professionals who operate warehouse management system (WMS) and warehouse control system (WCS). In this environment, the management of intra-logistic activities is a balancing act in which the logistics supervisor moves between the fragmentary data accessible.

7.2.7 SCM

SCM is the process of coordinating and controlling the flow of commodities, information, and money between different partners in a SC. According to a report by Gartner, SC management comprises all activities linked to the flow of goods and services from supplier to the customer (Tirkolaee et al., 2021). (Tirkolaee et al., 2021). This means that the entire process, from initial order placement to ultimate delivery, is part of SCM.

7.2.8 BENEFITS OF ML ON SCM

Every link in the SC, from sourcing to production to inventory management to distribution to customer support, can benefit from ML.

To begin, businesses that adopt an AI-driven approach to their SC operations can save time and energy by automating a variety of routine processes (Ariwala, 2022). Management based on warehouse and inventory stockpiles is often thought of as the epitome of effective SC planning. ML, equipped with the most recent demand and supply data, can enable continual improvement in a business's attempts to provide the required level of customer care at the lowest possible cost. The models, methodologies, and forecasting aspects of ML in SC can also address the issue of under- or overstocking, thereby revolutionizing your warehouse management (Ariwala, 2022). The complexities of production planning can be greatly reduced with the help of ML. To better pinpoint potential sources of inefficiency and waste in production, complex algorithms can be trained using ML models and methodologies and preexisting production data. Businesses can benefit greatly from ML because it yields actionable insights that streamline and speed up decision making. Executives can swiftly weigh the benefits and drawbacks of various scenarios. The purpose of ML is to help business executives make better decisions by providing them with recommendations for ideal solutions based on complicated algorithms. According to (Bokhan, 2020). Inventory analysis, for instance, can reveal when a product is becoming less sought after and is thus nearing the end of its useful retail life. Analysis of prices in relation to SC expenses and retail profit margins helps determine the optimal pricing strategy for a given level of demand (Bokhan, 2020). As a result of the speed and accuracy with which ML algorithms and their accompanying apps can analyze massive, varied datasets, demand forecasting accuracy has increased. Predicting the future demand for output is a major obstacle in SCM. Existing methodologies range from basic statistical analysis techniques including moving averages to advanced simulation modeling. ML is proving to be particularly successful at taking into account factors conventional approaches have no way of measuring or quantifying over time. The complexity of production planning can be greatly reduced with the help of ML. To better pinpoint potential sources of inefficiency and waste in production, complex algorithms can be trained using ML models and methodologies and preexisting production data. ML's application in the SC, resulting in a more flexible setting that can quickly adjust to new circumstances, is also significant.

Each company can benefit from ML algorithms' ability to sift through massive amounts of data and identify relevant trends to prevent fraud. In the SC, for instance, ML aids in the detection of fraudulent transactions, the prevention of credential misuse, the acceleration of fraud investigations, and the automation of anti-fraud procedures. Moreover, with ML, SC specialists can automate the process of monitoring if all parts as well as finished goods match the quality or safety standards (Bokhan, 2020).

SC managers can keep their businesses running smoothly with the help of clever ML tools by optimizing inventory and locating the most suitable suppliers. From its many benefits to completely capitalizing on the massive volumes of data collected by warehouses, transportation networks, and industrial logistics, ML is attracting a growing number of companies' attention (Ariwala, 2022). It can also aid businesses in developing a fully mechanized SC model, which is essential for lowering costs, gaining better insights, and increasing output on a worldwide scale. ML is being used by a growing number of business-to-consumer firms to minimize costs and enhance customer satisfaction by automating reactions to fluctuations in customer demand and stock levels. SC managers can save time, and money, and increase productivity by using ML algorithms to analyze and learn from real-time data and historical delivery records and then optimize the route for their fleet of trucks. Moreover, administrative and operational costs in the SC can be decreased by enhancing communication with various logistics service providers and unifying freight and warehouse procedures.

SC firms can make use of ML as a powerful analytical tool to analyze massive amounts of data. With the help of advanced technologies such as telematics, IoT gadgets, and intelligent transportation systems, ML in the SC is able to process enormous amounts of data while also guaranteeing that this data is processed with the greatest possible variety and unpredictability. Businesses in the SC can benefit greatly from this since it improves their ability to foresee the future. McKinsey found that using AI and ML in the SC may cut forecasting errors by half. Risk assessment is another area where ML and big data analytics have found use. The two most popular ML approaches that have demonstrated acceptable promise in modeling for risk assessment are artificial neural networks (ANNs) (Ni et al., 2019).

Without having to go out and acquire any new data, businesses may use data augmentation to greatly expand the variety of data used in model training. Different types of data call for different augmentation strategies in deep learning applications (Bokhan, 2020). Depending on the complexity of the application, many augmentation techniques can be used on unstructured data types such as photographs and text. With the ability to automate inspections and audits, as well as conduct real-time analysis of findings to spot abnormalities or divergence from usual patterns, ML algorithms have the potential to improve product quality while simultaneously lowering the risk of fraud. Privileged credential misuse is a major contributor to security failures all along the global SC, but it may be prevented with the help of ML techniques.

Incremental learning is a ML technique that can be used to train a model without a massive amount of initial data. Instead, novice learners are presented with a highly simplified model, one that predicts the mean plus or minus a given amount. A model can be "trained" to produce more precise predictions when additional data samples are introduced by a data scientist (Bokhan, 2020). Today, ML is being successfully used to the task of forecasting the demand for new items, including the causative elements that most drive new sales. From the pragmatic ways of asking channel partners, indirect and direct sales teams how many of a new product they will sell to utilizing fancy statistical models, there is a considerable difference in how organizations anticipate demand for a next-generation product. Factors influencing demand that were previously unknown are being taken into account with great success thanks to ML (Bendoly, 2016). Over time, the volume of datasets is good enough to produce credible estimates. The efficiency of last-mile delivery is crucial to many different aspects of the SC, including customer satisfaction and product quality. By analyzing a variety of factors, such as how customers enter their addresses and how long packages take to arrive at their destinations, ML can open up exciting new possibilities in the SC. ML can also offer essential assistance in improving the process and providing clients with more accurate information on the shipping status.

RL is one of three basic ML approaches alongside supervised learning and unsupervised learning. It employs rewards and punishment as signals for positive and negative conduct. RL is applied in robotics and industrial automation to help the robot develop its own effective adaptive control system by learning from its own actions and experiences (Bokhan, 2020). Management based on warehouse and inventory stockpiles is often thought of as the epitome of effective SC planning. ML, equipped with the most recent demand and supply data, can enable continual improvement in a business's attempts to provide the required level of customer care at the lowest possible cost. ML-based inventory management strategy helps companies track goods' location and storage conditions, the number of involved employees who handle order preparation, etc. ML here applies to companies with more than one warehouse in different parts of the world. Chief executive officers (CEOs), transport, and procurement officers leverage this technology to better synchronize operations and apply novel optimization tactics.

The models, methodologies, and forecasting functions of ML in the SC can help you avoid under- or overstocking, and they can also improve the efficiency of your warehouse management. With ML, businesses can speed up the analysis of large datasets and eliminate the errors introduced by human analysts. ML helps understand where a package is in the entire logistics cycle. It allows SC professionals to track the location of goods during transportation. The use of sensors allows stores to track data such as humidity, vibration, temperature, and more. In addition, ML is useful for improving travel plans in real time. Keeping tabs on the road and weather conditions, it suggests ways to shorten the trip. Trucks can be redirected to take the most economically viable route at any point in their journey. ML allows for the early detection of quality concerns in production lines. As an example, computer vision can be used to ensure that the final appearance of products meets standards. If there are flaws in the products, they can be found before they are shipped to consumers.

Equipment predictive maintenance is another common application of ML in the SC. With ML, you can rest assured that your equipment will be serviced both proactively and reactively, according to the condition of its assets at the moment rather than according to some fixed schedule. SC managers can save a ton of money on repairs by focusing on preventative care (Bokhan, 2020). More non-functioning item (NFF) situations can be fixed with the assistance of ML. A NFF is a piece of machinery that has been taken out of service due to a reported problem. If no problem is found, the unit is put back into service without any adjustments being made. The fewer accidents there are during production, the better it goes (Bokhan, 2020).

7.3 DISCUSSION

The purpose of this chapter was to provide an introduction to the use of ML methods in the SC. The goal of semi-supervised learning is to make better use of all the data available, not just the labeled data available in supervised learning. Using an unsupervised learning algorithm, we first group pieces of information that are similar; then, we use those clusters to assign labels to previously unlabeled data. Since labeled data is acquired at a higher cost than unlabeled data, this is the reason why (Javatpoint, 2022). Using evidence from Bokhan (2022), Javatpoint (2022) explained that RL is a feedback-based process that allows an AI agent (A software component) to automatically explore its surroundings by hitting and trailing, acting on what it discovers, learning from its mistakes, and getting better over time. Since the ideal answer is initially unknown to the system, RL requires iterative solution discovery. Generally speaking, this mechanism favors rational approaches while punishing erroneous ones. This strategy allows the system to potentially account for, and respond to, a wide variety of external factors. By use of RL and punishment, the system arrives at its own conclusions (Gentsch, 2018). The purpose of a RL agent is to maximize the rewards it receives for performing good actions and minimize the punishments it receives for performing poor ones. The use of ML in the SC has already caused significant changes for both retailers and their suppliers. ML is a subfield of AI that entails gathering and analyzing data to train a model that can learn and adapt to new circumstances with little to no human intervention. This allows the machine to gradually refine its own algorithms through self-education.

According to the Great Learning Team (2023), ML is utilized extensively in the management of SC in a variety of sectors. Managers in the SC might greatly broaden their employment prospects by acquiring a working knowledge of ML. For SCM, ML can be utilized to develop smart systems with the ability to analyze data and draw conclusions. This has the potential to aid businesses in their decision making, operational efficiency, and product and service development and delivery. Analysis and display of data are greatly aided by ML. Insights and patterns can be extracted from massive datasets, enabling SC managers to get a deeper understanding of complex systems and make more educated decisions (Bertolini et al., 2021).

7.4 IMPLICATION

ML has the potential to improve supplier competitiveness, efficiency, and resource availability, but only if firms make the long-term investment in ML and similar technologies. ML allows computers to acquire knowledge, retain it, and produce reliable results. It has helped businesses make well-informed choices that have been crucial to improving SCM, procurement, and project management. Such data-driven decisions aid businesses across all sectors in optimizing existing operations and exploring new ways to reduce the burden of order-taking, inventory management, and other back-office tasks.

Discovering reliable clients and suppliers is still a key obstacle in the field of SCD. This is truer than ever before in light of increasing internationalization and rapid technological advancement. Mori et al. (2010) apply ML approaches based on company profiles and transaction linkages to streamline the process of identifying new probable business partners. Subsequently, we examined the most crucial aspects of SCM, including supplier selection, supplier segmentation, SC risk prediction, demand estimation, inventory management, transportation, sustainable development, and circular economy. The purpose of this chapter was to give readers an overview of the ways in which ML techniques are being used in the SC. In this context, after a quick overview of popular ML techniques, supervised, unsupervised, and semi-supervised approaches to SCM were described. According to Tirkolaee et al., the most crucial aspects of SCM include supplier selection, supplier segmentation, SC risk prediction, demand estimation, inventory management, transportation, sustainable development, and circular economy (2021). Increased SC effectiveness is largely due to the contributions of ML. It makes it simpler to handle challenging forecasting and volatility in supply networks. Businesses need a long-term plan that includes investing in ML and related technologies if they want to reap the full benefits of AI.

7.5 FUTURE OF ML

ML is projected to integrate with AI and blockchain, as some qualities complement each other in both techs. Among these features are a transparent and immutable ledger that is maintained in a decentralized manner. Several companies can benefit from blockchain, the technology that underpins cryptocurrencies such as Bitcoin. This system eliminates the need for a third party to keep track of transactions by keeping a public ledger of all of them. After being added to the distributed ledger, blockchain transactions cannot be undone or altered in any way.

7.6 CONCLUSION

Despite the vast literature on both ML and SCM in isolation, the attention dedicated to the use of ML algorithms in SCM management has been insufficient. The purpose of this essay was to give readers a bird's-eye view of how ML methods are being used in the logistics industry. In SCM, there are a plethora of uses for ML. Their services aid businesses in enhancing their operations, boosting production, and cutting expenses. These innovations have just recently been used in SCM, but they are already having a significant impact on companies all over the globe. In this context, after a quick survey of popular ML techniques, supervised, unsupervised, and semi-supervised approaches to SCM were described. Any business would benefit greatly from a more streamlined SC. Companies that operate on razor-thin profit margins might benefit greatly from any changes made to the way they go about their business. The use of cutting-edge tools such as ML helps global SCs meet the issues of uncertainty and demand forecasting. By using algorithms that can swiftly identify the most relevant aspects to a supply network's success while continuously learning, ML makes it possible to detect patterns in SC data. If new patterns can be found in a company's SC data, it could completely transform that company. These novel patterns in SC data are being discovered every day by ML techniques, without requiring human participation or the development of taxonomy to guide the investigation. Data is queried iteratively by the algorithms, with many employing constraint-based modeling to hone in on the most predictive elements. The current dynamic in the SC ecosystem is great because of the digitalization of businesses and industries. This is a major step forward for the industry as a whole, and ML is at the heart of this transformation. Among the various ways in which it has transformed business is through the dissemination of new forms of communication, the mechanization of previously manual tasks, the ascent of computerized record-keeping and reporting, etc. SC management is becoming a key differentiator in an era of declining profits and more demanding customers. Fact-based SC decision making at the strategic, tactical, and operational levels is necessary for its management and optimization. ML methods and techniques have many practical uses in this information-rich setting for making SC decisions. Businesses today cannot avoid implementing some form of ML technology into nearly every facet of operations. In highly competitive markets, this becomes much more apparent. Despite its limitations, ML is a valuable tool for improving business operations and marketing. Businesses have integrated technology so deeply into their operations that they cannot function without it, from product development and quality assurance to marketing and public relations. ML has been implemented in a variety of real-world scenarios for SC choices in recent years.

7.7 THE PATH FORWARD FOR RESEARCH

Future studies can employ structural equation modeling to examine the complete ML framework's applicability in certain fields. Although ML has been around for the past fifty years, it is just now beginning to gain traction in the SCM sector, and there is a dearth of study into the specific issues of AI for the various SCM sectors. We propose more research into the use of RL approaches in real-time pricing based on anticipated trends in ML studies. Most attempts to apply AI methods to SCM have so far been restricted to more straightforward, well-defined, operational, and tactical issues. There are many nebulous but strategic SCM problems that could be addressed by applying ML approaches (particularly agent-based systems).

KEYWORDS

- **machine learning**
- **SCM**
- **technology**
- **supply chain**

REFERENCES

Abadi, M.; Barham, P.; Chen, J.; Chen, Z. *Proceedings of OSDI '16: 12th USENIX Symposium on Operating Systems Design and Implementation* [ebook]; Berkeley, 2016.

Ariwala, P. 9 Ways Machine Learning Can Transform Supply Chain Management, 2022. https://marutitech.com/machine-learning-in-supply-chain/

Badwi, M. The Future, Now: 8 Ways Machine Learning Transforms Warehousing. *SC Junction*, 2022. https://www.scjunction.com/blog/ai-and-machine-learning-transform-warehouse

Bendoly, E. Fit, Bias, and Enacted Sensemaking in Data Visualization: Frameworks for Continuous Development in Operations and Supply Chain Management Analytics. *J. Bus. Logist.* **2016,** *37* (1), 6–17.

Bertolini, M.; Mezzogori, D.; Neroni, M.; Zammori, F. Machine Learning for Industrial Applications: A Comprehensive Literature Review. *Expert Syst. Appl.* **2021,** *175*, Article ID 114820.

Biba, J. 4 Types of Machine Learning to Know 29 Sept 2022. https://builtin.com/machine-learning/types-of-machine-learning

Bokhan, K. Machine Learning in Supply Chain: 8 Use Cases That Will Impress You. NiX, 2020. https://www.n-ix.com/machine-learning-supply-chain-use-case.

Bowles, M. *Machine Learning in Python: Essential Techniques for Predictive Analysis*; John Wiley and Sons: Hoboken, 2015

Brownlee, J. 14 Different Types of Learning in Machine Learning, 11 Nov 2019. https://machinelearningmastery.com/types-of-learning-in-machine-learning/

Copeland, M.; What's the Difference between Artificial Intelligence, Machine Learning, and Deep Learning? [online].

Dey, A. Machine Learning Algorithms: A Review. *Int. J. Comput. Sci. Inf. Technol.* **2016,** *7* (3), 1174–1179.

DHL. Artificial Intelligence in Logistics2018 (PDF, 45 pp.; no opt-in).

Emeritus. 4 Types of Machine Learning and How to Build a Great Career in Each, 5 Aug 2022. https://emeritus.org/blog/types-of-machine-learning/

Gentsch, P. Künstliche Intelligenz für Sales, Marketing und Service. Mit AI und Bots zu einem Algorithmic Business—Konzepte, Technologien und Best Practices [e-book]; Wiesbaden: Springer Gabler, 2018.

Géron, A. Hands-on Machine Learning with Scikit-Learn and TensorFlow. Concepts, Tools, and Techniques to Build Intelligent Systems [e-book]; O'Reilly, 2017.

Great Learning Team. What Is Machine Learning? Definition, Types, Applications, and More, 9 Jan 2023. https://www.mygreatlearning.com/blog/what-is-machine-learning/

Haponik, A. 10 Use Cases of AI and Machine Learning in Logistics and Supply Chain (update: May 2021). Addepto, 18 May 2021. https://addepto.com/blog/use-cases-ai-machine-learning-logistics-supply-chain/

Javatpoint. Types of Machine Learning, 2021. https://www.javatpoint.com/types-of-machine-learning.

Jayantakut. AI/ML Use Cases for Supply Chain Management (SCM), 12 July 2022. https://www.analyticsvidhya.com/blog/2022/06/ai-ml-use-cases-for-supply-chain-management-scm/

Kirste, M.; Schürholz, M. Entwicklungswege zur KI. In: Künstliche Intelligenz. Entwicklungswege zur KI; Wittpahl, V., Ed.; Springer: Berlin Heidelberg, 2019; pp 25–26.

Mori, J.; Kajikawa, Y.; Sakata, I.; Kashima, H. Predicting Customer-Supplier Relationships Using Network-Based Features. In: *2010. IEEE International Conference on Industrial Engineering and Engineering Management (IEEM)*; Piscataway, 2010; pp 1916–1920.

Ni, D.; Xiao, Z.; Lim, M. K. A Systematic Review of the Research Trends of Machine Learning in Supply Chain Management. *Int. J. Machi. Learn. Cybern.* **2019,** 1–20.

Potential. What Is Machine Learning: Definition, Types, Applications and Examples, 2022. https://www.potentiaco.com/what-is-machine-learning-definition-types-applications-and-examples/#:~:text=These%20are%20three%20types%20of,unsupervised%20learning%2C%20and%20reinforcement%20learning.

Puri, S. Machine Learning in Supply Chain Management; C1India, 11 Nov 2022. https://c1india.com/machine-learning-in-supply-chain-management/

Sareen, P. Machine Learning and Supply Chain Management—A Conceptual View. *Int. J. Innov. Res. Technol.* **2022,** *9* (1), 60–64.

Singh, R. The Role of Machine Learning in Revolutionizing the Supply Chains, 2022. https://cocolevio.com/machine-learning-revolutionizing-the-supply-chains/

Steinbach, P. Wo noch nie eine CPU gewesen ist. In: *2018. iX Developer 2018—Machine Learning: Verstehen, verwenden, verifizieren*, 2018; pp 32–37.

Tirkolaee, E. B.; Sadeghi, S.; Mooseloo, F. M.; Vandchali, H. R.; Aeini, S. Application of Machine Learning in Supply Chain Management: A Comprehensive Overview of the Main Areas. *Math. Probl. Eng.* **2021,** 1476043. https://doi.org/10.1155/2021/1476043

Unext Editorial Team. Role of Artificial Intelligence and Machine Learning in Supply Chain Management, 2022. https://www.jigsawacademy.com/blogs/ai-ml/role-of-artificial-intelligence-and-machine-learning-in-supply-chain-management/

CHAPTER 8

The Influence of Information Communication Technology (ICT) Practices on Procurement Performance: An Analysis of Volta River Authority/ Northern Electricity Distribution Company (VRA/NEDCo)

MOHAMMED MAJEED[1], ANASS ISSAH[2], and DAVID INUSAH OFFEI[3]

[1]*Marketing Department, Tamale Technical University, Tamale, Ghana*

[2]*Northern Electricity Distribution Company, Ghana*

[3]*Automotive Engineering Department, Tamale Technical University, Tamale, Ghana*

ABSTRACT

Public procurement plays a crucial role in the delivery of services and the effective operation of government entities around the globe. The primary aim of this research was to assess the influence of information communication technology (ICT) on procurement performance (PP). A quantitative research methodology was used to gather data from a sample of 350 questionnaires using a purposive sampling technique. The data collection was facilitated by the use of a self-administered questionnaire. The software used for the analysis consisted of IBM SPSS, version 25.0, and AMOS, version 24.0. The study revealed that the use of IoT, RPA, AI, and blockchain technologies has shown robust, affirmative, and statistically significant associations with PP. The findings indicate that all dimensions of

New Age Technology in Supply Chain Management: Digital Transformation Tools in Perspective. Mohammed Majeed (Ed.)

ICT have a significant impact on PP. The study's findings indicate that ICT tools have a significant role in enhancing procurement efficiency within buyer–supplier interactions. Among these tools, the Internet of Things (IoT), Robotic Process Automation (RPA), Artificial Intelligence (AI), and blockchain technology were identified as the most influential. However, it was observed that these technologies have a very limited impact on the PP of the Volta River Authority (VRA) and the Northern Electricity Distribution Company (NEDCo) in Ghana.

8.1 INTRODUCTION

8.1.1 BACKGROUND OF THE STUDY

The integration of ICT in procurement has ushered in a transformative period in public procurement, effectively resolving the longstanding issues associated with manual procurement processes that the nation has previously encountered. The implementation of this system would enhance the management and monitoring of the whole procurement process, including activities from procurement initiation and planning through final payment. E-purchase facilitates the procurement of products and services in a way that is fair, equitable, competitive, and cost-effective. This approach guarantees that all procurement activities are made transparent to the public, allowing people to see the transparency of the process (Bittok, 2017). According to an article published in The Daily Nation newspaper on March 11, 2015, the implementation of this system is expected to enhance the connection between the government and its suppliers. This will be achieved by the provision of convenient access to relevant information and paperwork, streamlining the bidding process, and ultimately resulting in cost savings for the government and taxpayers. In the context of the highly competitive global business landscape, the integration of technology-based procurement has transitioned from being a secondary consideration to being an imperative for both public and private entities. In contemporary business practices it has become imperative for organizations to provide their clientele cost-effective comprehensive solutions, while simultaneously enhancing customer satisfaction via the implementation of new concepts and methodologies. The advent of technology has compelled organizations to transition from old operational methods to embrace e-business, e-procurement, and e-supply chain principles as a means of ensuring their continued viability (Lee et al., 1997).

Efficiency in expenditure has the potential to significantly enhance Ghana's economic performance. Therefore, the capacity to decrease budgets and governmental expenditures with the aim of enhancing savings, generating wealth, and alleviating poverty. Improvement of the public sector procurement system may facilitate the attainment of this objective. Ghana has had difficulties pertaining to its public expenditure and has undertaken endeavors to address these concerns. In order to enhance the efficiency of public sector procurement, a range of measures, including the implementation of various financial and legal mechanisms, have been implemented. One of the most significant measures in this regard has been the enactment of the Public Procurement Law, 2003 (Act 663). The enactment of this legislation was undertaken with the aim of preempting deficiencies in the procurement of goods and services, as well as other forms of public expenditure, notably within governmental entities. After engaging with its development partners, the Ghanaian government recognized the necessity of revitalizing the public procurement system. The objective was to instill confidence in the system, as it had been widely perceived by the public to be plagued by issues such as corruption and malpractice.

In 1996, the implementation of a Public Financial Management Reform Program (PUFMARP) was initiated. The primary aim was to ensure that all expenditures on products and services within the public sector were justified, with the intention of eliminating fraudulent practices from the system. Furthermore, the enhancement of public sector PP will be seen. The operations of the Public Procurement System Monitoring and Review Panel (PUFMARP) have exposed several fundamental faults within the public procurement system. One of the identified shortcomings was the lack of a comprehensive and meticulously outlined public procurement policy. Furthermore, a notable deficiency was seen in the absence of a centralized entity including individuals with specialized knowledge and skills in the field of procurement. Additionally, the entities responsible for procurement lacked well-defined duties and responsibilities. One crucial aspect to note is the absence of a legislative framework to provide guidance for public procurement. Finally, it should be noted that there was a lack of laws and regulations in place to effectively guide and oversee public buying activities. The Public Procurement Reform Program (PUFMARP) was assigned the responsibility of providing guidance for the development of a comprehensive initiative aimed at facilitating the reform of the public procurement process. The draft was prepared and eventually, on 31 December 2003, a public procurement legislation was adopted by September 2002. Numerous developing nations around the globe, particularly in Africa and Asia, encounter comparable obstacles in the realm of public procurements, and Ghana is no exception to this trend. (Kumaraswamy, 1994; Aniekwu and Okpala, 1988; Rwelamila et al., 1999). The public procurement process is characterized by a complex interplay of issues. Corruption is a very significant issue that plagues the system and necessitates comprehensive measures to address it. The implementation of suitable measures is of utmost importance in order to mitigate this regrettable circumstance.

8.2 PROBLEM STATEMENT

The performance of procurement is a perpetual and comprehensive process that needs ongoing evaluation and improvement. Procurement serves as the central hub for operational efficiency in both public and commercial institutions, necessitating the implementation of a rigorous system. The process of PP measurement involves the establishment of criteria by procurement, which are derived from strategic planning objectives, in order to assess the outcomes and quality of its actions. The process entails the development of a straightforward and efficient framework for assessing the extent to which the purchase is achieving its intended goals (Wanyonyi and Muturi, 2015). The aforementioned activities include the monitoring of outcomes, the comparison of such outcomes to established benchmarks and best practices, the evaluation of the effectiveness and efficiency of the process, the control of any deviations, and the implementation of required improvements to the process (Kerzner and Kerzner, 2017).

Despite the significant contribution of the manufacturing sector to the economic well-being of the nation, empirical data suggests that the industry is confronted with a multitude of obstacles, including legal and financial aspects (Anzetse, 2016; Ogot, 2014). Moreover, scholarly research has shown that the manufacturing sector has difficulties in its procurement procedures, which subsequently impact its PP (Moenga, 2011; Osoro, 2016). There is a need for increased attention from industry stakeholders and academics toward this sector, which plays a crucial role in the country's economy. The objective should be to identify the problems that are impeding its development. The objective of this research was to investigate the many elements that influence PP, which is considered a precursor to sector development, inside manufacturing enterprises, with a specific focus on Nzoia Sugar Company Limited. The literature extract presents evidence indicating that manufacturing firms in Ghana have encountered a range of difficulties. Anzetse (2016) asserts that these firms are comparatively underdeveloped in Ghana, as their growth has consistently lagged behind that of the overall economy. Ogot (2014) posits that micro-enterprises in the informal sector that are associated with the manufacturing industry have many difficulties, including insufficient capital, high production costs, and intense rivalry.

In an investigation carried out by Moenga (2011) regarding the procurement and supply chain strategies and outcomes within the small-scale tea sector in Ghana, findings revealed that the difficulties experienced by this industry included issues related to procurement efficiency and supply chain transparency, increasing customer expectations, managing risks, the impact of globalization, and maintaining cost controls. To achieve maximum procurement success, organizations must consider many criteria. The majority of accessible resources are from wealthy nations, and the limited selection fails to adequately address the specific topics of my research. The research was conducted within the setting of Ghana in order to address the existing gap. With respect to the aforementioned, the objective is to address the existing disparity by developing novel insights to enhance the operational efficacy of the energy industry in Ghana, particularly pertaining to the procurement practices of these enterprises. The field of public procurement has considerable economic and political implications, underscoring the need to establish a dependable and cost-effective method. It is imperative for all major stakeholders involved in the public procurement process to possess a comprehensive understanding of the principles behind ICT as well as the procurement procedures. This knowledge is essential for ensuring the optimal functioning and effectiveness of the process. The public procurement process in many government organizations is often characterized by secrecy, inefficiency, and corruption (Nyakundi et al., 2012).

8.3 OBJECTIVES OF THE STUDY

8.3.1 MAIN OBJECTIVE

The primary aim of this research was to assess the effect of ICT on the efficiency with which purchases were made.

8.3.2 SPECIFIC OBJECTIVES

The following specific objectives support answering the main research question.

1. To the influence of blockchain technology on its PP of VRA–NEDCo.
2. To the influence of IoT on its PP of VRA–NEDCo.
3. To the influence of AI on its PP of VRA–NEDCo.
4. To the influence of RPA on its PP of VRA–NEDCo.

8.4 RESEARCH QUESTIONS

8.4.1 THE MAIN RESEARCH QUESTION

What is the effect of ICT on PP?

8.4.2 SPECIFIC RESEARCH QUESTIONS

The following specific questions guided the formulation of the research questionnaires which facilitated data collection to arrive at the correct conclusion.

1. What is the influence of blockchain technology on its PP of VRA– NEDCo?
2. What is the influence of IoT on its PP of VRA–NEDCo?
3. What is the influence of AI on its PP of VRA–NEDCo?
4. What is the influence of RPA in its PP of VRA–NEDCo?

8.5 SIGNIFICANCE OF THE STUDY

The results of this research shed light on the impact that ICT procurement has on supply chain efficiency in Ghana's energy industry. It was expected that other businesses would get a deeper appreciation for the role that ICT plays in supply chain management (SCM). The study's results might be used as a resource for academics and researchers. Additionally, the study will serve as a foundation for future studies.

The study's suggestions can be used as a road map to increase productivity in the purchasing process. If the study's suggestions are put into action, the organization will be able to reduce its procurement costs and gain a competitive edge. Researchers may utilize the study's findings to guide their own literature evaluations, and the document report can be a useful resource for many students learning about ICT and procurement outcomes. Academics will be able to use the study findings as a guide to swiftly identify unexplored areas of procurement. They might utilize the results of this analysis to identify research gaps in the literature.

8.6 LITERATURE REVIEW

8.6.1 EMPIRICAL LITERATURE REVIEW

8.6.1.1 PROCUREMENT

Procurement is an integral component of a business, including the many purchasing procedures that take place inside a corporation, including both direct and indirect expenditures (van Weele, 2014). The field of procurement has become more significant in recent years as organizations have recognized the substantial cost-saving opportunities associated with expenditure. Vollmer and Murphy (2017) assert that a significant proportion, namely 65%, of a company's overall value in terms of its goods and services may be attributed to its suppliers. The Accenture Operations report from 2017 highlights the growing significance of effective procurement in strategic decision-making. There is a common misconception about the distinction between procurement and buying, as well as the potential confusion with related concepts like sourcing or supply management. Nevertheless, according to van Weele (2014), there is an argument that both words may be used interchangeably, but there are opposing viewpoints held by many other scholars. Procurement may be seen as a broader function, including buying as one of its constituent components (buying Insight Ltd, 2018). Procurement encompasses a range of tasks, as outlined by Purchasing Insight Ltd (2018), which include both strategic elements such as supplier assessment and negotiation, as well as operational aspects involved in the ordering and receipt of products. In contrast, the act of purchasing alone encompasses the operational aspect (Purchasing Insight Ltd, 2018) and may be characterized as the transactional component of procurement, as stated by Lim (2014). Nevertheless, a lack of universally accepted definitions for these two words exists, leading to variations in their use across various organizations, and contexts.

8.6.2 PROCUREMENT'S ROLE IN AN ORGANIZATION

In the past, the strategic importance of procurement within organizational contexts has often been overlooked (Vollmer and Murphy, 2017). The rationale behind this occurrence can be clarified through the renowned value chain framework introduced by Porter (1985). This model portrays procurement as an auxiliary operation. As outlined by Magnusson (2018), ancillary activities have historically been regarded as sectors that do not directly contribute to value creation, thus offering avenues for substantial cost reductions. Fundamentally, it becomes crucial to optimize these responsibilities for economic effectiveness. As Magnusson (2018) expounds, the credit for the current elevated status of procurement in modern corporations can be assigned to Porter. The value chain concept has been widely adopted by numerous companies and academic institutions, functioning as an instructional tool for a multitude of professionals to proficiently manage procurement, as endorsed by Porter. Consequently, procurement is predominantly perceived as a facet that should emphasize cost-efficiency rather than being acknowledged for its strategic importance. The absence of procurement participation in research and development is a prevalent issue in several firms, despite the potential significant advantages it may provide if implemented at an early stage (Vollmer and Murphy, 2017). Consider a hypothetical scenario involving the creation of a novel product, whereby the team is presenting their ultimate design idea. However, they get communication from the procurement department indicating that one of the required components cannot be obtained from any currently available supplier. Consequently, the team's efforts over the last several months seem to have been rendered futile.

8.6.3 ICT ADOPTION AND USE

To address contemporary operational obstacles, managers are increasingly using ICT as a means to increase client, company, and tourist services, as well as to optimize internal operations by reducing expenses and boosting efficiency. According to Abouzeedan and Busler (2002), the executives are now constructing scalable communication infrastructures with the aim of improving economic growth, attracting new customers and enterprises, and ultimately providing exceptional services to consumers. As per Kirungu (2011), the employment of manual procedures in Ghana has been pinpointed as a notable element leading to ineffectiveness in overseeing and executing the specified task. The integration of ICT is imperative to ensure the streamlined and proficient functioning of the procurement mechanism. This involves more than just automating the system; it also encompasses the adoption of expandable communication technologies.

Given the phenomenon of globalization and the widespread availability of internet access, there arises a need to enhance and expand the operations in Ghana. The traditional practices used in doing business include buyers overseeing projections and conveying their demands to suppliers using telephonic, facsimile, and electronic mail communication channels. The exchange of spreadsheets and handwritten reports occurs between the trade partners. The manual procedures exhibit a lack of efficiency and are burdensome. Contemporary demand-driven firms are not adequately supported by them. Thomson and Jackson (2007) assert that supply chain procurement experts allocate a significant amount of their work toward addressing immediate issues and responding to everyday challenges. The individuals in question seem to be facing challenges in allocating sufficient time to cultivate strategic alliances with suppliers and implement enhanced operational procedures aimed at mitigating shortages. There are many obstacles that impede the spread of ICT in developing countries. These issues include infrastructural limitations, challenges in the business environment (including financial and legal elements), social factors such as poverty, illiteracy, urbanization levels, educational considerations, and the cultural context. The use of ICT for the acquisition of products, works, and services is gaining prominence on a global scale. This practice has the capacity to significantly alter procedures, enhance market accessibility, and foster transparency and ethical practices in public procurement. Research conducted in several nations has shown that ICT plays a crucial role in enhancing the effectiveness and efficiency of procurement systems.

Kramer et al. (2007) have documented the utilization of ICTs by the Government of Chile to streamline the procurement process for small businesses. This implementation of a novel business model has yielded favorable outcomes, particularly following the integration of online services into the procurement system. The improvement in information access has been significant as a result of this. If the system in Ghana is effectively enhanced via the integration of ICT, it has the potential to generate these advantages as well. The practice of procurement encompasses a wide range of approaches, ranging from the simple act of putting certain data, such as tender announcements, onto a website, to the implementation of very intricate systems that include the whole of the procurement process. Regardless of the level of complexity shown by an ICT system, its use inherently has the capacity to promptly render information accessible to the public, thus augmenting transparency.

8.6.4 ICT IN SUPPLY CHAIN

In its most comprehensive interpretation, electronic procurement encompasses "business-to-business (B2B), business-to-consumer (B2C), and business-to-government (B2G)" transactions involving the acquisition and exchange of goods, services, and infrastructure, including data networks and information systems. This pertains to the process of exchanging information and coordinating schedules (Muhia and Afande, 2015). E-procurement encompasses many components, including electronic contracts, data management, order processing, and sourcing activities. E-procurement refers to the practice of integrating and optimizing procurement procedures inside an organization (Muhia and Afande, 2015). Lysons and Farrington (2012) posit that Electronic Data Interchange (EDI) is a method that relies on established standards to enable the exchange of business transactions in a uniform electronic format, automating the process from one computer application to another. The directory provides descriptions of data items and codes that pertain to the message standard used, therefore enabling electronic trading between organizations.

Monczka et al. (2009) assert that an enterprise resource planning (ERP) system is a comprehensive system that combines transaction processing and reporting functionalities. Various software tools and kinds of ERP facilitate the re-engineering of company processes. In more accessible language, ERP solutions facilitate the monitoring and management of many components inside an organization, such as personnel, procedures, and technological assets. The system functions as a fundamental component of the organization, facilitating the provision of necessary information and assistance for decision-making processes.

ERP solutions enhance the functionality of an organizational information system by including process logic, therefore, establishing a crucial framework for managing business operations. In contrast to previous practices when managers and employees enjoyed autonomy in decision-making inside their respective functional domains, the implementation of ERP systems compels individuals to engage in collaborative interactions within a unified system. ERP systems facilitate the establishment of process logic that connects various interconnected domains. In research carried out by Monczka et al. (2015) pertaining to Procurement and Logistics Management, it was determined that EDI effectively substituted conventional documentation employed by purchasers and vendors for business transactions. This transition resulted in improved record keeping, expedited information retrieval, and enhanced information sharing among business entities. Furthermore, the sharing of reorder level information with potential suppliers has resulted in a reduction in wait times, since it enables prompt response to inventory requirements. Ultimately, this will result in a reduction in inventory costs and facilitate the implementation of the Just-In-Time (JIT) approach, hence enhancing customer service.

8.6.5 PUBLIC PROCUREMENT ACT, 2003 (ACT 663), GHANA

In 2003, the Government of Ghana implemented the Public Procurement Act, 2003 (663) with the aim of establishing regulatory measures for the procurement process within the public sector of Ghana. The document establishes overarching principles and protocols that regulate the procurement process.

8.6.6 PROCUREMENT STRUCTURES

8.6.6.1 PUBLIC PROCUREMENT AUTHORITY (PPA)

The establishment of the PPA in Ghana serves as a constitutional advisory entity responsible for the coordination, direction, and enhancement of public procurement practices and processes. The purpose of this measure is to guarantee the constant adherence of all public institutions to the rules and regulations outlined in the Act. The primary goals of the Act are to establish consistent processes, enhance transparency, and ensure accountability in all procurement activities, with the ultimate aim of achieving optimal value for money. The topic involves the traditional acquisition process, commencing with procurement strategizing and culminating in contract completion, along with the comprehensive evaluation of procurement effectiveness. The uniform application of the legislation by governmental bodies is essential for attaining and elevating efficacy, productivity, openness, and uniformity in records and determinations, as envisaged.

8.6.6.2 PROCUREMENT ENTITY (PE)

The legislation defines PE as any entity or individual authorized by legal or administrative means to engage in procurement activities.

8.6.6.3 HEAD OF PROCUREMENT ENTITY (HE)

The person in the position of HE holds the responsibility for ensuring adherence to the regulations and guidelines specified in the legislation. As per the legislation, it becomes obligatory for the HE to establish a Procurement Division and recruit capable professionals possessing pertinent skills and knowledge to effectively supervise the procurement operations conducted on behalf of the organization. The procurement duties encompass the assessment and approval of agreements proposed or presented by either the Procurement Division or the Tender Assessment Panel. Additionally, the individual undertakes the role of Chairman for the Entity Tender Committee (ETC) or participates as a member in cases involving the Tender Review Board. They are granted the authority to affix their signature on agreements on behalf of the entity and are tasked with addressing or reevaluating grievances raised by aggrieved bidders (suppliers, contractors, or advisers) in accordance with Section 79 of the legislation.

8.6.6.4 PROCUREMENT UNIT (PU)

A PU is a department inside a PE that is in charge of making purchases and overseeing the procurement process.

8.6.6.5 ETC

As stipulated in Section 1 of the Legislation, it is obligatory for every PE to establish a Tender Panel tasked with assessing, modifying, and giving approval to procurement strategies presented by the Procurement Division. The panel is also responsible for declining a proposal and furnishing reasons for disapproving contract allocations within the confines of its authorized limit. These propositions can be initiated or recommended by either the Bidding Appraisal Board or the Procurement Division.

8.6.6.6 TENDER EVALUATION PANELS

An ad hoc group consisting of no more than five individuals is established to support the efforts of the ETC via the evaluation of tenders. The individuals must possess the necessary expertise, knowledge, and experience that are pertinent to the procurement requisites.

8.6.7 PROCUREMENT PRINCIPLES

Both public and private procurements must adhere to fundamental principles that serve to fulfill the ultimate goal of all such endeavors. Public procurement must adhere to the values of professionalism, value for money, competition, accountability, fairness, efficiency, ethics, and separation of duties, as outlined in Act 663.

8.6.7.1 PROFESSIONALISM

In order to ensure informed purchase choices within every purchase entity, it is essential that the management of procurement activities be entrusted to professionals who possess the necessary competencies, knowledge, skills, and qualifications.

8.6.7.2 TRANSPARENCY

Public procurement is often conducted in a manner that ensures fairness and transparency, whereby consistent methods and information are uniformly applied to all potential tenderers seeking to engage in business with the government.

8.6.7.3 VALUE FOR MONEY (ECONOMY)

The aforementioned premise has significant importance for evaluating the efficacy of the procurement process, including both inputs and outputs. The assessment of the whole life cost and quality of procurement that aligns with users' expectations or demands is considered the optimal approach. Organizations are required to attain optimal cost-effectiveness for all commodities acquired or throughout their procurement procedures. In the past, organizations had the belief that the most effective way to get value for money was to simply accept the lowest tender price offered by a potential provider. At present, the determination of value for funds in procurement relies on a thorough assessment of the entire lifespan expenditure associated with the acquired product. This encompasses the expenditure linked to the apparatus, its setup, maintenance, and various non-financial factors.

8.6.7.4 COMPETITIVENESS

The legislation mandates that organizations promote increased involvement of suppliers in procurement procedures. In order to reduce costs and expand the pool of possible suppliers, procurement professionals are advised to use various strategies such as advertising, sourcing reviews, pre-qualifications, and transparent processes. These measures aim to foster fair and transparent competition among suppliers.

8.6.7.5 ETHICAL APPROACH

This pertains to the convictions and values around moral judgments and ethical standards. It exercises control over behaviors and choices.

8.6.7.6 SEPARATION OF DUTIES

In all governmental organizations, it is crucial for the Chief of Entity to firmly adhere to the principle of function segregation, backed by the assistance of the purchasing executive or project supervisor (in instances involving projects). This measure serves to mitigate any disruptions in the public procurement procedures. In circumstances characterized by limited staffing resources, it is advisable for management to prioritize the assignment of procurement responsibilities to individuals with a background or expertise in procurement.

8.6.8 PP

The subject under consideration revolves around procurement effectiveness. The effectiveness of procurement holds a pivotal role in the triumph of a manufacturing enterprise, as it facilitates the competitive attainment and acquisition of premium goods. This subsequently empowers the organization's offerings to secure a competitive edge within the marketplace. Nevertheless, there have been instances wherein insufficient PP has yielded financial setbacks for the corporate sector. These financial setbacks can be attributed to the supply of subpar materials, compromised value for money, and inflated expenditures. The deterioration in the profitability of the corporate sector was also shaped by underwhelming PP (Juma, 2010). Migai (2010) contends that inadequate PP significantly hampers the growth of corporate entities within the private sector. This is primarily due to its link to delayed deliveries, heightened defect rates, the provision of substandard products, or even complete non-delivery (Barsemoi et al., 2014).

Barsemoi et al. (2014) affirm that the corporate sector has encountered hurdles concerning performance, which can be ascribed to diverse elements. These factors encompass the presence of unskilled personnel, adherence to conventional procurement protocols, reluctance to embrace e-procurement practices, insufficient coordination of procurement undertakings, the dearth of quality assurance policies, and inadequate regulatory frameworks (Juma, 2010). Canon (2000) asserts that the absence of well-defined procurement legislation in Ghana is a significant factor contributing to a substantial 61 percent of losses incurred in procurement bidding processes. Furthermore, the topic of procurement is rather nascent, and there is a dearth of comprehensive development in areas such as training and ethical principles within this domain. The current circumstances have exacerbated the problem, particularly within the private sector, prompting the need for an investigation into the many elements that impact PP in Ghana's private sector. The objective of this research is to enhance PP via a comprehensive analysis.

8.6.9 TYPES OF TECHNOLOGIES USED IN SCM

8.6.9.1 BLOCKCHAIN

The definition of blockchain, as provided by Gartner (2018b), pertains to the sequential storage of value exchange transactions inside blocks, which are then recorded in a distributed ledger. Every individual block is connected to the preceding block, so forming a sequential chain. This establishes an unchangeable decentralized network, based on cryptographic protocols and agreement processes. The behavior of the blockchain network may be adjusted to accommodate various implementations. According to Christidis and Devetsikiotis (2016), a network platform that utilizes cryptology allows for secure peer-to-peer transactions without requiring trust between peers. The technology further facilitates the tracing of transactions from their inception to the genesis of the networks, hence enhancing transparency inside the network. The data pertaining to the transactions is maintained in a decentralized manner inside the distributed ledger, ensuring that it is accessible to all users within the network. Currently, its primary use is in the realm of digital currency, namely cryptocurrencies like as Bitcoin and Ether.

The notion of blockchain technology was initially presented in 1991 in an essay written by Stuart Haber and W. Scott Stornetta, which found publication in the Journal of Cryptology with the title "Methods for time-stamping digital documents" (Narayanan et al., 2016). In that era, the phrase "blockchain" had not yet come into play; instead, it was denoted as a cryptographically safeguarded sequence of blocks. The origin of the concept behind blockchain dates back to 2008 when it was initially formulated by Satoshi Nakamoto, who is widely acknowledged as the architect behind the digital currency Bitcoin (Baghla, 2017). It is important to note that Satoshi Nakamoto is not a verifiable individual, but rather a pseudonym attributed to either an individual or a collective entity. Bitcoin was established in response to a lack of confidence in traditional banking institutions, which was exacerbated by the global financial crisis. Its primary objective is to remove middlemen from transactions. In essence, exclusive ownership of Bitcoins would be confined only to the individual user, hence eliminating any involvement of financial institutions or any other intermediary entities in the transactional process. Currently, the predominant use of blockchain technology is mostly associated with various cryptocurrencies. However, it is widely anticipated that the potential advantages of using this technology across diverse sectors and enterprises would be significant (Busby, 2018).

According to Christidis and Devetsikiotis (2016), a blockchain refers to a decentralized system that stores information in blocks. Although it may not first seem enticing, the concept of information utilization and storage exhibits significant variations. In the present scenario, when a corporation intends to exchange information with another company, both entities would typically own a single copy of the shared data, which is kept inside their respective server systems. According to Christidis and Devetsikiotis (2016), in a blockchain system, data is kept inside the network, namely in the blockchain, and may be accessed by other participants in the network.

8.6.9.2 AI

The use of algorithms facilitates computer systems in comprehending pertinent facts and using such data to autonomously make judgments. The term "artificial" encompasses several sub-technologies, including machine learning, deep learning, and NLP. Through the use of these technologies, a computer has the capability to comprehend many forms of data, such as pictures, written text, and speech. Cognitive computing is a concept that is sometimes misunderstood or erroneously conflated with AI. However, it is important to note that cognitive computing specifically refers to an undertaking spearheaded by IBM, with the objective of developing a computer system capable of emulating human thought processes and behaviors (Kelly, 2015). The phrase "artificial intelligence" (AI) was first used by John McCarthy at the Dartmouth Conference in 1956 (Garnham, 1988). McCarthy's definition of AI included the creation of computers that exhibit behaviors akin to human intellect (Ertel, 2011a). In the field of computer science, a software agent refers to a program that utilizes user input data to generate corresponding output data (Ertel, 2011a). One example of this may be a basic mathematical computation, in which an input is converted into an output. This agent operates using user interactions as its foundation.

The field of study was first established by notable figures like as Alan Turing, Kurt Gödel, and Alonso Church. However, it is worth noting that at their time, computers were not yet in existence. It was not until the 1950s that computers with enough computational capabilities were developed, enabling the simulation of rudimentary human thought processes (Ertel, 2011a). The Dartmouth Conference is widely regarded as a pivotal event in the emergence of the field of AI. In their seminal work, Newell and Simon presented the Logic Theorist, a groundbreaking system capable of autonomously proving theorems. This significant development demonstrated the capacity of computers to handle not just numerical data, but also symbolic information. As previously stated, McCarthy also invented a programming language known as LISP, with the intention of processing symbolic structures. According to the source cited, these programs exhibited the ability to edit their own code. The first definition of AI proposed by McCarthy was deemed too restrictive since it only focused on computers exhibiting intelligent behavior, without considering their capacity to effectively address complex real-world challenges (Ertel, 2011a).

In this research, the definition of AI as proposed by Gartner (2018a) will be used due to its contemporaneity and its focus on the specific aims of

AI, as well as its distinguishing features from RPA. The provided definition encompasses the concept of acquiring knowledge, so indicating that machine learning is an integral component of AI. This assertion is further substantiated by Techopedia (2018). Another significant component of AI, as stated by Gartner (2018a), is its ability to facilitate the substitution of people in jobs that are not regular. This juncture represents the divergence between RPA and AI. According to Accenture Operations (2017), the primary objective of RPA is to automate repetitive and predictable processes. Conversely, tasks that are non-routine in nature need a greater degree of intelligence, which falls within the purview of AI.

8.6.9.3 IOT

According to Gubbi et al. (2013), the definition proposed by Kevin Ashton in 1999 remains applicable despite the evolving use of the technology. Computer autonomy refers to the capacity of a computer system to perceive and gather information without any need for human intervention. In essence, it may be said that things possess the ability to establish direct communication with a computer in an automated manner. It is worth noting that the concept of the IoT does not include the specific actions performed by computers with the provided information. This technology facilitates the establishment of a connection between computational devices and tangible entities. The process involves the placement of sensors on tangible entities in order to collect data (Gubbi et al., 2013). These sensors have the potential to provide data on the deterioration of an item. By giving this information, the production will get prior knowledge of the impending breakdown, enabling timely replacement to avert its occurrence. While the IoT facilitates such processes, it is important to note that the technology itself does not directly execute these tasks. The function of this technology is to establish connections between tangible entities and the internet via the use of sensors and/or processors (Xia et al., 2012).

The phrase "Internet of Things" was introduced by Kevin Ashton in 1999 during a presentation at Procter & Gamble, as documented by Gubbi et al. (2013). The subject under discussion was to the influence of Radio Frequency Identification (RFID) technology on the supply chain, as explored by Gubbi et al. (2013). In general, the IoT leverages a variety of established technologies, including temperature sensors, RFID, and barcodes. The IoT technology facilitates internet connectivity. By using this approach, it facilitates the activation of many automated functionalities. Since that time, there have been several use cases of the IoT that include a wide range of applications, including the optimization of heavy industries and the automation of residential environments (Gubbi et al., 2013). Moreover, the IoT facilitates novel capabilities for several developing technologies, with blockchain serving as a notable example.

8.7 THEORETICAL REVIEW

8.7.1 DYNAMIC CAPABILITY THEORY

According to Teece (2007), the dynamic theory posits that a firm's success is primarily derived from its capacity to consistently adapt, renew, and reconfigure its skills and competencies. According to Eisenhardt and Martin (2000), dynamic capacities refer to the organizational and strategic routines used by enterprises to attain new resource configurations in response to the emergence, collision, division, evolution, and decline of markets. The Resource-Based View (RBV) places emphasis on the careful selection of resources, whereas the Dynamic Capabilities Theory (DCT) focuses on the development and evolution of resources (Teece, 2007). This is considered crucial due to two key processes: resource acquisition and capacity enhancement within the organizational learning cycle. Therefore, according to the DCT, it is essential for organizational resources to possess the qualities of adaptability, renewability, and reconfigurability in order to establish and maintain a sustainable competitive advantage (Teece, 2007). Dynamic capabilities are often linked to dynamic environments, in which organizations must continually adapt their resources to align with the organization's strategy in certain circumstances (O'Connor, 2008). In varying circumstances within the corporate environment, several forms of dynamic capabilities are required. This study incorporates the concept of dynamic capacities from several perspectives. Specifically, it examines the inclusion of both internal and external factors in the development of the strategic agility taxonomy. The scholarly discourse revolves around the precise definition of dynamic capabilities. Consequently, scholarly works such as the review and research agenda on dynamic capabilities conducted by Wang and Ahmed (2007) and the study titled "Dynamic Capabilities: What Are They?" by Eisenhardt and Martin (2000) contribute to the ongoing debate in the literature. Winter (2003) conducted a study on the comprehension of dynamic capacities. According to Hassabis (2016), the definition suggests that dynamic capabilities pertain to the adaptation to a dynamic environment and the cultivation of organizational strengths in alignment with environmental changes. The competitive advantage of organizations is shown via their capacity to effectively respond to various challenges and opportunities. According to Wang and Ahmed (2007), dynamic capabilities are inherent in processing, namely in the form of explicit structures composed of resource combinations that may be flexibly modified in response to changes in the environment. Therefore, capabilities may be defined as the organizational ability to reallocate resources and modify processes in order to effectively integrate and adapt to the surrounding environment. According to Eisenhardt and Martin (2000), dynamic capacities may be seen via recognizable activities like as product creation, strategic decision-making, and partnerships. According to Teece et al. (2007), the competitive advantage of an organization is determined by the procedures, places, and pathways that are accessible to it.

8.8 CONCEPTUAL REVIEW

8.8.1 ICT PRACTICES INFLUENCE PROCUREMENT EFFICIENCY

In the current dynamic economic landscape, companies encounter intense rivalry, swiftly changing client preferences, and a quick rate of technology advancements (Ganguly et al., 2009). According to Overby et al. (2006), it is crucial for a corporation to possess the capability to perceive shifts in the market and promptly adapt to these changes in order to achieve success. Due to the prevailing business environments, the notion of ICT practices has undergone development, presenting firms with a chance to navigate uncertain and volatile markets. Consequently, beverage companies must possess the ability to swiftly and effectively modify their business processes in accordance with evolving business conditions and customer demands (Aitken, et al., 2002; Christopher, 2000). Therefore, the use of ICT practices, which includes both rapidity and adaptability, is increasingly seen as a crucial instrument for fostering innovation and enhancing competitive performance within modern corporate landscapes. The field of ICT practices encompasses intricate topics that have been extensively examined within several academic disciplines.

The concept of ICT practices draws from prior research on flexibility within economics (Mathiyakalan et al., 2005) and has been further developed within the context of agile manufacturing. The operational strategy of the supply chain and the utilization of ICT practices are linked to customer responsiveness and supply chain flexibility (Prates et al., 2001). The ability of an organization to adjust and thrive by perceiving and responding to changes in its external environment has gained immense significance in today's fiercely competitive and volatile business landscape. This capability is widely acknowledged as a pivotal factor influencing a company's competitiveness and its potential to enhance overall performance (Mathiassen and Pries-Heje, 2006).

A notable advantage of adopting supply chain and ICT practices is the rapid access to information, facilitating efficient management of operations that function on an "on-demand" basis. The field of SCM has undergone substantial transformations with the integration of IT, as evidenced in scholarly research (Ghiassi and Spera, 2003; Shore, 2001). Conventional EDI systems and ERP systems have given way to Internet and Intranet technologies, which now play a pivotal role in supporting SCM operations (Pant et al., 2003; Shore, 2001).

The fusion of information systems serves as the cornerstone for promoting information sharing and exchange within organizations (Auramo et al., 2005; Yusuf et al., 2004). Patnayakuni et al. (2006) contend that limited information exchange and insufficient information hinder supply chain coordination, leading to heightened operational inefficiencies. The successful implementation of an integrated information system demands the seamless integration of communication, data, and application components (Muller et al., 2007; Ross, 2003). This integration is critical in enabling constant and real-time connectivity across functional units along supply chains (Rai et al., 2006). However, it is essential to recognize that information systems alone lack the inherent capability to offer enduring performance or value (Powell and Dent-Micallef, 2007). Therefore, it is imperative for beverage companies to effectively incorporate resources and align them within their social and cultural context (Barua et al., 2004) to bolster operational efficiency and streamline workflow coordination (Rai et al., 2006).

In this particular context, the fundamental dynamics associated with the utilization of information technology (IT) in businesses, which play a substantial role in addressing the growing global competition, encompass various factors such as technological, economic, political, cultural, and environmental aspects, as well as alterations in business management (Çağlar et al., 2006). IT is a critical implementation that is gaining growing significance in the areas of data gathering, processing, preservation, and transmission. Therefore, IT serves as a valuable tool for organizations, providing them with innovative methods to outperform their competitors and get a competitive advantage. Porter and Millar (2005) assert that IT has a significant impact on the cost structure of businesses and offers avenues for differentiation. In the present environment, IT exerts its influence on competitiveness via three primary mechanisms: altering the industry's structure, fostering competitive advantages, and generating employment opportunities (Porter and Millar, 2005). In addition, Whiteley (2006) posited that IT can serve as a strategic tool for gaining a competitive advantage, enhancing operational effectiveness and performance, optimizing business management and organization, and fostering the emergence of novel business prospects. This is achieved through the provision of substantial opportunities for business and management innovation. The use of IT applications has been shown to have a favorable influence on company performance in isolation. The majority of organizations are unable to maintain their commercial operations without the assistance of IT. The collection, retention, and analysis of data are vital in enhancing the operational efficiency and overall performance of organizations via the facilitation of informed decision-making (Güleş et al., 2003).

In addition to enhancing operational efficiency, organizations also use IT to facilitate cooperation with suppliers, sales channels, and customers, with the aim of meeting consumer demands in the most efficient and expeditious manner (Gunasekaran and McGaughey, 2002). IT also facilitates the monitoring of operational and organizational performances, as well as the management of complex processes such as product creation (Whiteley, 2006). The acquisition and use of information are of paramount importance for organizations operating in the contemporary and rapidly evolving business landscape. The ability to get and analyze information is crucial for organizations to maintain their competitive edge in the current demanding business landscape (Caglar et al., 2006). Drawing from the previously discussed explanations, one can argue that the realm of IT significantly influences the competitive landscape of a particular industry by facilitating innovative product and service advancement, improving decision-making procedures, nurturing collaborations between organizations, minimizing operational costs, and integrating seamlessly with existing offerings. The pivotal role of IT extends to the optimization of SCM operations. To elevate efficiency within the supply chain, businesses can implement diverse strategies, including the restructuring of customer and supplier affiliations, refinement of operational workflows, meticulous performance monitoring, and amplification of data visibility throughout the entire supply chain (McLeod and Rubin, 2000).

8.8.2 BLOCKCHAIN AND PP

Through the examination of blockchain technology, one may ascertain the potential ramifications it may have on many businesses. Currently, the practical applications of blockchain technology remain limited, and the challenge of expanding its implementation is a significant concern (Maltaverne, 2017). In order to maximize the potential benefits derived from the use of this technology, it is essential to secure the participation and investment of other stakeholders within the supply chain. The implementation of an internal blockchain just inside the confines of a single organization might provide some advantages. However, when juxtaposed against the possible benefits offered by this technology, such an endeavor would be deemed superfluous. Hence, establishing a strong and mutually beneficial connection with suppliers is crucial in order to incentivize their participation in the network. Alternatively, if suppliers are not sufficiently motivated to provide information, they may fail to recognize the significance and benefits associated with the use of the technology (Kaipia and Hartiala, 2006). Subsequently, due to the inherent reliability of all data stored on the blockchain, the significance of the link will be diminished (Christidis and Devetsikiotis, 2016).

Nonetheless, it is apparent that the potential for blockchain technology to augment supply chain effectiveness within four core spheres is conspicuous when contrasted with prevailing technologies. These mentioned spheres encompass reliance, safeguarding, openness, and dealings (Williams, 2017). The unchangeable nature of the blockchain guarantees swift identification of any endeavor to manipulate data within a block (Loop, 2016). The interplay of trust among stakeholders would lose significance as they collectively possess mutual understanding concerning the credibility of the data (Christidis and Devetsikiotis, 2016). Hence, it becomes plausible to follow the sequential blocks along the supply chain to pinpoint the origin of the primary material employed in the ultimate product (Maltaverne, 2017). As previously indicated, this information could be seen as entirely reliable.

The security of the Bitcoin framework is heavily reliant on the pair of cryptographic codes (public and private) allocated to every participant within the system (Christidis and Devetsikiotis, 2016). These codes are intricately designed passphrases that have so far proven impervious to hacking endeavors. One inherent drawback of the Bitcoin mechanism pertains to the potential loss of a private code, which renders the associated Bitcoin(s) inaccessible and unusable. Put otherwise, these Bitcoins would become permanently inaccessible. Given that the entire supply of Bitcoin is capped at 21.4 million, it follows that the overall quantity of Bitcoins will be limited.

The inherent fixed supply of Bitcoins and the fluctuating nature of investor participation contribute to the currency's inherent volatility, rendering it untrustworthy. This characteristic is seen in many cryptocurrencies. Hence, it is improbable that the tokenization of assets in this manner will be used for industrial applications in the near-term future.

The inherent anonymity of the network makes it very difficult to establish a direct correlation between public keys and specific individuals. Consequently, several criminal activities have been associated with the use of cryptocurrencies. As shown, the online marketplace facilitates the sale of both weaponry and drugs, using Bitcoins as a medium of exchange (Bloomberg, 2017). In the context of transactions, blockchain technology facilitates near-instantaneous transaction processing, significantly reducing the time required compared to traditional intermediaries, which can take several days to complete transactions. This expedited processing allows stakeholders to make timely decisions based on up-to-date information (Byström, 2016). Currently, the process of upscaling presents challenges that result in elevated transaction costs. However, it is anticipated that in the future, transaction costs inside a peer-to-peer system might be eradicated (Gupta, 2017). In essence, the ability to conduct instantaneous transactions worldwide would be accompanied by minimal costs.

Furthermore, each transaction would be assigned a unique identifier (hash) that is maintained throughout the distributed ledger. In essence, any transaction involving money or information inside the blockchain network would be accessible to all participants at any given moment (Maltaverne, 2017). One much-debated topic in the realm of blockchain technology is its potential for scalability (Maltaverne, 2017). Hence,

"H1: There is a significant positive relationship between blockchain and PP."

8.8.3 IOT AND PP

One of the benefits of the IoT is the potential to access real-time data. This particular characteristic has a wide range of applications, particularly in the context of SCM. According to Christidis and Devetsikiotis (2016), the capability to track the real-time location of commodities facilitates the planning process for firms. By incorporating sensor data into program codes, there exists the potential for the sensor data to indirectly initiate autonomous reactions, contingent upon the information sent by the sensor.

The IoT often serves as a crucial conduit for several other technologies. The use of IoT data has some significant attributes that are also applicable to other technologies. One example is the potential of RFID tags to facilitate the identification of commodities (Lindman, 2018), a crucial need for the use of blockchain technology in the context of tracing items to their source within a supply chain (Christidis and Devetsikiotis, 2016). An additional example pertains to the use of historical IoT data in the context of machine learning algorithms to facilitate the prediction of future events (Abu Alsheikh et al., 2014). This research also highlights the potential of machine learning in facilitating the selection of relevant IoT data for retrieval. This exemplifies the mutual benefits derived from the integration of several technologies. The phenomenon of servitization, which entails the transition from a mostly product-oriented organizational model to one that emphasizes the provision of services, is being seen as a prevalent trend across several sectors and industries. IoT sensors serve as a significant facilitator for several sectors. According to GE Digital (2017), sensors have the capacity to detect the gradual deterioration of machines or their individual components. Through the use of IoT technology, the aforementioned sensors would transmit the gathered data to a centralized database. By means of this data transmission, the corporation would be enabled to proactively replace or do maintenance on the machine or component in question, prior to its failure.

Hence,

"H2: There is a significant positive relationship between IoT and PP."

8.8.4 ROBOT PROCESS AUTOMATION (RPA) AND PP

RPA is seen as a distinct subject matter by some individuals, but others characterize it only as a collection of algorithms. According to Wright et al. (2017), RPA refers to the use of computer-coded and rule-based automation techniques to substitute human involvement in the execution of repetitive operations. Furthermore, it is vital to note that RPA does not refer to physical robots capable of walking and talking. According to Accenture Operations (2017), a distinction may be made between AI and RPA. RPA often deals with structured data and operates based on predefined rules, while AI handles unstructured data and relies on judgment-based decision-making. The demarcation between the two notions, however, remains ambiguous, and it is likely that mixtures or integrated technologies, known as blended technologies, are prevalent (Accenture Operations, 2017).

A pure RPA may be likened to the aforementioned instance of a basic chatbot. While an AI-enhanced chatbot utilizes natural language processing (NLP) to comprehend a wide range of conversations, a basic chatbot operates by responding to certain words based on a predetermined set of rules. The proposed chatbot may be classified as a RPA solution since it is designed to handle repetitive tasks by pre-programming precise replies to user inquiries. RPA may be seen as a simplified iteration of AI, primarily focused on handling fewer complex jobs (Willcocks, 2016). Despite the presence of distinctions between the two ideas, there are no inherent disparities that justify the inclusion of a distinct section on RPA, despite its significance and basic role in enhancing overall PP.

"H3: There is a significant positive relationship between RPA and PP."

8.8.5 AI AND PP

When discussing the benefits of AI, it is common to highlight the many possible areas of use. The examination of digital assistants, medical diagnosis, and fraud detection reveals many noteworthy cases that have potential benefits for corporations, people, and society at large (Rao and Verweij, 2017). Nevertheless, the true benefits of AI are in its impacts. AI has the potential to decrease the level of human intervention necessary, particularly in jobs that entail repetition, resulting in time and cost savings (Guszcza, 2018). According to Goldberg (2017), the integration of AI and RPA has the potential to significantly decrease the error rate. Nevertheless, it is important to note that total elimination of errors is not feasible, since computers, like people, are also prone to making mistakes. According to Brynjolfsson and McAfee (2017), the enhancement of AI may be achieved with relative ease. Furthermore, once AI reaches a higher level of proficiency, it does not regress to its former state of knowledge. AI solutions demonstrate consistency in their performance when given with same data, resulting in improved procurement outcomes.

One notable feature of AI/RPA technologies is their ability to operate continuously without the need for sleep, relaxation, or sustenance (Daisy, 2017). According to Guszcza (2018), the use of automation technology in completing repetitive tasks may result in remarkable gains in productivity and time efficiency. When examining the drawbacks associated with AI/RPA solutions, a prevalent area of concern is the financial implications (Goldberg, 2017). The implementation of new technology is often associated with high costs; however, it has the potential for significant savings when used effectively. Hence,

"H4: There is a significant positive relationship between AI and PP."

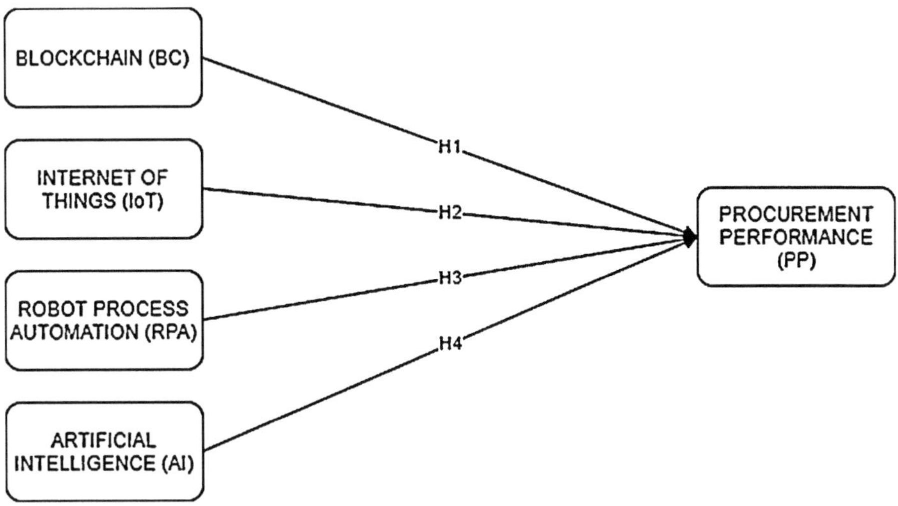

FIGURE 8.1 Conceptual model 34.

8.9 RESEARCH METHODOLOGY

8.9.1 RESEARCH DESIGN OF THE STUDY

Based on a thorough examination of existing literature, it is evident that the study of ICT practices in SCM has traditionally been approached with equal emphasis on qualitative and quantitative methodologies. However, recent scholarly investigations have shown a growing inclination toward quantitative research, as evidenced by studies conducted by Cleme et al. (2007), Olsson and Gall (2012), Narteh (2013), and Farah (2017b). Therefore, this study employs a quantitative approach. The optimal strategy involves using sophisticated and rigorous statistical analyses to establish the facts by defining trends and interactions between the variables being examined, namely the influence of ICT practices and PP. Furthermore, a substantial quantity of data is necessary to empirically evaluate the postulated theory and ascertain its validity or refutability. In order to provide the most effective approach for obtaining answers to the research question, it is recommended to use a quantitative research design. This recommendation takes into account the study's goals, as well as other relevant factors discussed earlier.

8.9.2 DATA COLLECTION SOURCES

According to Saunders et al. (2009), there are two major sources from which researchers might collect data, namely primary and secondary data sources.

8.9.2.1 PRIMARY DATA

Primary data refers to original material collected by researchers for the purpose of a specific study (Kothari, 2004), with a primary focus on the most recent investigation (Zikmund et al., 2010). The publication includes many types of data collection methods such as reports, interviews, and questionnaires (Kothari, 2004). The questionnaire comprises a series of predetermined questions designed to gather information from a selected group of participants on the topic of research (Hair et al., 2007). The selection of this particular strategy by the researchers was motivated by its cost-effectiveness and its ability to accurately target respondents while also ensuring a large and diverse sample size (Kothari, 2004). The researcher successfully used the questionnaire to collect relevant data pertaining to the topic of study. The questionnaire was specifically prepared to assess the acceptance and utilization of Virtual Reality Applications (VRA) among workers of the NEDCo in Ghana. The survey was administered in a physical format, consisting of concise words with a straightforward structure that facilitated effortless participation from the participants without encountering any challenges. Furthermore, it was essential for the researchers that the participants show a predisposition to engage in thoughtful introspection and accurately express their emotions when completing the surveys.

8.9.2.2 SECONDARY DATA

Secondary data refers to publicly available information that has been acquired by others. Acquiring it is often cost-effective or even free, making it a valuable foundation for any study endeavor, provided one have the knowledge to discover and evaluate its relevance and value. Prior to incorporating secondary data into a research project, it is essential to address many crucial elements. In cases where the researcher has not collected the data, it is imperative for them to acquire a comprehensive understanding of the dataset. This includes familiarizing themselves with the methods employed to collect the data, the nature of responses obtained for each question, the potential necessity of applying weights during the analysis, and the potential need for stratification within the sample population, among other relevant considerations. One of the primary advantages associated with the use of secondary data is its potential for cost-effectiveness.

The existing data has been previously acquired by other researchers, hence obviating the requirement for the current researcher to allocate time, financial resources, and energy toward the data collection procedure. The importation of the secondary data set is necessary, and it is very likely that the associated expenses are comparatively cheaper than the costs incurred in developing a comparable data collection from scratch. The latter often entails expenditures related to travel, salary, accommodation, equipment, office space, and other operational costs. The researcher shows a strong commitment to use contemporary, relevant, and dependable evidence in support of the study. According to Zikmund and Al (2010), secondary data plays a crucial role in providing substantiating evidence for facts, consumer behavior, trends, and market conditions. Secondary evidence has significant value for researchers behavior to its cost-effectiveness and time efficiency since it offers the potential for generating novel ideas (Hair et al., 2007). Additionally, it aids in the gathering of data, delineating research inquiries, and conducting analyses on a broader scope (Collins, 2010).

8.9.3 RESEARCH DESIGN

A sample size of 350 was selected from six areas operating in VRA–NEDCo Ghana. The researchers used probabilistic techniques in the selection of survey participants for the study, ensuring their inclusion in the sample. Random sampling procedures were used in order to choose all of the components. Primary data for the study was acquired via the administration of individual questionnaires to respondents. In addition, data pertaining to the general characteristics of consumers was gathered. The data that was gathered was subjected to analysis via the use of descriptive statistics. The survey data underwent coding, verification, and cleansing processes before being inputted into the SPSS program for analysis. In order to facilitate comprehension, the study's results were presented via the use of appropriate tables and charts. A total of 350 questionnaires were gathered.

8.9.4 SAMPLING TECHNIQUE

According to Ngembe (2019), probability sampling technique is described as the systematic procedure used by researchers to pick a representative sample of individuals from a given community by random selection. According to Ngembe (2019), the method is suitable for the purpose of sampling in quantitative research, ensuring that every participant has an equal probability of being chosen. The chance of selecting responses from the population is a known quantity. The objective of this research is to collect data pertaining to service quality within the higher education sector. The use of both probability and nonprobability sampling methods will be considered appropriate. The data will be collected using a convenience sampling approach.

8.9.4.1 NONPROBABILITY SAMPLING

Nonprobability sampling involves the selection of units from a population without providing every unit with an equal chance of being picked (Saunders et al., 2016). Etikan and Bala (2017) as well as Etikan et al. (2016) have classified five distinct nonprobability sampling strategies. The sample techniques mentioned in the study conducted by Saunders et al. (2016) include quota, purposive, convenience, self-selection, and snowball sampling.

8.9.5 DATA COLLECTION

The major data gathering tool used by the researcher was a questionnaire using a Likert scale. Kothari (2004) asserts that the use of a self-administered questionnaire is the only method for obtaining self-reported data pertaining to individuals' opinions, attitudes, beliefs, and values. The questionnaire was partitioned into several parts that corresponded to the different factors that were chosen for examination. The selected study used both closed-structured and open-ended questions in each part, aiming to capture the perspectives, opinions, and attitudes of the respondents that may not have been fully caught by the researcher. The survey questions were created with the intention of gathering both qualitative and quantitative data. The open-ended questions provided respondents with full latitude to provide their answers. The survey was conducted using a drop-and-pick approach with the procurement managers/supply chain managers or their equivalents at VRA–NEDCo in Ghana.

8.9.6 DATA ANALYSIS

For the analysis, IBM SPSS version 25.0 and AMOS version 26.0 were utilized as the software tools. The assessment of convergent and discriminant validities, along with instrument reliability, was carried out through the utilization of measures such as Cronbach's alpha, composite reliability (CR), and average variance extracted (AVE). These evaluations also gauged the internal consistency of the research instrument. The researcher not only conducted confirmatory factor analysis (CFA) but also performed exploratory factor analysis (EFA), evaluated factor loadings, and generated descriptive statistics.

The data was also analyzed with the method of Structural Equation Modeling (SEM). The research investigated the SEM in light of two primary advantages. Firstly, there exists an estimate of many interconnected dependencies. One additional benefit is the capacity to depict latent constructs inside these associations and accommodate for inaccuracies in measurement during the estimate procedure (Hair et al., 2000). The researchers used mean scores to assess and evaluate the degree of satisfaction among respondents about the utilization of ICT at VRA–NEDCo in Ghana, as well as its impact on PP.

8.10 DATA ANALYSIS AND RESULTS

8.10.1 DEMOGRAPHICS CHARACTERISTICS OF RESPONDENTS

Table 8.1 displays the demographic characteristics of the student responders. The research primarily focuses on the pertinent demographic factors. According to the researcher, the factors that were considered were gender, age, marital status, program of study, and institution of study of the student. As a result of the COVID-19 pandemic and the subsequent restrictions imposed on university operations, a modified approach was taken in administering the questionnaire. Specifically, one-third of the questionnaire was administered during the period spanning from April 7th, 2020 to August 30th, 2020, when only final-year students were allowed on campus. The remaining two-thirds of the questionnaire was administered between September 1st, 2020 and

September 9th, 2020, when first to third-year students were permitted to return to campus to complete the academic year. According to the data shown in Table 8.1, it was found that a majority of the respondents, namely 215 individuals or 61.4% of the total sample, were male students. The remaining 135 respondents, accounting for 38.6% of the sample, were identified as female students. In terms of the age distribution of the respondents, it is seen that 0.9% of the participants are below the age of 18. Additionally, 17.7% fall within the age range of 18 to 30 years, while 38.0% are between 31 and 40 years old. Furthermore, 32.3% of the respondents are aged between 41 and 50 years, and the remaining 11.1% are 50 years old or older. In terms of the marital status of the participants, it is worth noting that just 73 respondents, accounting for 20.9% of the sample, reported being married. Conversely, the majority of participants, namely 277 respondents, representing 79.1% of the sample, reported being single.

TABLE 8.1 Demographic Characteristics of Student Respondents.

Demographic parameter	Groupings	Frequency	%
Sex/Gender	Male	215	61.4
	Female	135	38.6
	Total	350	100.0
Age	Less than 18 years	3	.9
	18–30 years	62	17.7
	31–40 years	133	38.0
	41–50 years	113	32.3
	>50 years	39	11.1
	Total	350	100.0
Marital Status	Married	73	20.9
	Single	277	79.1
	Total	350	100.0

Source: Field survey, 2021

8.10.2 LOADINGS

As per the findings of Steenkamp and Geyskens (2006), it is essential for the factor loadings of the confirmatory model to exhibit statistical significance at a level of 0.01, while also surpassing a threshold of 0.5 points.

TABLE 8.2 Factor Loading.

		1	2	3	4	5
Blockchain	BC1	0.73				
	BC2	0.76				
	BC3	0.82				
	BC4	0.88				
IoTs	IoT1		0.76			
	IoT2		0.78			
	IoT3		0.73			
	IoT4		0.80			
	IoT5		0.87			
RPA	RPA			0.76		
	RPA			0.79		
	RPA			0.89		
	RPA			0.83		
AI	AI				0.77	
	AI				0.81	
	AI				0.72	
	AI				0.90	
	AI				0.82	
Procurement performance	PP1					0.74
	PP2					0.85
	PP3					0.76
	PP4					0.81
	PP5					0.77

Source: Field Work (2021)

8.10.3 TOTAL VARIANCE EXPLAINED

Table 8.4 presents the Principal Component Analysis, a statistical technique often used for exploratory component analysis. Based on the findings, the cumulative variation accounted for amounts to 61.64%. The numbers shown in the fifth column represent the cumulative percentage of the variance of the variables that can be accounted for by the primary components.

TABLE 8.3 Total Variances Explained.

Component	Initial Eigenvalues			Extraction Sums of Squared Loadings			Rotation Sums of Squared Loadings		
	Total	% of Variance	Cumulative %	Total	% of Variance	Cumulative %	Total	% of Variance	Cumulative %
BC	4.216	10.282	41.661	4.216	10.282	41.661	5.222	12.736	27.635
IoT	3.439	8.389	50.050	3.439	8.389	50.050	4.262	10.396	38.031
RPA	2.763	6.739	56.789	2.763	6.739	56.789	3.791	9.247	47.278
AI	1.928	4.701	67.293	1.928	4.701	67.293	3.356	8.186	64.116
RP	1.558	3.800	71.093	1.558	3.800	71.093	2.860	6.976	71.093
8	.982	2.396	73.489						
9	.837	2.041	75.530						
10	.813	1.983	77.513						
11	.770	1.878	79.391						
12	.671	1.637	81.028						

Extraction Method: Principal Component analysis.

8.10.4 RELIABILITY

This research employed a reliability assessment utilizing Cronbach's alpha (α) with a stipulated cutoff point of 0.70 or higher (Henseler et al., 2016). Moreover, the evaluation encompassed the AVE, adhering to a standard of 0.50 or superior, and the assessment of (CR), which was conducted with a minimum requirement of 0.70 and beyond (Bagozzi and Yi, 1988; Hair et al., 2014). Additionally, factor determinacy (FD) was scrutinized at a threshold of 0.70 (Bagozzi and Yi, 1988) in order to establish reliability (Hair et al., 2014; Henseler et al., 2016; Ringle et al., 2005). The alpha coefficient (α) exhibited a spectrum of values ranging from 0.82 to 0.92, signifying a notable degree of internal consistency. Similarly, the CR demonstrated a range of values from 0.77 to 0.91, further supporting the internal consistency of the constructs and items used in data collection. Additionally, the AVE shows a range of values between 0.58 and 0.71, providing further evidence of construct validity. Overall, these findings suggest that the measures employed in this study had satisfactory levels of internal consistency and validity. Therefore, all the ICT and PP components were maintained in the research for further analysis.

TABLE 8.4 Reliability.

Constructs	α	CR	AVE
Blockchain	0.92	0.77	0.67
IoTs	0.91	0.78	0.71
RPA	0.82	0.87	0.59
AI	0.91	0.88	0.65
PP	0.87	0.91	0.58

Source: Field Work (2021)

8.10.5 CORRELATION

In order to guarantee uniform comprehension of the findings in this study: A positive correlation is characterized by a correlational coefficient that falls within the range of more than 0 but less than 1, hence indicating a tight relationship between the variables (Dziak, 2016). A negative correlation is characterized by a correlational coefficient that falls between −1 and 0, indicating that an increase in one variable is accompanied by a reduction in the other (Dziak, 2016). In conclusion, a correlational coefficient of 0 or close to 0 suggests a high probability that the variables under consideration are not significantly connected. The results were graphed and subjected to analysis in order to provide scientific predictions (Dziak, 2016). Discriminatory validity refers to the extent to which the measurements of distinct constructs exhibit a weak correlation, so indicating that they are not assessing the same underlying concept (Blanco et al., 2010). As per the research conducted by Fornell and Larcker (1981), for the purpose of demonstrating distinct validity, it is anticipated that the square root of the mean extracted variance (AVE), indicated by the elements along the diagonal in Table 8.5, should surpass the correlations with different constructs (elements off the diagonal). The primary objective of the current investigation was to evaluate the potential violation of conventional method bias and the assumptions of linearity. The assessment of the intensity and orientation of the link between the variables was executed utilizing Pearson's coefficient of product-moment correlation. The researcher scrutinized the connection among the study variables through the utilization of Pearson's product-moment correlation (r), and the results are presented in the provided tabular format.

8.10.6 DESCRIPTIVE STATISTICS

Descriptive statistics are used to delineate the main characteristics of the outcomes of research. The provided service provides expedited synopses of the given sample and its corresponding metrics. According to Tronchim (2006), basic graphical analysis, combined with quantitative data analysis, is the fundamental basis for most analytical processes. Descriptive statistics were used to provide the mean and standard deviation of the collected data pertaining to the elements influencing effective ICT procurement practices at VRA–NEDCo, located in Ghana. The majority of the participants emphasized that the VRA–NEDCo extensively uses Blockchain technology in PP, as shown by a mean score of 4.09. Additionally, the usage of IoT is also very prevalent, as evidenced by a mean score of 3.54. The remaining participants likewise shown proficiency in contributing to procurement performance, with respective scores of 3.37 for RPA, 4.34 for PP, and 3.33 for AI. The findings indicate a significant utilization of computers within the procurement department of VRA–NEDCo, in contrast to the very limited usage of the internet.

The discriminant validity of the square root of AVE is assessed by comparing its similarities with other constructs. The findings, which demonstrate the uniqueness of the constructs, are shown in Table 8.5. Discriminant validity is shown when the square root of AVE is larger than the correlations with the other latent variables, as proposed by Fornell and Larcker (1981). It is evident that the existing measuring model fulfills this criterion, so indicating that the new model also successfully satisfies the discriminant validity assessment.

TABLE 8.5 Discriminant Validity and Descriptive Statistics.

	Mean	SD	AVE	BC	IoT	RPA	AI	PP
BC	4.09	0.78	0.67	0.82				
IoTs	3.54	1.17	0.71	0.65	0.84			
RPA	3.37	1.05	0.59	0.71	0.54	0.77		
AI	3.33	1.49	1.65	0.65	0.62	0.73	0.81	
PP	4.34	0.65	0.58	0.43	0.54	0.47	0.51	0.76

The findings demonstrate a considerable favorable association between blockchain technology and procurement efficacy, as confirmed by a correlation coefficient of 0.43. Furthermore, a distinct constructive correlation between the IoT and procurement efficacy is apparent, indicated by a correlation coefficient of 0.54. Moreover, a beneficial correlation is detected between procurement efficiency and both RPA and AI, supported by correlation coefficients of 0.47 and 0.51 correspondingly. This finding demonstrates a favorable association between the performance of procurement activities and the use of ICT (namely e-procurement) within VRA–NEDCo.

8.10.7 GOODNESS OF FIT (GOF)

Considering the substantial importance assigned to the decision-making process of adopting or rejecting a particular framework, numerous metrics have been formulated to elucidate the extent of alignment between the measurement approach and the observed data (Teo et al. 2014). Scholars specializing in Structural Equation Modeling (SEM) classify fit indices primarily into two fundamental categories: "absolute fit" and "incremental fit." The comprehensive fit indices offer initial insights into the degree to which the theoretical structure corresponds with the empirical outcomes. On the other hand, incremental fit indices, occasionally denoted as relative or comparative fit indices, evaluate the relative appropriateness or GoF of a proposed model by contrasting it with a simpler model that lacks pathways

(Teo et al., 2013; Iacobucci, 2010). The Chi-square (Δ2) and Root-Mean-Square Error of Approximation (RMSEA) represent two absolute indices frequently utilized to oversee measurement accuracy (Jackson et al., 2009).

It is widely acknowledged in the existing body of literature that the X2 was first devised as a metric for assessing the performance of models (Hooper, 2008). The assessment of model fitness and the statistical testing of structural equation models (SEM) proposed by Bagozzi and Yi (2012) provides a straightforward and conspicuous evaluation. As previously mentioned, when the value of Δ2 is less relative to the degree of freedom, it suggests that the model is more appropriate for the data. Conversely, a negligible Δ2 suggests that the model is a good match for the data. The credibility of Teo et al.'s (2013) approach for assessing model adequacy may be called into question due to its almost substantial nature, which suggests a low level of fitness (Iacobucci, 2010). Based on this premise, a number of appropriate metrics have been formulated and more measures of model validity have been suggested as feasible (Teo et al., 2013). Hair Jr et al. (2016) assert that RMSEA is the preferred absolute fit index due to its ability to quantify the extent of lack of fit. In order to address potential issues related to sample error and model misspecification, Teo et al. (2013) might consider using confidence intervals in their analysis to assess the quality of the RMSEA estimations. The Standardized Root Mean Square Residual (SRMR) is a widely used measure in research, which has been strongly recommended by Teo et al. (2013) as an integral absolute index. The SRMR index, as proposed by Weston and Gore Jr. (2006), is derived from the residual covariance and serves as a measure of the extent to which observed data deviates from the model. According to Iacobucci (2010), SRMR demonstrates a substantially lower vulnerability to violations of distributional assumptions.

The presence of various absolute indices, in conjunction with other forms of fit indices, pertains to the challenge of comparing a target model to a constrained baseline model, such as an independent model. An example of this may be seen in the Normed Fit Index (NFI), which was first introduced as an incremental fit index (IFI) by Bentler and Bonett in 1980. It is crucial to acknowledge that the nonresponse rate (NFI) might have an impact on the sample size and has shown a propensity to underestimate the adequacy of samples below 200 (Hooper et al., 2008; Bentler and Bonett, 1980). A modification of the NFI to include considerations for the size of the sample. According to Jackson (2003), the Comparative Fit Index (CFI) has been proposed as a more advanced indication compared to other indices. In a similar vein, Hu and Bentler (1999) argued that the CFI should be the preferred index when comparing it to the NFI. It is important to note that there exist other indexes; however, the CFI stands out due to its comprehensive analysis and widespread use among academics (Teo et al., 2013; Hu and Bentler, 1999). Fit indices have garnered growing interest from many researchers (Hair et al., 2017).

In contrast, scholars contend that it is important to provide the model chi-square and its corresponding p-value for all tested models (Kline, 2015). Furthermore, Bagozzi and Yi (2012) assert that RMSEA, NNFI, CFI, and SRMR are widely acknowledged and suggested indicators of functional fit. Therefore, there are no universally applicable guidelines for assessing the adequacy of the model's fit. According to Hooper et al. (2008), there is no universally accepted threshold for fit indices that can definitively distinguish between excellent and poor models (Wong, 2013). In the context of model analysis. Several scholars argue that several factors, including those mentioned in the previous paragraph, should be considered simultaneously when evaluating the adequacy of a model (Byrne, 2016; Cangur and Ercan, 2015; Smith and McMillan, 2001; Hu and Bentler, 1998). In their study, Hu and Bentler (1998) suggest a two-index presentation technique for ML (maximum likelihood) and GLS (generalized least squares) approaches. They advocate using the SRMR (standardized root mean square residual) together with one of the other indices, either TLI (Tucker–Lewis index), RNI (relative noncentrality index), CFI, or RMSEA (root mean square error of approximation). The model fit indices are shown in Table 8.6.

TABLE 8.6 Model Fit Indices.

Measure	CMIN	DF	CMIN/DF	CFI	SFMR	RMSEA	P-Close
Estimation	1256.995	736	1.708	0.957	0.066	0.045	0.974

a. Predictors (Constants): ICT. b. Dependent Variable: Precurement performance in manufacturing firms

The χ-square divided by degrees of freedom ($\chi 2$/df) demonstrates a score of 1.953, which falls beneath the threshold of 3. The root mean square error of approximation (RMSEA) stands at 0.040, a value below the significance level of 0.05. Calculated at 0.904, the GoF index (GFI) is determined, accompanied by a normalized fit index (NFI) of 0.909. Furthermore, the IFI registers at 0.954. CFI, however, remains unspecified in the provided text. The provided text lacks mention of the CFI. TLI and CFI values, measuring 0.948 and 0.953, respectively, surpass the 0.9 threshold. This data implies that the model showcases an exceptional overall fitness level.

8.10.8 HYPOTHESIS TESTING/PATH ANALYSIS

Following the successful completion of tests on the measurement model aimed at evaluating the constructs' reliability and validity, the final stage involved conducting route analysis utilizing SEM to explore the research hypotheses. The match indices of the measurement model correspond to those of the model fit indicators. The indices of GoF indicate a strong alignment between the sample data and the model, signifying the model's suitability for further scrutiny. The study's aim was to gauge the extent to which the independent variables influenced the dependent variables. The computation of the coefficient of determination was executed, as demonstrated in Table 8.7. The depiction of pathways necessitates adhering to the utilization of beta coefficients and p-values. Specifically, beta coefficients should reside within the 0 to 1 spectrum, while p-values are required to demonstrate significance below the 0.05 threshold. A comprehensive statistical assessment of all proposed pathways has been carried out, and the outcomes are outlined in Table 8.7.

TABLE 8.7 Path Analysis.

Paths	Hypothesis	β	t-value	p-value	Results
BC → PP	H1	0.35	11.36	0.001	Supported
IoTs → PP	H2	0.56	12.62	0.000	Supported
RPA → PP	H3	0.42	9.71	0.002	Supported
AI → PP	H4	0.62	14.35	0.005	Supported

Source: Field Work (2021)

Based on the data shown in Table 8.7, it can be deduced that all hypotheses of the research have been corroborated. The relationships between Blockchain (BC), AI, RPA, and IoT on PP have been found to be strong, positive, and statistically significant. This is supported by the beta coefficients (β) of 0.35 for BC, 0.56 for AI, 0.42 for RPA, and 0.35 for IoT, as well as the corresponding t-values of 11.36, 12.62, 9.71, and 14.35, and the p-values of 0.001, 0.000, 0.002, and 0.005, respectively. The findings indicate that all dimensions of ICT have a significant impact on PP.

8.11 SUMMARY OF FINDINGS

The results suggest that all hypotheses proposed in the research have been corroborated. The study found strong, positive, and significant relationships between "Blockchain (BC) ($\beta = 0.35$; $t = 11.36$ and $p = 0.001$), AI ($\beta = 0.56$; $t = 12.62$ and $p = 0.000$), RPA ($\beta = 0.42$; $t = 9.71$ and $p = 0.002$), and IoT ($\beta = 0.35$; $t = 14.35$ and $p = 0.005$) on PP." The findings indicate that all dimensions of ICT have a significant impact on PP.

8.12 CONCLUSION

As per the study findings, the utilization of advanced technologies is prominent within the Volta River Authority–Northern Electricity Distribution Company (VRA–NEDCo). This encompasses contemporary innovations like the IoT, RPA, AI, and blockchain. The VRA–NEDCo, situated in Ghana, has effectively integrated ICT across various phases of the procurement procedure. This includes using ICT for activities such as announcing notices, managing contracts, preparing tender documents, and planning procurement. Additionally, the VRA–NEDCo has utilized ICT for tasks such as calculating contract value and classification, as well as opening and evaluating tenders. This integration of ICT has significantly contributed to the efficiency and accuracy of the procurement process within the organization.

The research findings also indicate that the use of ICT at several stages of VRA-procurement NEDCo, such as contract and advertising placement, tender assessment, tender aggregation, and tender definition, significantly impacts the efficiency of the procurement process in Ghana. This suggests that ICT tools have a significant role in enhancing procurement efficiency, particularly in service sectors such as VRA–NEDCo. The widespread use of ICT tools in these industries has led to the recognition of ICT's crucial role in procurement inside organizations. Based on the research results, the use of ICT resources within an organization to effectively attain strategic goals such as enhancing customer happiness and maximizing profitability via cost management has shown to be a viable and successful approach. The integration of IoT, RPA, AI, and blockchain technology platforms has been shown to enhance PP by incorporating diverse business processes. The use of ICT aspects has enhanced the flexibility and effectiveness of procurement processes. The use of IoT, RPA, AI, and blockchain technology supplier connections has facilitated corporations in attaining a competitive edge in material management. This has resulted in increased adoption of these technological breakthroughs by a growing number of organizations.

Diverse elements impact the procurement effectiveness of VRA–NEDCo in Ghana, encompassing supplier assessment, supplier connectivity, and the fusion of brand and procurement operational methods. Furthermore, the establishment of supplier pick and enhancement strategies, initial-phase brand engagement, and the dissemination of information (comprising records, reporting, and correspondence), along with the monitoring and evaluation of supplier performance, collectively exert substantial influence over the organizational PP. The influence of technology on the procurement process has affected vendors' procurement criteria, including their responsiveness to requests for quotes, delivery dates, and accuracy in fulfilling orders. The use of technology in the field of procurement has resulted in enhanced productivity. The availability and accessibility of timely information play a crucial role in SCM. Companies may enhance their service levels, save costs, and minimize lead times by relying on trustworthy and prompt information.

As per the report, the VRA–NEDCo encountered various obstacles including expensive delays and inaccuracies, elevated maintenance expenditures, inadequate IT infrastructure, insufficient resources for facilitating e-procurement, utilization of multiple ERPs that may lack compatibility, and absence of the requisite digital format for e-procurement systems. The aforementioned problems have a significant impact on several aspects of the supply chain, including inventory management, distribution processes, plant operations, and design considerations for recycling and reuse. Additionally, they also influence the procurement function by imposing constraints on waste reduction and defect prevention. Based on the research results, it has been determined that ICT tools play a significant role in enhancing procurement efficiency within buyer–supplier partnerships. Among these tools, the IoT, RPA, AI, and blockchain technology have been identified as the most influential contributors. Conversely, it has been observed that these technologies have a relatively lower impact on the PP of VRA–NEDCo in Ghana.

8.13 RECOMMENDATIONS

The suggestions presented in this study are based on the results, findings, and conclusions.

ICT plays a pivotal and indispensable role in ensuring the effectiveness and efficiency of the procurement departments within the VRA and the NEDCo.

The research indicates that it is important for firms to maintain awareness of the dynamic market climate that shapes the competitive landscape within which they operate. Consequently, the use of ICT may provide organizations with a competitive advantage, enabling them to thrive in a highly competitive global environment. The use of ICT plays a crucial role in achieving a harmonious equilibrium between fulfilling the needs of both businesses and consumers within the supply chain, while effectively managing expenses to optimize financial gains.

VRA–NEDCo should establish mechanisms to address the barriers impeding the implementation of electronic procurement. When establishing e-procurement processes with the aim of enhancing resource productivity, it is essential to take into account the environmental issues pertaining to performance criteria. According to VRA–NEDCo, it is essential for the automated procurement process to exhibit specificity in several aspects, including requisitions, tenders, contract warding, and payment. The primary objective of using ICT in procurement processes is to enhance the quality of services provided, while concurrently ensuring the provision of timely, transparent, and dependable financial and accounting information. Furthermore, it is recommended that the organization has a readily accessible information system that is user-friendly for all suppliers. This measure would effectively mitigate the social disapproval associated with electronic procurement, hence fostering more adoption and utilization of this method among individuals and organizations. In conclusion, it is recommended that VRA–NEDCo undertakes frequent efforts to enhance their internal procedures in order to mitigate bureaucratic tendencies and enhance overall performance.

KEYWORDS

- **IoT**
- **AI**
- **RPA**
- **blockchain**
- **performance**
- **technology**

REFERENCES

Abu Alsheikh, M.; Lin, S.; Niyato, D.; Tan, H.-P. Machine Learning in Wireless Sensor Networks: Algorithms, Strategies, and Applications. *IEEE Commun. Surv. Tutor.* **2014,** *16* (4), 1996–2015.

Allianz Global Corporate & Specialty. Allianz Risk Barometer 2016—Top Risks in Focus: Digitalization, 2016. http://www.agcs.allianz.com/insights/expert- riskarticles/top-risks-in-focus-digitalization/ (accessed 23 April 2018).

Andersson, P. Nuläge: Blockchain. Medium, 22 Feb, 2018a.

Arnoux, P.-H.o.a. Using Cognitive Computing to Gain Deeper Individual Insights, u.o.: IBM Watson, 2016.

Arpe, J. Globalization and Its Complexity. The Economic Risks of Globalization, Expert and Public Opinion Survey Results, Issue Global Choices 1 | Bertelsmann Stiftung, 2012.

Averstad, J. o.a. Digital Transformation, u.o.: QVARTZ, Microsoft, 2017.

Baccala, M. et al. 2018 AI Predictions—8 Insights to Shape Business Strategy, s.l.: PwC, 2018.

Baghla, S. Origin of Bitcoin: A Brief History from 2008 Crisis to Present Times. *Anal. India Mag.*, 19 March 2017.

Bagila, A. Understanding Blockchain Consensus Models, u.o.: Persistent Systems, 2017.

Bhadeshia, H. K. D. H. Additive Manufacturing. *Mater. Sci. Technol.* **2016,** *32* (7), 615–616.

Blomkvist, P.; Hallin, A. *Method for Engineering Students*; Studentlitteratur AB: Spanien, 2015.

Bloomberg, J. Using Bitcoin or Other Cryptocurrency to Commit Crimes? Law Enforcement Is Onto You, 2017. https://www.forbes.com/sites/jasonbloomberg/2017/12/28/using-bitcoin-orother- cryptocurrency-to-commit-crimes-law-enforcement-is-onto-you/#4921792a3bdc (accessed 7 May 2018).

Blum, T. Digitalisation for Purchasing [Interview] (26 Feb 2018).

Brynjolfsson, E.; McAfee, A. *The Business of Artificial Intelligence*; Harvard Business Review: Boston, 2017.

Busby, M. Blockchain Is This Year's Buzzword—But Can It Outlive the Hype. *The Guardian*, 2018.

Buterin, V. On Public and Private Blockchains, 2015. https://blog.ethereum.org/2015/08/07/on-public-and-private-blockchains/ (accessed 4 April 2018).

Carlsson, S. Allt du velat veta—Om artificiell intelligens med Stefan Carlsson [Podcast]. s.l.:Fritte Fritzson, 2016.

Chin, T. A.; Tat, H. H.; Sulaiman, Z. Green Supply Chain Management, Environmental Collaboration and Sustainability Performance. *Procedia CIRP* **2015,** *26*, 695–699.

Christidis, K.; Devetsikiotis, M. Blockchain and Smart Contracts for the Internet of Things. *IEEE* **2016,** *4*, 2292–2303.

Cook, M. Convergence: Big Data + IoT + Artificial Intelligence = Your Time Has Come, 2018.

Copeland, B. Encyclopaedia Britannica—Artificial Intelligence, 2018. https://www.britannica.com/technology/artificial-intelligence/Expert-systems (accessed 31 Jan 2018).

Daisy, C. 8 Pros and Cons Of Artificial Intelligence | You Must Be Aware Of!, 2017. https://www.csestack.org/pros-cons-artificial-intelligence/ (accessed 4 April 2018).

DeepMind. The Story of AlphaGo So Far, 2017a. https://deepmind.com/research/alphago/ (accessed 28 Mar 2018).

DeepMind. AlphaGo Zero: Learning from Scratch, 2017b. https://deepmind.com/blog/alphago-zero-learning-scratch/ [Accessed 28 March 2018]. Deloitte LLP. The Fourth Revolution Is Now: Are You Ready? Future of Operations, 2017.

Dobson, D. The Four Types of Blockchain Networks Explained, 2018. https://www.linkedin.com/pulse/4-types-blockchain-networks-explained-debdobson/ (accessed 4 April 2018).

Ertel, W. *Introduction I: Introduction to Artificial Intelligence*; Springer: London, 2011a; pp 1–14.

Ertel, W. *Machine Learning and Data Mining. I: Introduction to Artificial Intelligence*; Springer: London, 2011b; pp 161–220.

Friessnig, M.; Karre, H. Induscript: Creativity Techniques. Graz, Institute for Industrial Management and Innovation Research—Graz University of Technology, 2016.

Geitgey, A. Machine Learning is Fun Part 6: How to do Speech Recognition with Deep Learning. Medium, 23 Dec. GEP, 2017. How Emerging Technologies are Reshaping Procurement. s.l.; Smart by GEP & My Purchasing Center, 2016.

GEP. *GEP Outlook: Procurement 2018—The Impact of the Most Important Trends in Global Business and Technology*; GEP: Clark, 2018.

Gilster, P. Artificial Intelligence Is Now Part of Our Daily Life. Are We Too Dependent on It? *The News & Observer*, 6 Nov 2017.

Goldberg, A. What Are the Advantages & Disadvantages of Artificial Intelligence? 2017. https://www.quora.com/What-are-the-advantages-disadvantages-ofartificial- intelligence (accessed 4 April 2018).

Gubbi, J.; Buyya, R.; Marusic, S.; Palaniswami, M. Internet of Things (IoT): A Vision, Architectural Elements, and Future Directions. *Fut. Gener. Comput. Syst.* **2013,** *29* (7), 1645–1660.

Gupta, V. The Promise of Blockchain Is a World Without Middlemen. *Harv. Bus. Rev.—Int. Bus.* 2017, Issue March 6.

Guszcza, J. Smarter Together: Why Artificial Intelligence Needs Human-Centered Design. *Deloitte Rev.* **2018,** *22*.

Hassabis, D. AlphaGo: Using Machine Learning to Master the Ancient Game of Go. *The Keyword* (Google), 27 Jan 2016.

Heimbuch, J. 7 Major Ways We're Digitizing Our World, and 3 Reasons Why We Still Want Hard Copies, 2010. https://www.treehugger.com/clean-technology/7-major- ways-were-digitizingour-world-and-3-reasons-we-still-want-hardcopies.html (accessed 22 Feb 2018).

Hoffenberg, S. IBM's Watson Answers the QUestion, "What's the Difference Between Artificial Intelligence and Cognitive Computing?" 2016. http://www.vdcresearch.com/News-events/iot-blog/IBM-Watson-Answers-QuestionArtificial-Intelligence.html (accessed 2 April 2018).

Lee, H. L.; Padmanabhan, V.; Whang, S. Information Distortion in a Supply Chain: The Bullwhip. *Manag. Sci.* **1997,** *43* (4).

Magnusson, J. Master Thesis—Digitalisation Overview [Interview] (20 Feb 2018).

Magnusson, J.; Nilsson, A. *Enterprise System Platforms—Transforming the Agenda*, 1st ed.; Studentlitteratur AB: Spain, 2014.

Maltaverne, B. Blockchain: What Are the Opportunities for Procurement? *Medium*, 17 July 2017.

Marcotte, A. Airbnb Has Permanently Changed the Way People Travel, 2017. https://www.salon.com/2017/02/16/airbnb-has-permanently-changed-the-waypeople- travel/ (accessed 22 Feb 2018).

Marks, F.; Vos, R.; Kemps, D. Servitization: Service Is the Future of Manufacturing; u.o.: ABN AMRO, 2017.

Mearian, L. What Is Blockchain? The Most Disruptive Tech in Decades. *Computer World*, 18 Jan 2018a.

Mearian, L. Spending on Blockchain Technology to Double This Year to $2.1B, 2018b. https://www.computerworld.com/article/3251505/financial-it/spending-onblockchain-networks-to-double-this-year-to-21b.html (accessed 20 April 2018).

Mitchell, T. *Machine Learning*; McGraw Hill: New York, 1997.

Mohan, B.; Khan, B.; N, V. *Blockchain in the Real World—The Promise, the Progress and the Hype*; GEP: Clark, 2018.

Morgan, B. 10 Things Robots Can't Do Better Than Humans. Forbes—CMO Network, 16 Aug 2017.

Murphy, K. The Key Steps in the Purchase Order Process, 2017. https://www.purchasecontrol.com/blog/purchase-order-process/ (accessed 26 Jan 2018).

Narayanan, A. et al. *Bitcoin and Cryptocurrency Technologies: A Comprehensive Introduction*; Princeton University Press: New Jersey.

Neocapita. The Logical Components of Blockchain, 2018. https://medium.com/@neocapita/the-logical-components-of-blockchain870d781a4a3a [Accessed 3 April 2018].

Nguyen, M.-H. How Artificial Intelligence & Machine Learning Produced Robots We Can Talk to, 2017. http://www.businessinsider.com/what-is-chatbot-talking- airobot-chat-simulators-2017-10?r=US&IR=T&IR=T (accessed 2 April 2018).

Nyakundi, E.; Kombo, C.; Omari, R.; Mongare, O. Challenges Facing Procurement Committees in Implementing the Procurement Act; A Case Study of Secondary Schools Procurement Committees in Kisii County, Kenya. *Elixir Int J.* **2012,** 9186–9191.

The Daily Nation News Paper 11th March 2015, Keynya.

Petersen, A. Master Thesis—Digitalisation Overview [Interview] (12 Feb 2018).

Poelstra, A. Distributed Consensus from Proof of Stake Is Impossible, u.o.: u.n, 2014.

Thai, K.V. *Introduction to Public Procurement (IPP)*; National Institute of Government Purchasing (NIGP): Washington, DC, 2004.

Titah, R.; Shuraida, S.; Rekik, Y. Integration Breach: Investigating the Effect of Internal and External Information Sharing and Coordination on Firm Profit. *Int. J. Prod. Econ.* **2016,** *181*, 34–47.

Vaidya, K. *J. Public Procurement* **2006,** *6* (1&3), 7099.

Ward, J.; Peppard, J. *Strategic Planning for Information Systems*; Wiley: Chichester, 2003.

Weele, A. J. *Purchasing and Supply Chain Management*; Cengage Learning EMEA: Hampshire, 2010.

CHAPTER 9

The Effects of Electronic Procurement Adoption on Supply Chain Management: The Mediating Role of Regulatory Environment

KWASI NKAYI[1], MOHAMMED MAJEED[2], JONAS YOMBOI[3], CLEMENT NANGPIIRE[4], and GORDON SABUTEY TERKPEH[5]

[1]*Tamale Teaching Hospital, Tamale, Ghana*

[2]*Tamale Technical University, Tamale, Ghana*

[3]*University for Development Studies, Tamale, Ghana*

[4]*SDD University of Business and Integrated Development Studies, Tamale, Ghana*

[5]*University for Development Studies, Tamale, Ghana*

ABSTRACT

This study examined the impact of e-procurement (EP) implementation on supply chain management (SCM), with a special emphasis on 29 public and private hospitals within the five Northern regions of Ghana, in consideration of the regulatory environment. The research is a cross-sectional study and employed a quantitative approach due to its design. Our findings show that EP and SCM are directly linked, with the regulatory environment serving as a moderating factor. However, EP implementation is a difficult journey for the reason that it involves overcoming numerous barriers, and the costs of adoption limit overall organizational success. From the study results, the policy implications are discussed: Ghana's public hospitals should revamp EP.

New Age Technology in Supply Chain Management: Digital Transformation Tools in Perspective. Mohammed Majeed (Ed.)

The management should adopt EP to promote openness, fairness, and responsibility for effective and efficient operations. Government agencies most especially should help public hospitals embrace EP to reap its advantages.

9.1 INTRODUCTION

Historically, purchasing was done by either physically going to a store and completing the steps required to place an order, or else by looking through catalogs and placing an order over the phone. This method has historically involved physical processes and management of procurement transactions has at some stage, been through relaxed centralized processes (Barngetuny and Kimutai, 2015). Procurement's primary objective is to acquire the appropriate goods or services at the appropriate time and place, in the appropriate condition, and at the appropriate price, in order to efficiently and effectively complete the purchasing process (Calipinar and Soysal, 2012). In the procurement process, EP utilizes an internet-based approach to complete any or all processes, such as searching, purchasing and negotiating, ordering, receipting, and reviewing purchases after they have been made (Barngetuny and Kimutai, 2015).

EP is based on the traditional procurement system. Since the invention of the internet and technological advances, industries began to shift their procurement practices to the internet, realizing that if all procurement procedures are completed properly and accurately, they save money (Brandon-Jones and Kauppi, 2018). EP, according to Johnson (2011), is an effective tool for increasing transparency, accountability, efficiency, and money well spent on goods, services, and construction of projects. EP, particularly in the public sector, is still in its infancy in Ghana. The proliferation of the internet as a platform for commercial activities has brought about a sea change in the functioning and standing of organizational procurement (Johnson, 2011). Most developing countries, including Ghana, are increasingly adopting and promoting EP in healthcare delivery (Ofori and Fuseini, 2020). Despite its rapid implementation, the use of EP is still very much in its infancy in the public sector, especially in the healthcare industry. Hospitals and health centers in Ghana lack well-trained procurement staff, rendering financial oversight of healthcare procurement processes insignificant. Similarly, as seen in the research that was carried out by Sarpong et al. (2017), there is substantial inefficiency in the government's procurement processes, which hinders the effective use of the government's economic resources in infrastructure procurement in getting a better value for money.

To better understand this, Sarpong et al. explain that the most common types of corruption are unjustified personal enrichment and various forms of bids being bought out with money, ineffective work, deliberate deceit when personal information is compromised, incompetence, documents being overvalued, dubious schemes, and illicit means of procurement by participants. Kusi, Antwi, et al. (2016) research report confirmed some of the challenges connected with procurement. His results indicate that the majority of those charged with procuring capital are inept. Due to these challenges, the EP process was developed, to make sure that all procurement processes are completed electronically, eliminating the need for any manual intervention. EP according to Domfeh (2020) is a useful tool for promoting accountability, productivity, transparency, and money spent well on goods and services. Historically, public sector procurement in Ghana has been characterized by delays and long procurement processes, less transparency, lack of professionalism, significant human interference, state interference, and prejudicial treatment in the awarding of government contracts in particular (Sarpong et al., 2017). With the purpose of eradicating or at the very least minimizing public procurement corruption, looking up to value for money, increasing efficiency, and procuring procedures among others, Ghana has gone through various phases of procurement development (Domfeh, 2020). Both the Public Procurement Amendment Act (Act 914) which was updated in 2016 and the Public Procurement Act (Act 663) that was adopted in 2003 were important modifications to the law. The practice of Act 663 has reduced the costs of buying supplies for various businesses and institutions in the country, adding sanity to the procurement environment, and has compelled some procurement professionals to call for the country's first EP legislation (Public Procurement Authority (PPA), 2010). However, the primary aim of the Public Procurement Act of 2003 (Act 663) is to accomplish a prudent, economical, and effective use of state resources in public procurement, as well as to make sure that public procurement is carried out fairly, transparently, non-discriminatorily and in a competitive manner.

The bottlenecks mentioned above have heightened the interest of academics and procurement professionals alike to examine how public bodies are responsible for Public Procurement Act 2003 (Act 663) implementation. Additionally, many scholars assessed the importance and challenges of the public EP framework and argued that it provides an innovative way to mitigate the many challenges of Ghana's traditional procurement system (Abagna Azanlerigu and Akay, 2015). However, less has been researched on the effects of EP adoption. The few works done on Ghana's case are EP adoption barriers in retrospect (Sarpong et al., 2017), Electronic Government Procurement Adoption in Ghana (Ofori and Fuseini, 2020), and EP: is Ghana ready? (Bulletin, 2010), as a result of the scanty literature on this subject, the investigation of electronic procurement is the primary emphasis of this research (EP) adoption effects on SCM. We also looked at the mediating by regulatory environment at the Tamale Teaching Hospital of Ghana.

The study has a number of important contributions to make. To begin, many studies have been conducted on the Public Procurement Act 663 and on the effects of EP adoption in order to enhance the procurement system in the public hospitals in Ghana and to ensure that proper administration and institutional arrangements are made. However, not a lot of research has been done on how EP adoption affects SCM moderated by the regulatory environment within public hospitals in Ghana. This is something that needs to be addressed in order to improve the procurement system in public hospitals This research is significant because it attempted to investigate the implications of EP adoption on SCM inside public hospitals in Ghana, and it did so through the lens of the regulatory environment. This research is essential because it intended to uncover the impacts of the implementation of EP on SCM inside public hospitals in Ghana and how such effects were mediated by regulatory environments.

Secondly, for those who are interested and involved in the field of science, the current study is considered a significant guide. The findings of the research will not only assist in determining the extent to which the regulatory environment plays a role in determining whether or not public institutions adopt EP, but they will also allow for an analysis of how the implementation of electronic procurement has impacted the management of supply chains. The present research enables those participating in the procurement procedures in both public and private hospitals to understand both the benefits and difficulties associated with EP. Once again, the results of this research will enable us to comprehend the mediating function that the regulatory environment plays in the adoption of EP and the impact that it has on the management of supply chains. In addition, the research offers suggestions to public sector organizations about the crucial role that the regulatory environment plays in the use of EP technologies to enhance SCM, which will ultimately result in value for money. In conclusion, the study will contribute to the previously existing body of scientific information on the study factors, and it will be of great use to scholars in the years to come.

The other parts of the study are structured as follows: the very next section discusses the literature review and the formulation of the hypothesis, and then the following section discusses the design and methods of the research. In the last part of the presentation, the results, a discussion of the findings, and the conclusions were given.

9.2 LITERATURE REVIEW AND HYPOTHESIS DEVELOPMENT

9.2.1 EP AND SCM

Owing to the fact that sourcing is an essential component of the supply chain. In order to have a solid understanding of the phenomena being studied, this study employs these aspects as constructs in order to explore the connection between EP and the regulatory environment on supply chain efficiency. According to Jain et al. (2018) and Smith and Flanegin (2014), EP is not limited to just doing a search and making a purchase of items via the internet; rather, it connects companies and their business processes with suppliers directly while managing any and all partnerships that may occur between them. Khuan and Swee (2018) stipulate that when EP is effectively implemented, it reduces costs, produces high responsiveness, and allows rapid reactions via the supply chain, making the supply chain more agile. A good EP installation will improve an organization's supply chain by eliminating paper orders, receipts, and invoices. Customer expectations and high competitiveness costs in today's market have driven enterprises to analyze their supply chain practices and capitalize on indirect spending reductions (Nurmandi and Kim, 2015).

It is less expensive, more adaptable, and has enhanced tactical uniformity with these systems. The vast majority of publications on EP reveal considerable SCM savings. With EP, the end-user is integrated into the process of procurement, with an automated multi-vendor catalog, and process gaps in the supply chain for indirect goods are addressed (Zsidisin, 2002). EP, according to Sahu (2016), refers to the process of controlling supply chains in the context of the acquisition of indirect goods via the use of information systems and e-markets that are accessible through the internet. EP made it possible for the supply chain to undergo five significant modifications, according to Ateto et al. (2013): protecting managers' budgetary oversight, providing robust process efficiency with fewer delays, offering much greater clarity and usability through the whole process, enhancing management knowledge which goes a long way to strengthening user compliance and improving system stability.

Hypothesis 1 (H1): *EP positively and significantly influences SCM*

9.2.2 REGULATORY ENVIRONMENT AND EP

EP according to Rotchanakitumnuai (2013a) is essential to solve functional problems that might arise in the supply chain process. Regulatory environment (RE) has a significant positive relationship with EP. It is for instance clear that the relationship between SCM and EP in the healthcare industry is moderated by RE. RE ensures that there is smooth implementation of EP which goes a long way to affect SCM as products and services in different healthcare industries are networked given a clear indication that, relationships among RE and EP are important in the SCM (Awadallah and Saad, 2018).

Lee et al. (2020) examined the correlation between RE and EP and concluded that RE improves EP leading to competitiveness and flexibility in the procurement mechanism. Furthermore, there is a connection between the RE and EP as the RE helps manage key procurement information proactively and make better procurement decisions in a company, which boosts efficiencies and generates value for money throughout the entire procurement process (Lee et al., 2020). On the contrary, Asare, Evelyn Nsiah and Prempeh (2017) explore the relationship between the RE and EP and conclude that the two are unconnected. However, Kusi (Kusi et al., 2016), looked at the impact of the RE on EP in Ghana and found that the RE has positive impact on EP. The authors conclude that the correct implementation of EP can bring significant direct and indirect benefits if regulatory bodies do not lose guard. According to the research that has been done, the RE has a beneficial effect on supply chain management, and SCM also has a favorable effect on EP. The question of whether or not there is a connection between the RE and EP is one that is currently being debated. As a consequence of this, this research investigated the implications of the RE on EP, with a particular emphasis on the function that it plays as a mediator.

Hypothesis 2 (H2): *RE (EP) positively and significantly influences EP*

9.2.3 THE MEDIATING ROLE OF RE ON EP AND SCM

Many scholars have pointed out that there is a correlation between regulatory settings and the implementation of EP, and these connections are important to consider. It has been noted that government agencies and corporations alike will have to go past current legislative, regulatory, and organizational impediments with a view to gaining a foothold in EP implementation (Jain et al., 2018). There are still quite a few countries on earth that have not adopted any kind of EP regulation into the country's legislative structure, including Ghana (European Union, 2012).

Despite the fact that the country is not yet ready or prepared to adopt this scheme, data suggests that the government is working to prepare the country for this new procurement revolution. Among these initiatives are the e-Ghana project, which aims to develop internet connectivity across the country in all public offices; the Ministry of Communications' establishment of Information Centers in communities to facilitate convenient public access to the internet; and the World Bank's budgetary funding of two million US dollars for the establishment of EP under the e-Ghana project (PPA, 2010). Government Agencies, Legal and Regulatory Bodies, and Certain Key Stakeholders are the Primary Elements that determine the strength levels of SCM and EP. The Public Procurement Act 2003 as amended Act 2016 stipulates that compliance with its provisions is mandatory for all agencies, organizations, and establishments run by the government or in which it has a controlling interest. Teaching hospitals, for instance, are independent institutions that function according to their own organizational framework when it comes to the purchase of products and services.

RE positively and significantly affects SCM. According to the procurement handbook, one of the responsibilities of the Ministry of Health is to ensure that the appropriate level of financial and executive support is provided for procurement activities carried out within the Ministry and its divisions (2004). In addition, the Medical and Dental Council, the Nursing and Midwifery Council, as well as the Pharmacy Council, are all regulatory entities that fall under the Ministry of Health. It is the responsibility of these semi-autonomous agencies, which fall under the Ministry of Health, to safeguard the standards of professional practice in their respective professions. Due to the fact that these establishments are within the Ministry of Health, the procurement procedure that is outlined in this handbook is applicable to them. The individual in charge of a regulatory body is accountable for all procurement-related operations. According to the Public Procurement Act, the utmost responsibility for procurement is with the head of the body doing the purchasing (Act 663). For this reason, the goal of this research is to investigate the RE's potential function as a mediator in order to look into how EP affects the supply chain data gleaned from Ghana's Public Health Hospitals, namely the Tamale Teaching Hospital. As a result, the research contends that the RE has a favorable and considerable impact on EP and SCM in the capacity of a mediator function.

Hypothesis 3 (H3): *RE (EP) positively and significantly mediates EP and SCM*

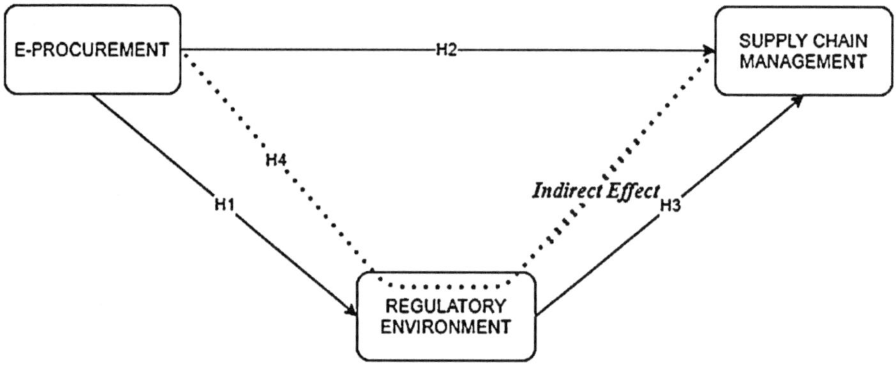

FIGURE 9.1 Conceptual model and hypothesis.

9.3 RESEARCH METHODOLOGY

9.3.1 STUDY POPULATION, AREA, SAMPLING, AND DATA COLLECTION

The population of this research consists of 364 of the staff of Hospitals within the five Northern regions: Savana region, Upper West, North East, Northern, and Upper East region of Ghana which was further grouped into two (2), that is, management group and senior staff group especially people who are directly engaged in the processes of purchasing goods and services.

The purpose of the research sample technique was to choose individuals whose backgrounds and experiences were the most relevant to the primary focus of the study. The study used a quantitative approach to determine the sample size by using the PLS-SEM "10 times law" technique. This enabled the researcher to achieve sample adequacy (Jr et al., 2010; Peng and Lai, 2012). According to the "10-times rule," the minimum sample size for research must be more than "10 times the largest number of links to the inner or outer model leading to either of the model's constructs." This is the minimum sample size that may be considered acceptable (Saunders and Lewis, 2012). EP is the model's most successful construct in terms of indicators, according to the study model (7 indicators). As a consequence of this, the "10-times rule" dictates that the research must have a minimum sample size of seven times ten, which equals seventy. For the purposes of this research, a minimum of 70 participants are necessary to respond. This research sent questionnaires to 245 participants and retrieved 243 questionnaires, which was sufficient to satisfy the "10-times rule" minimum criteria for the size of the sample. It was suitable to adopt a sampling approach to help in the gathering of data after the minimum sample size required to carry out this analysis had been reached. This minimal sample size was necessary in order to undertake this analysis. As a result, this research used a non-probability sampling approach in conjunction with a strategy known as purposive sampling to identify appropriate individuals for the study. The reason for using this method is that it has the benefit of obtaining information that is both rich and detailed on the primary concerns that are being investigated. Purposive sampling is appropriate for selecting respondents subjectively and based on their unique traits, experiences, attitudes, or views; hence, the necessity to choose personnel who are closely related to hospital procurement processes (Rotich and Okello, 2015) stated that scientists use purposive sampling to choose individuals who supply rich or enough information and exhibit expertise of the study subject and issue they are asked to answer.

TABLE 9.1 Sampling Frame for the Study.

Officers	Population	Sample
Chief Executive officer	1	1
Medical superintendent	28	28
Procurement managers	31	29
Accountants	70	38
Administrators	43	35
Supply officers	38	31
Planning managers	8	5
Estate managers	33	30
Heads of units/Depts	112	46
Total	364	243

Source: Field survey (2020).

Again, purposive sampling was chosen because it is suitable for answering a variety of research questions and eliminates individuals who are unsuitable for the sampling study, so only the most suitable participants are retained. Participants provide sufficient information for the study through purposeful sampling (Yin and Quazi, 2018; Yomboi et al., 2021). A purposive sampling technique enables investigators to use their own decisions to choose participants who appropriately answer the questions to meet the research objectives. On the other hand, convenience sampling also called haphazard or accidental sampling, was also used in selecting officers especially the senior staff based on criteria of availability of respondents at an appointed time, easy accessibility, and willingness to part-take in the study. It means in convenient sampling, researchers select participants who are easy to reach (Barngetuny and Kimutai, 2015). In this particular study, the researchers observed that the strategy of convenient sampling was effective in order to enhance the probability of the total number of respondents. In addition, convenient sampling was employed because of how straightforward and useful it is when it comes to performing research. The questionnaire was the primary tool for data collection.

9.3.2 CONSTRUCTS, VARIABLES, AND MEASURES

This study took into account three latent variables (constructs) based on our research model (Fig. 9.2):

(1) EP, (2) RE, and (3) SCM. Table 9.2 gives details about the constructs and their indicators used in this study.

TABLE 9.2 Constructs and Sources of Data.

Sn	Latent Variable	Indicator	Acronym
1a	EP	Enhanced quality, Harmonization, and Product standardization.	EP1
1b		Reliability of spending information and reduced administrative cost.	EP2
1c		At each and every step of the procurement process, there is a level playing field provided for any and all prospective bidders.	EP3
1d		The majority of our acquisition operations are carried out in a way that is competitive, and the user rate of the goods, projects, and services that we have acquired is acceptable.	EP4
1e		When it comes to our purchasing decisions, we take great care to employ only personnel who are both knowledgeable and skilled.	EP5
1f		Issues of procurement transparency, accountability, and professionalism.	EP6
1g		Lack of trust in the system by suppliers, unreliable energy supply, and government interference.	EP7

TABLE 9.2 *(Continued)*

Sn	Latent Variable	Indicator	Acronym
2a	Regulatory Environment	There is a government agency that regulates procurement activities in the organization.	RE1
2b		Legal and regulatory control are of standards.	RE2
2c		EP initiatives have been started by regulatory agencies.	RE3
2d		EP is of interest to legal and regulatory organizations, and they want to see it implemented.	RE4
2e		The RE positively impacts EP adoption.	RE5
2f		Our procurement activities are regulated by PPA.	RE6
3a	SCM	Our organization has a well-built warehouse.	SCM1
3b		Inventory management (monitory) is done online.	SCM2
3c		Tracking of goods and services is carried out online.	SCM3
3d		End-users make requisitions online.	SCM4
3e		Forecasting of procurement needs is easy with EP.	SCM5

9.3.3 DATA ANALYSIS

In the field of information science (IS), structural equation modeling, sometimes known as SEM, is a method of multivariate data analysis that is frequently used for validating constructs and examining the interactions between constructs (Gefen et al., 2000). In this particular investigation, the PLS-SEM approach was used. This was partly due to the fact that PLS-SEM, unlike CB-SEM, is an approach to SEM that does not make any assumptions about the distribution of the data (Vinzi et al., 2010). In other words, the PLS-SEM method is beneficial in research projects that have a limited number of respondents and a skewed distribution of the data (Wong, 2011). In addition, the researchers decided to employ PLS-SEM since the goal of the study was to determine the nature of the link between dependent constructs and independent constructs by determining the magnitude of the effect and the predictive significance of the data.

The independent variable shown in Figure 9.1 is EP. EP, which is the independent variable, has a direct influence on SCM, which is the variable that is being studied, which is the dependent variable. The dependent variable is influenced in some way by the independent variable (SCM). The RE serves as the overarching variable, which functions as a bridging factor to influence both the independent and dependent variables.

9.4 RESULTS AND DISCUSSION

9.4.1 MEASUREMENT MODEL EVALUATION

A reflective model assessment was done as well as testing of indicator reliability loading, convergent validity, discriminant validity, and internal consistency reliability. The convergent validity of the outer model is checked by examining the Factor Loading Rate and AVE (Average Variance Extracted) Rate as shown in Tables 9.2 and Figure 9.2. Reflective loadings of 0.708 and above are recommended. Indicators EP5 and SCM1 were deleted after running the model because they did not load significantly at the minimum threshold requirement of 0.708 to their corresponding latent variables. Table 9.2 indicates that factor loading for all indicators are greater than 0.7, indicating that all indicators are accurate in terms of composite reliability. Further, all latent variables have AVE rates greater than 0.5, implying that all latent variables are valid in terms of convergent validity. The outer model can be said to have validated by loading factors on the same scale, as well as AVE parameters. This, accordingly, establishes that latent variables (EP implementation, RE, and SCM) are considered reliable and valid as shown in Table 9.2 and Figure 9.2. To measure discriminant validity, we primarily used the Fornell and Larcker (1981) criteria. They argue that a latent variable can share more variation with its variables than any different latent variable in order to achieve discrimination. Table 9.3 shows that the many of the latent variables have a greater amount of variation with their respective assigned indicators compared to the other hidden variables. This is indicated by bolding the numbers. As shown in both rows and columns, the bold numbers indicate the highest values.

TABLE 9.3 Construct Reliability and Validity.

Construct	Composite reliability	AVE
EP	0.968	0.836
RE	0.978	0.881
SCM	0.927	0.762

TABLE 9.4 Discriminant Validity (Fornell and Larcker Criterion).

Constructs	E-procurement	Regulatory environment	SCM
EP	**0.914**		
RE	-0.545	**0.939**	
SCM	-0.183	0.63	0.873

In addition, the reliability discriminant validity of the outer model is analyzed by performing a discriminant validity test on the cross-loading phase, making use of factor loading rates for each predictor in the latent variable. This allows one to determine the outer model's reliability discriminant validity. As can be seen in Table 9.4, cross-loading across factor loading rates of each predictor in latent variables led to greater cross-loading rates than cross-loading across factor loading rates of latent variables did, resulting in higher overall cross-loading rates.

TABLE 9.5 Discriminant, Cross-Loading.

Items	E-procurement	Regulatory environment	SCM
EP1	**0.929**	-0.396	-0.034
EP2	**0.908**	-0.529	-0.326
EP3	**0.914**	-0.598	-0.231
EP4	**0.956**	-0.587	-0.191
EP6	**0.889**	-0.383	-0.046
EP7	**0.889**	-0.36	-0.015
RE1	-0.653	**0.954**	0.71
RE2	-0.497	**0.926**	0.551
RE3	-0.553	**0.834**	0.345
RE4	-0.297	**0.943**	0.553
RE5	-0.531	**0.983**	0.657
RE6	-0.478	**0.984**	0.649
SCM2	0.005	0.293	**0.723**
SCM3	-0.349	0.612	**0.892**
SCM4	-0.236	0.607	**0.982**
SCM5	-0.019	0.6	0.875

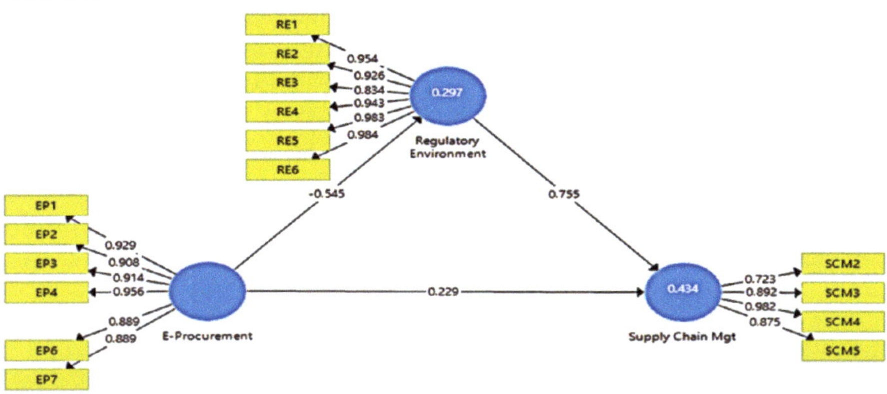

FIGURE 9.2 Outer loadings. Indicators removed; EP5 and SCM1 were deleted after running the model because they did not load significantly at the minimum threshold requirement of 0.708 to their corresponding latent variables.

9.4.2 STRUCTURAL MODEL EVALUATION

The Structural models were first calculated for the path coefficients significances. Given the assumption of an interval with a confidence level of 95 percent and a minimum critical value of 1.65 and above is strongly suggested for a 10% (two-tailed) significance stage (Hair et al., 2011). Of the three hypotheses formulated, all were supported as they met the minimum threshold of 1.65 (t-values of 2.083, 5.625, and 7.490). This is shown in Table 9.5. The R^2 value is used to evaluate the goodness-of-fit of an inner model in the goodness-of-fit test. R^2 values presented in Figure 9.2 and Table 9.6 show that EP adoption explicates about 29.7% of the variations in the RE. Collectively, EP adoption and RE explain 43.4% of the variations in SCM.

TABLE 9.5 Hypotheses Testing for Direct Effect.

Hypothesis	Paths	Std. beta	Std. error	t-value	Decision	95% CI LL	95% CI UL
Direct effects							
H1	EP → RE	-0.549	0.097	5.625**	Supported	-0.699	-0.373
H2	EP → SCM	0.222	0.110	2.083**	Supported	0.039	0.404
H3	RE → SCM	0.754	0.101	7.490**	Supported	0.603	0.917
Indirect effect/Mediation							
Hypothesis	**Paths**		**B**	**t-values**	**p-values**	**Decision**	
H4	EP → RE → SCM		0.267	5.234	0.000	Supported	

In testing the direct effect, H1 was formulated for the purpose of determining the impact of EP on the RE. It was found that there is a substantial amount of favorable impact of EP on RE ($\beta = 0.097$; $t = 5.625$ and $p < 0.001$), hence, hypothesis 1 was supported. Hypothesis 2 looks at the influence of EP on SCM ($\beta = 0.110$; $t = 2.083$ and $p < 0.001$). It was found that EP has both a significant and positive influence on SCM, hence, hypothesis 2 was supported. Hypothesis 3 looks at the influence of RE on SCM ($\beta = 0.101$; $t = 7.490$ and $p < 0.001$). It was discovered that RE has a significant positive influence on SCM, hence, hypothesis 3 was supported. Finally, the analysis of the indirect paths shows that RE mediates the influence of EP on SCM, which is significant and positive ($\beta = 0.097$; $t = 5.625$ and $p < 0.001$), hence, hypothesis 1 was supported. Hypothesis 2 looks at the influence of EP on SCM ($\beta = 0.267$; $t = 5.234$ and $p < 0.000$).

TABLE 9.6 R Square (R^2).

Constructs	R square	R square adjusted
RE	0.297	0.287
SCM	0.434	0.417

TABLE 9.7 Effect Size (f^2).

Constructs	E-procurement	Regulatory environment	SCM
EP		0.423	0.065
RE			0.706
SCM			

9.4.3 GOODNESS-OF-FIT TEST FOR INNER MODEL

The R^2 value is used to evaluate the goodness-of-fit of an inner model in the goodness-of-fit test. The test procedure is carried out using SmartPLS, and the outcomes are shown in Table 9.6. RE has a variance (R^2) of 0.297 and SCM of 0.434, as shown in Table 9.6. Since the R^2 condition has been met, it has been determined that the internal model is appropriate for usage, and it may be put to the test of hypotheses.

9.5 DISCUSSION OF FINDINGS

After doing the analysis, a number of discoveries were made from the findings. Foremost, our study demonstrates that both EP adoption and RE account for 43.4% of the change in SCM. It is very clear that these two factors play an important part to the success of SCM. Though, both EP adoption and RE account for 43.4% of the variance in SCM, however, to achieve full success in SCM effectiveness, e-procurement and RE play a very significant role. Nonetheless, other factors account for the remaining 56.6% our study highlights the critical importance of EP adoption and RE in SCM and this should not be underestimated. The mediating role of RE was also found to be positive and significant, confirming the significant role of RE.

Second, our findings show that the RE is a critical factor in the effective deployment of EP accounting for 29.9% of the variance in the RE. Despite the fact that RE has a low impact on e-procurement implementation a public institution should listen to the call by PPA and implement EP to ease procurement processes. the recently enacted Public Procurement Amendment Act (Act 914) does not take into consideration the use of electronic transactions in the procurement process. According to the PPA, Ghana was the first nation in the West African sub-region to implement an EP system for the public sector in 2019, however, some public institutions have still not implemented it. Even though EP has its challenges, its benefits as shown in this research cannot be overemphasized, it is, therefore, paramount that regulatory agencies help to support the call of PPA.

Lee et al. (2020) explored the correlation between the RE and EP and concluded that the RE improves EP leading to competitiveness and flexibility in procurement mechanism. Furthermore, there is a connection between the RE and EP as the RE helps manage key procurement information proactively and make better procurement decisions in a company, which boosts efficiencies and generates value for money throughout the entire procurement process (Lee et al., 2020). On whether or not the RE positively influences SCM, our findings support the hypothesis. The study is consistent with Desmond et al. (2019) studies which reveal that public procurement officials complied with laws in the execution of their duties. This is true because our findings indicate a positive relationship between the RE and SCM. This was due to compliance with the legal framework by public procurement officials.

Furthermore, the study discovered that EP has a major impact on SCM. This study supports the findings of Leonard and Baum (2005), who claim that EP can make a company's supply chain more effective by allowing orders, receipts, and invoices to be processed without paper. Increasing costs, rivalry, and consumer pressure would force businesses to rethink in their supply chain processes and take advantage of the tremendous savings potential of indirect spending. The research revealed a positive association between EP and SCM which could be alluded to in some studies (e.g. Nawi et al., 2017). This may be due to the status of hospitals and the design in which these experiments were conducted. The key benefits of EP, according to (Smith and Flanegin, 2014), include cost savings, process re-organization, and increased contract fulfillment, among others. The authors elaborate further by explaining that EP helps the government save money because it reduces the time and resources needed to process purchase orders, which can now be managed electronically, as well as the costs associated with maintaining inventory and the amount of time required to fulfill orders. Governments and other public agencies that have implemented the EP process have reaped numerous benefits, including increased transparency, contract award alerts, online bid submission, and increased participation by tenderers as a result of better information and access to opportunities, according to a 2013 Asian Development Bank Report. This study, therefore, agrees with the Asian Development Bank Report (2013), therefore, management of hospitals are advised to embrace EP fully to ensure transparency, fairness, and accountability for effective and efficient EP processes.

Finally, results from our PLS analysis suggest that the RE positively mediates the association between EP adoption and SCM. This leads one to believe that the implementation of EP will, in the context of a regulated framework, result in an improvement in the management of supply chains on a worldwide scale. This underscores the need for enterprises to explore the use of EP as a means to strengthen excellent procurement processes for the purpose of realizing value for money.

9.6 CONCLUSIONS AND RECOMMENDATIONS

The implementation of EP has the potential to be a fruitful idea for the performance of any business provided that it is correctly executed. It opens the way for better procurement procedures, brings about effective monitoring, improves communication, enhances the capacity to coordinate distant activities, and helps save both time and money via an effective and efficient procurement approach. According to the findings of the study, the role of RE plays in this discussion has provided more insight that deepens the discourse. Second, our research is one of just a handful that focuses on the mediating role of the RE in the EP adoption-SCM nexus. Basically, our study can support policymakers in understanding the effects of EP adoption on SCM. Second, our study suggests that EP adoption directly affects SCM through the RE. The relevance of this study also stems from the problem that it discusses, which is very important for other organizations interested in EP implementation. In addition, the study provides ideas for government institutions on how to maximize the use of EP to improve SCM which will lead to value for money via the gargantuan role of RE.

Therefore, a facelift should be given to EP schemes as well as procurement experts and policymakers should be empowered to make sure that the RE is enhanced to reap the benefits of EP adoption in Ghana's public hospitals. Furthermore, as EP is heavily influenced by technology, it is therefore fair to recommend that a concerted attempt should be made to ensure that service providers (suppliers) are well-equipped through the provision of secure connectivity hubs and educated as well as maintaining a strong IT infrastructure to meet the needs of public hospitals employees.

The purpose of this study was to do two things: (a) evaluate the effects that the RE has on the nexus between EP adoption and SCM at the global level, and (b) assess the effects that the adoption of EP has on SCM. Results from our

PLS analysis showed that RE positively influenced SCM at the global level. Also, the mediating effects of RE on the nexus between EP adoption and SCM were supported. Our study is limited by the use of primary data though we had control over the definition of the variables in the study. The researchers were unable to conduct a data collection exercise across multiple countries because it was not feasible for us to do so because of resource constraints. However, the data used for the study was found to be very reliable. Future research may consider introducing other mediating variables such as political influence, organizational culture, etc. in the relationship between EP adoption and SCM. Furthermore, future studies may extend this cross-sectional study to a longitudinal one when much data becomes available.

CONSENT

Respondents' written consent has been gathered and preserved by the authors in accordance with international and university standards.

KEYWORDS

- **electronic**
- **procurement**
- **SCM**
- **regulatory environment**

REFERENCES

Abagna Azanlerigu, J.; Akay, E. Prospects and Challenges of E-Procurement in Some Selected Public Institutions in Ghana. *Eur. J. Bus. Manag.* **2015,** *7* (29). www.iiste.org ISSN; www.iiste.org

Asare, E. N.; Prempeh, K. B. An Empirical Assessment of Factors That Influence the Implementation of E-Procurement in Technical Universities in Ghana. *Munich Personal RePEc Arch.* **2017,** *6* (9), 52–60. https://doi.org/10.5923/j.logistics.20170602.03

Ateto, D.; Ondieki, S.; Okibo, W. The Effect of E-Procurement Practices on Effective Procurement in Public Hospitals: A Case of KISII Level 5 Hospital. *Am. Int. J. Contemp. Res.* **2013,** *3* (8). www.aijcrnet.com

Awadallah, N.; Saad, S. G. E-procurement as a New Trend in Hospitality Industry: A Descriptive Study in Egyptian Hotels. *Astra Salvensis* **2018,** *6*, 321–332. https://doi.org/10.4172/2169-0286.1000168

Barngetuny, D. C.; Kimutai, G. International Academic Journals Effects Of E-Procurement On Supply Chain Management Performance in Elgeyo- Marakwet County International Academic Journals. *Int. Acad. J. Procurement Supply Chain Manag.* **2015,** *1* (5), 99–120. www.iajournals.org

Brandon-Jones, A.; Kauppi, K. Examining the Antecedents of the Technology Acceptance Model Within E-Procurement. *Int. J. Operat. Prod. Manag.* **2018,** *38* (1), 22–42. https://doi.org/10.1108/IJOPM-06-2015-0346

Bulletin, E. *E-Procurement: Is Ghana Ready?* **2010,** *1* (4), 1–13.

Calipinar, H.; Soysal, M. E-Procurement: A Case Study About the Health Sector in Turkey. *Int. Jo. Bus. Soc. Sci.* **2012,** *3* (7), 232–244. www.ijbssnet.com

Desmond, A.; Osei Tutu, E.; Kissi, E.; Tutu, S. O.; Kissi, E.; Osei-Tutu, E.; Desmond, A. Evaluating Critical Factors for the Implementation of E-Procurement in Ghana. *Article Int. J. Procurement Manag.* **2019,** *12* (1), 1–14. https://doi.org/10.1504/IJPM.2019.10018011

Domfeh, K. A. *The Role of Pooled Procurement Programme in the Quality Improvement of Medicines of the National Catholic Health Services (Nchs) in Ghana.* 10166654, 2020. http://ugspace.ug.edu.gh

Gefen, D.; Straub, D.; Boudreau, M.-C. Structural Equation Modeling and Regression: Guidelines for Research Practice. *Commun. Assoc. Inf. Syst.* 2000. https://doi.org/10.17705/1cais.00407

Jain, M.; Abidi, N.; Bandyopadhayay, A. E-procurement Espousal and Assessment Framework: A Case-Based Study of Indian Automobile Companies. *Int. J. Technol. Manag. Sustain. Dev.* **2018,** *17* (1), 87–109. https://doi.org/10.1386/tmsd.17.1.87_1

Johnson, M. Public Sector E-Procurement: A Study of Benefits from E-Markets in the Local Government Sector. *Int. J. Serv. Technol. Manag.* **2011,** *16* (1), 1–27. https://doi.org/10.1504/IJSTM.2011.041975

Jr, J. H.; Babin, B.; Anderson, R. *A Global Perspectivie*, 2010. http://sutlib2.sut.ac.th/sut_contents/H139232.pdf

Khuan, L. S.; Swee, M. F. S. H. Technologies for Procurement: Current Trends and Emerging Trends. *Emerg. Technol. Supply Chain Manag.* **2018,** 45–61. https://www.academia.edu/download/58971642/Ch2_Emerging_Technologies_for_Supply_Chain_Management_Robiics_in_SC20190420-115343-1qe5whi.pdf#page=53

Kiprono, R. Challenges of E-Procurement Adoption in the Kenyan Public Sector: A Survey of Parastatals in the Ministry of Finance. *School Hum. Resour. Dev.* **2013,** *1* (1), 26–83. http://www.academia.edu/download/60699177/challenges_of_e-procurement_adoption20190925-38550-1gafudb.pdf

Kusi, B.; Antwi, H. A.; Nani, G.; Mensah, S. O.; Akomeah, M. O.; Road, X. Modeling an Effective E- Procurement System for Ghana‘s Healthcare Sector : A Critical Review and Proposal. *Academia.Educ* **2016,** *2* (6), 641–652. http://www.academia.edu/download/51631954/2121.pdf

Kusi, B.; Asante Antwi, H.; Nani, G.; Mensah, S. O.; Akomeah, M. O. Adoptive Deficiencies and E-Procurement Lag among Hospitals in Ghana : A Logistic Regression Analysis. *Academia.Edu.* https://www.academia.edu/download/51631962/2122.pdf

Lee, S. A.; Allen, D.; Wilkins, C. Patent Application Publication. In: *United States Patent Appl.* 2020. https://patents.google.com/patent/US20020156695A1/en

Leonard, C. L.; Baum, S. R. Research Note: The Ability of Individuals with Right-Hemisphere Damage to Use Context Under Conditions of Focused and Divided Attention. *J. Neurolinguistics* **2005**. https://doi.org/10.1016/j.jneuroling.2005.03.001

Nawi, M. N. M.; Deraman, R.; Bamgbade, J. A.; Zulhumadi, F.; Riazi, S. R. M.; Nasrun Mohd Nawi, M.; Deraman, R.; Adewale Bamgbade, J.; Zulhumadi, F.; Riazi Mehdi Riazi, S.; Nawi, M. N. M.; Deraman, R.; Bamgbade, J. A.; Zulhumadi, F.; Riazi, S. R. M. E-Procurement in Malaysian Construction Industry: Benefits and Challenges in Implementation. *Int. J Sup. Chain. Manag.* **2017,** *6* (1). http://excelingtech.co.uk/

Nurmandi, A.; Kim, S. Making E-Procurement Work in a Decentralized Procurement System: A Comparison of Three Indonesian Cities. *Int. J. Public Sector Manag.* **2015,** *28* (3), 198–220. https://doi.org/10.1108/IJPSM-03-2015-0035

Ofori, D.; Fuseini, O. I. Electronic Government Procurement Adoption in Ghana: Critical Success Factors. *Adv. Res.* **2020,** *21*, 18–34. https://doi.org/10.9734/air/2020/v21i330191

Peng, R.; Lai, H. DRE-specific wikis for Distributed Requirements Engineering: A Review. *Proc. Asia-Pac. Softw. Eng. Conf., APSEC* **2012**. https://doi.org/10.1109/APSEC.2012.72

Rotchanakitumnuai, S. Impact of E-Procurement on Procurement Practices and Performance. *Benchmarking: Int. J.* **2013a,** *7* (3), 330–344. https://doi.org/10.1108/TG-01-2013-0004

Rotchanakitumnuai, S. The Governance Evidence of E-Government Procurement. *Transf. Govern.: People, Process Policy* **2013b,** *7* (3), 309–321. https://doi.org/10.1108/TG-01-2013-0004

Rotich, G. K.; Okello, B. Analysis of Use of E-Procurement on Performance of the Procurement Functions of County Governments in Kenya. *Int. J. Econ. Comm. Manag.* **2015,** *II I*(6), 1381–1398. http://ijecm.co.uk/

Sahu, G. P. E-Procurement Implementation: Critical Analysis of Success Factors' Impact on Project Outcome. *Papers.Ssrn.Com*. 2016. https://doi.org/10.2139/ssrn.2019575

Sarpong, P. B.; Du, J.; Antwi, H. A.; Udimal, T. B.; Musah, A.-A. I.; Khan, H. S. E-Procurement Adoption Barriers in Retrospect: a Structural Equation Analysis of Ghanaian Hospitals. *Can. J. Appl. Sci. Technol.* **2017,** *5* (2), 201–209. http://onlinejournal.org.uk/index.php/cajast/article/view/119

Saunders, M.; Lewis, P. *Doing research in Business & Management: An Essential Guide to Planning Your Project*, 2012. https://epubs.surrey.ac.uk/817620/

Smith, A. D.; Flanegin, F. R. E-Procurement and Automatic Identification: Enhancing Supply Chain Management in the Healthcare Industry. *Int. J. Electron. Healthcare* **2014,** *1* (2), 176–198. https://doi.org/10.1504/IJEH.2004.005866

Vinzi, V.; Chin, W.; Henseler, J.; Wang, H. *Handbook of Partial Least Squares*, 2010. https://link.springer.com/content/pdf/10.1007/978-3-540-32827-8.pdf

Yin, J.; Quazi, A. Business Ethics in the Greater China Region: Past, Present, and Future Research. *J. Bus. Ethics* **2018,** *150* (3), 815–835. https://doi.org/10.1007/s10551-016-3220-9

Yomboi, J.; Nangpiire, C.; Kutochigaga, E. A.; Majeed, M. The Impact of the Collapsed Banks on Customers in Ghana. *Asian J. Econ. Bus. Account., October*, 15–25. https://doi.org/10.9734/ajeba/2021/v21i1730487

Zsidisin, G. A. E-Procurement: From Strategy to Implementation. *J. Supply Chain Manag.* **2002,** *38* (3), 58. https://books.google.com/books?hl=en&lr=&id=UDaxAcoX1JQC&oi=fnd&pg=PP15&dq=(Neef,+2001)&ots=X2XXCDRIul&sig=ORQpKw1bXCQe9tOKGqDFzwoNurw

Index

M

N

P

R

S

T

U

V

W